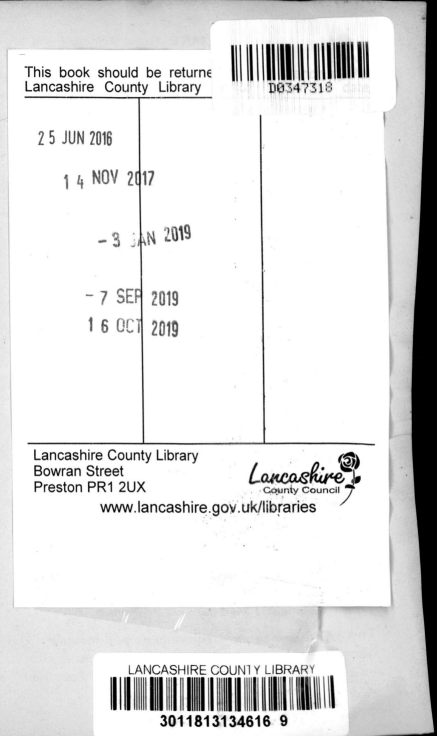

The book is f***ing **BRILLIANT**! **Mega!** Well done. – Bob Geldof

So Ellen's book is a riotous, **wildly enthusiastic** look back over a constantly changing m............ ....s who have dominated it. – *Express*

Hectic, quietly perceptive and in a writing style best described as **A d Wodehouse**. – *New Statesman*

Knowngly ridiculous and very funny. – *Independent on Sunday*

A cult al history of music fandom in a period of fascinating flux. – *MOJO*

Mark E n: the man with the best job ever! – *Elle*

A fantas read. – Simon Mayo

A treasu hest of funny and occasionally touching anecdotes . . . an u at **and immensely readable** account of a joyous addiction *Mail on Sunday*

The coll n of people who cross Ellen's path . . . is enough to keep y rning the page. Having such a **funny, charming** guide do hurt either. – *Independent*

A wry, fu book. – *Sun*

Mark Ell as us laughing all the way through. – *Stylist*

Your boo a joy. – Jeremy Vine, *BBC Radio 2 Arts Show*

Made me gh out loud. – Adam Boulton, *New Statesman*

Rock Star tole My Life reminds us that [pop music] can also be joyously ri ulous . . . Ellen relates a blessed life . . . with playful wit and **in efatigable good humour**. – *Guardian*

This year's most breezily entertaining pop memoir . . . Ellen sails through pop history with an infectious joie de vivre that sends **laughter tumbling from every page**. – *Daily Mail*

MARK ELLEN

Rock Stars Stole My Life!

A Big Bad Love Affair With Music

CORONET

First published in Great Britain in 2014 by Coronet
An imprint of Hodder & Stoughton
An Hachette UK company

First published in paperback in 2015

1

A CIP catalogue record for this title is available from the British Library

ISBN 9781444775518
Ebook ISBN 9781444775525

Printed and bound by Clays Ltd, St Ives plc

Typeset in Plantin Light by Palimpsest Book Production Ltd, Falkirk, Stirlingshire

Hodder & Stoughton policy is to use papers that are natural,
renewable and recyclable products and made from wood grown
in sustainable forests. The logging and manufacturing processes are
expected to conform to the environmental regulations of the country of origin.

Hodder & Stoughton Ltd
338 Euston Road
London NW1 3BH

www.hodder.co.uk

For Clare, Tom and Robbie, the classic line-up, and for my ninety-six-year-old mum. And for Dave Hepworth who was such a big part of this story.

Picture Acknowledgements

Most of the photographs are from the author's collection – with thanks to Q Magazine.

Additional acknowledgements:
© Anton Corbjin: 6 (middle right), © Virginia Turbett/ Redferns/ Getty Images: 8 (middle), © Chris Ridley: 9 (top), © NI Syndication: 11 (middle).

Acknowledgements

All hurrahs to the magnificent M&M (my editor Mark Booth and agent Mark Lucas) – and to my dear friend Nick Sayers for getting the whole thing started. Also to Vero Norton, Fiona Rose, Bea Long and Jason Bartholomew at Hodder, and Alice Laurent for the wonderful cover. Thanks, too, to Paul Du Noyer, Trevor Dann, Nick Leslie, Anton Corbijn and Neil Tennant for jogging my memory – and to Michèle Noach, Mark Billingham, Adam Boulton and Elizabeth Kinder for encouraging me to write it. And to Annabel Brog, who thinks this book should be called *How Mark Ellen Was Totally Washed Up Till His Career Was Saved By Annabel Brog From Elle Magazine* – which, to be fair, it was. And thanks for being the photographer all those years ago to Anji Hunter, Mary Ingoldby, Nick Sayers, Johnny Felton, Allyce Hibbert and Clare Belfield. And much love to Tommy Hibbs.

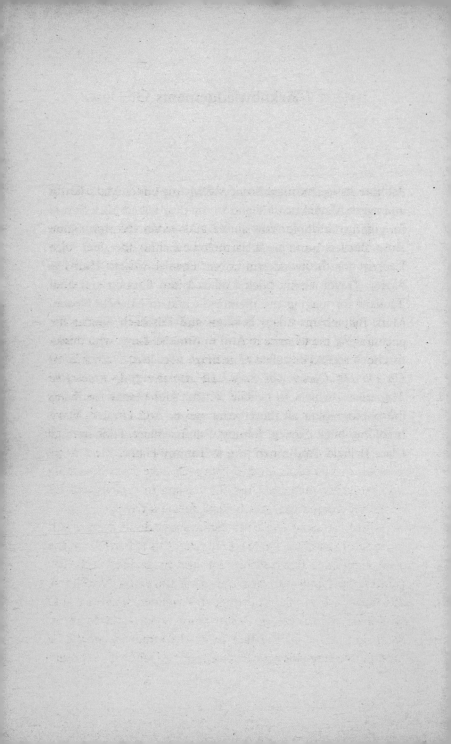

Bloody Marys At The Gates Of Dawn

It's five in the morning somewhere over Greenland and the noise is beginning to fade.

I lift my little window-shade and watch the dawn glow on a curved horizon, then melt back into the deep blue darkness. Is it day or night? Not even the Earth seems to know. It's the weekend and I've had four hours' sleep since Tuesday.

The plane is heaving with bloggers, gossip hacks, journalists, DJs and TV presenters, and we've been hoofing down champagne on the people who manage and make records by Rihanna. It's November 2012, and their twenty-four-year-old pop siren is the hottest ticket on the globe below us. She's playing seven shows in seven countries in seven days, her band, their entourage, the press corps and a handful of fans all transported in a Boeing 777. When some marketing wonk cooked up this caper there might well have been whooping and punching of the air, but it's starting to unravel and it's costing three-quarters of a million dollars a day.

A hush descends and the cabin shuts down with a soft clicking of switches. There's only two of us still awake in the pale lamplight, filing pieces for our magazines' websites, mine tapped out with one quivering finger on an iPhone. It's thirsty work, this reporting, so I wander down the aisle to see if I can scare up some more booze, and there, in the gloom, I see a third face lit by the luminous glow of a laptop, a teenage blogger from Berkeley, California – pointy shoes, skinny jeans, big hair, a self-styled 'Rihanna nut'. I'd talked to him earlier.

'What did you think of the show?' I whisper.

'Didn't see it, man.' He doesn't look up. 'The whole thing was, like, fucked.'

'The whole thing? You *sure*?'

'I get to the venue, OK, and I'm supposed to have a seat but I, like, *don't*? Every time I sit down someone comes along and says it's reserved,' he shrugs, 'so obvy I go to the bar across the road and have a drink.'

'How many times did this happen?'

'Twice,' he says, stabbing at a computer game. 'Maybe three times. A whole bowl of wrong.'

He left and went to a bar?

'You left and went to a bar?'

'To a bar, *totes*.' Stabbing away. 'I'm, like, *outta* here!'

Now I'm thinking: Hang *on* a minute. This is the same guy, right, who boarded this tub in Los Angeles and was then flown to Mexico City and Toronto. And he's now en route to Stockholm, Paris, Berlin, London and New York with some $800-a-night hotel suites along the way. Total cost to him: nothing at all. On the same plane as the pop star he's 'totally mental' about, who's asleep in her pod up the sharp end, just the other side of that curtain. And when he first sank into his capacious seat he was given – we all were – a bulging gift bag containing clothes, books, perfume, a digital watch, an expensive set of headphones and a little bracelet with a rock in it. Not a *big* one, I grant you, but a genuine diamond nonetheless. Rihanna's show normally fills packed football stadia in a vast, cranked-up spectacle of sound and light but on the 777 Tour she's playing clubs, last night's a tiny Canadian music-hall with chandeliers and a moulded plaster ceiling. Hardcore supporters travelled thousands of miles in the hope of a ticket.

And he's walked out of her concert – *why*? Because he didn't fancy standing up to watch it.

At this point something snaps in the back of my head. Some rogue neurone kicks in and I find myself thinking, This kid's taken leave of his senses. For crying out loud, *what is the problem*? Was his champagne not quite chilled enough? Champagne, I might add, that was personally served him on the flight to Mexico by the smiling and powerfully attractive figure of Rihanna herself; champagne, I might *also* add, that's fifty dollars a glass and tipped from bottles that appear to be fashioned from pure gold. Did the cognac run out? Are we out of hot towels and sushi? Was there no square of speciality nougat on the counterpane in his hotel room, no linen napkin folded into the shape of a swan with a flower in its beak? I mean, *what*?

Look here, mate, I huff to myself. *We* fought this war for you, the wind-lashed foot-soldiers of the seventies! We bought the records, we queued for the tickets, we served in the dug-outs, we kept the ball rolling so that years later, in the twenty-first century, a highly refined, multi-billion-dollar industry could ferry massively over-served seventeen-year-olds like this guy, eighteen thousand miles round the planet to see his favourite act seven nights in succession for free!

Except he goes across the road for a drink.

I didn't say it out loud, of course. Had I actually delivered this monologue, it would have sparked hoots of derisive mirth. He'd probably have filmed me, too, and stuck the footage on the internet in pursuit of mass public humiliation. So, I give a crumpled smile and slink back to my seat, handing a chinking glass to my fellow reporter.

'How are you feeling?' she says.

'Great,' I say, poking a straw into a Bloody Mary and tapping my phone. And I *am*, I'm enthralled by everything. But when I switch off my light and try to close my eyes, I can't sleep. I keep thinking back to when *I* was seventeen and the music *I* was 'totally mental' about, and what a quaint, clunky, magical old world it seemed to be.

The creaking portals of my mind had opened and issued their mud-stained memories . . .

2

Tumbling Down The Rabbit Hole

If this was a movie, wavy lines would now appear and the screen dissolve into dust-flecked footage of two boys hitch-hiking through the floodplains of Clacton-on-Sea. It's the bank holiday weekend of August 1971 and my friend Will and I are heading for a flat slab of Essex farmland filled with scrub and puddles. Some bright spark's decided it's the perfect spot for a pop festival.

The two of us stood at the entrance to Weeley and watched the great army of hippies converge like some mass exodus from Middle Earth. Cranky old vans bumped down the cart tracks, the air rich with the smell of warm earth and hedgerows. Hairy men with big boots lolloped along, lugging canvas bags full of beer and corned beef. Skinny girls with peace signs on their foreheads carried guitars. It was as if some magnetic force had attached itself to anyone with a trench-coat and a packet of Rizlas. A certain slice of the populace was being drawn together to sit in noise-filled union at the feet of sonic adventurers like Van der Graaf Generator. Governments would be overthrown, the old world would come tumbling down and everyone would get a bit giddy and probably fall in a ditch.

Terrific, we thought. We desperately wanted to be a part of it.

Will and I were seventeen and ecstatic just to be away from our home turf of Fleet, Hampshire, a town of such skull-cracking tedium that you spent every waking hour plotting an escape from the place. There were two types of people in life, Will reckoned – you were either 'do-ey' or 'non-do-ey' – and we were 'do-ey': we *did* stuff. We'd told our parents we were 'off on an adventure', hitching round the southern counties, no mention of any festivals, and spent most of the week in damp lay-bys eating tinned sardines and vamping manfully on our harmonicas. We'd formed a blues band with a four-song set performed in the weather-beaten drawl of our stage characters, Ramblin' Will Thompson and 'Mississippi' Mark Ellen, pretending we were from the Deep South rather than a leafy suburb just outside Farnborough where practically everybody owned a lawnmower.

Will was blond, stubbly, had a suede jacket and looked annoyingly like Robert Redford. I had an army greatcoat and some maroon cord trousers. Our matted hair was full of burrs as we'd slept in a thistle patch near Colchester. We looked tremendous, we reckoned: wind-battered travellers on the road to discovery! Somewhere along the line, rock music had shown us a contract demanding our souls, our money and most of our attention span, and we'd simply said, 'Where do I sign?' We couldn't name the chancellor of the exchequer but we could quote whole chunks of sleeve notes from albums by Skin Alley and Tucky Buzzard. As far as we were concerned, the world was split into a pair of mutually exclusive enclaves: 'rock' and 'non-rock'. 'Non-rock' was a pallid, joyless vista filled with the lumpen rigours of real life – exams, washing-up, dull holiday jobs stacking shelves in supermarkets, and slightly crumpled men in cardigans who dropped round to visit our parents. But 'rock' was a magic portal through which you dived into daydreams sparked by no more than a cursory glance at a record sleeve. One squint at weathered prog-soldiers Atomic Rooster with their headbands, hand-stitched waistcoats and generous flares, and you fell into a warm reverie about a world of impossible freedom way beyond the painted picket fences of the Guildford borders. Once through the 'rock' window, pretty much everything was acceptable. Even the most clod-hopping rhythm section seemed a symphony of pure delight. Anything involving amplifiers and men with hair like an exploded mattress was A Good Thing. Anyone with a guitar round their neck was transformed into a sage-like prophet shepherding you to a sparkling new parallel universe bereft of rules, bores, number-crunching 'straights' and anyone over the age of thirty.

Like the rest of the steaming throng, Will and I had heard the clarion call and headed down to Weeley. We had a fiver between us, two sleeping-bags and a packet of Rothmans, and were overloading with excitement – though, obviously, we couldn't show it. We cultivated a look of cool, slightly glazed detachment as if enormously stoned and went to a festival every twenty minutes and this just happened to be the latest. Somewhere in the distance the soft throb of music reverberated from some scaffolding covered with planks and tarpaulins, and we picked our way through the crowd towards it. The whole place looked like a painting by Hieronymus Bosch only with denim and litter – pie-munching troglodytes, frail hippie chicks, lone idiot dancers, pale-faced inner voyagers and sunburnt bikers with knotted hankies on their heads asleep amid piles of empties. I found the strange rhythmic motion of one couple we stepped over slightly baffling until Will pointed out they were having sexual intercourse.

We staked out our square of plastic sheeting and set up camp, and soon learnt that you didn't dare move for the entire weekend or you lost your spot. Community spirit might be in the air but it could be fairly thin on the ground. Festival virgins would head out for a group wander, tripping over

7

rucksacks and people frying bacon, and return to find their space had been taken, along with their boots, their rug and all their Kraft Cheese Slices. People often just got lost. They'd skip off, barefoot, to buy an ice-cream in a burst of sunlight on the Friday morning and still be trudging forlornly through the mud days later, their feet in plastic carrier-bags, calling weakly for Dave or Kipper or Wally or Nod.

Generally, though, the mood was forgiving. There was a bonding sense of collective endurance. If you were more than a hundred yards away you could barely see the stage, especially as everyone had flags for the purpose of self-location or sales – 'PETE & SKAGGY'S BARMY ARMY' or 'ACID HERE!!' with an arrow pointing to the frazzled loon beneath it. And in a nasty crosswind you couldn't hear a great deal either so you sat rooted to the spot, pathetically grateful for whatever was lobbed your way in the name of entertainment. The more energetic crowd members built wobbling pyramids of beer cans and threw shoes at them, but most just dozed in their sleeping-bags, mildly distracted by the brave, mind-expanding excursions of Audience or Formerly Fat Harry rumbling on the horizon. Roof-free rock and roll wasn't easy for the bands either: if you wanted to get a crowd on its feet, first you had to get it to finish its sandwich, then climb out of bed and put its trousers on.

To ease the tedium of the long gaps in the running order, thrilling rumours would circulate through the multitude, allegedly started by someone who'd 'been backstage'.

'Hey, mate,' our neighbours shouted above the noise. 'Heard about Ronnie Wood? The Faces are playing without him.'

'Heavy!'

'He's totally bombed. Out of his tree. Clapton's going to replace him!'

'Far out!'

'And The Edgar Broughton Band could be a bit late on,' they added with a nudge and a wink. 'Old Edgar's copped off with a chick.'

'Nice one. Have some crisps!'

'And some guy's died, right. Electrocuted. He was pissing on a power cable. Unlucky.'

'Total downer!'

Every now and then some colossal stoner would wander on and make a mumbling stage announcement about how the cheerless people of Clacton eight miles away were complaining about the noise – *raucous applause* – or how 'Keith's old lady Arabella just had a baby, man!' – *waves of joy*. There was always a birth at festivals. It seemed a great way to open your account, being born during an encore by Sam Apple Pie. It was cheering that the population of your alternative global village was on the up, though if you factored in the bloke full of mescaline who'd fallen off the lighting tower you were pretty much back to square one.

Will and I passed the time honking on our harmonicas, eating sardine-and-Sunblest sandwiches and gawping in shiny-faced reverence at the colourful noodlings of King Crimson and Principal Edwards Magic Theatre, a shambling collective of strummers, dancers and tambourine-tapping girls in felt hats, who performed a courageous tribute to their home town of Kettering. Al Stewart played his bed-sit staple 'Love Chronicles' which included the line 'it grew to be less like fucking and more like making love' and we nodded sagely and exchanged knowing looks – 'Ain't it the truth!' – though we had no experience of either. Whole hours were lost in rounds of the much-loved parlour game What Are Our Favourite Rock Stars Doing Now? Even the lowliest musicians, we assumed, were impossibly glamorous, so what kind of dizzying lifestyle had chart success bestowed upon Weeley's headliners, Rod Stewart and Marc Bolan? To think they could be just the other side of that corrugated iron fence made me wobble with excitement. We gazed longingly at the backstage area, shaking our burr-filled heads in wonder.

I got the ball rolling. 'What, my old pal, is Rod Stewart doing now?'

'Old Rodders,' Will imagined, 'has probably just bowled up in an open-topped Bentley, bunged the chauffeur a fiver for fish and chips and said, "Keep the change, mate." Satin jacket, stripy trousers, glass of bubbly on the go, bird on his arm wearing . . .'

'*Two* birds . . .' I chipped in.

'. . . *two* birds, one on each arm, wearing hot pants. Tell you what,' he added, '*he* won't be up to his knees in empty cider bottles, listening to seventy-five minutes of Juicy Lucy. Your go . . . Marc Bolan?'

Bolan was a tricky one. A year earlier the leader of rambling hippie princelings Tyrannosaurus Rex had been writing lyrics about a siren called Debora who dressed like a conjuror 'clawed with mysteries of the Spanish Main'. Debate raged in our moist patch of the meadow as to whether he'd now 'sold out' by forming T. Rex and making pared-down boogie for girls who bought singles and had glitter on their eyelids. *Melody Maker* referred to him disdainfully as 'The Bopping Elf'. He'd done a bad thing and Weeley weren't going to let him forget it. We imagined he used to have a horse-drawn gypsy caravan full of cats and a bloke called Gandalf playing bongos, but this clearly needed updating.

'He's got rid of the caravan,' I reckoned, 'and he's steaming round the Colchester bypass in a brand-new Cadillac, shades on, smoking a ciggie. Six-foot scarf made out of pink feathers. Girlfriend called Marigold . . .'

'. . . or Coriander or maybe Starshine,' Will thought dreamily. 'Her nails are painted silver . . .'

News arrived on the grapevine that a backstage row had erupted about which act was going on last, and the Faces eventually appeared in the Saturday evening sunlight, swigging bottles of white wine and knocking out rollicking versions of 'Maggie May' and 'Gasoline Alley', Rod Stewart in a pink satin jacket and no shirt. And then darkness fell and a tiny pouting figure with a bushel of curls shimmied into the lights and a reedy little voice came across the PA, buffeted by the wind.

'Hi, I'm Marc Bolan. You've probably seen me on *Top of the Pops*.'

A mighty howl of disapproval rent the night sky. The heavens opened and plastic bottles full of warm wee spun down upon him, many with the tops off. I joined in lustily but felt a bit confused. I liked the conga-tapping whimsy of his early records but I also liked 'Hot Love' and 'Ride A White Swan' – though if I'd applauded either I'd have been accused of desertion, like the traitor Bolan himself, and probably set on fire by heavily bearded men with headbands. You were either with the Underground or the Mainstream. It seemed to be a crime to belong to both.

The Weeley wind brought with it the soft scent of salt and vinegar and the tang of old socks. But something else was in the breeze, a gentle sense of menace. Occasionally there'd be the stench of burning plastic as a bonfire raged out of control and a fire-engine clattered slowly round the edge of the crowd with its siren wailing. Now and again fights broke out or someone started selling 'pot' rather too obviously and a pair of uniformed officers would bustle into view, at which point we'd all scoff loftily and shout 'Fuck off!' from a safe distance.

But now a fresh set of rumours began doing the rounds: the Hells Angels had arrived. We had a local chapter back home, the Devil's Disciples, who were based in Aldershot, a.k.a. 'Sin City of the South'. A cartoonish bunch, they had wooden swords and horned Viking helmets, and the sum total of their criminal activity appeared to be stealing a life-size plywood replica of Colonel Sanders from outside the Kentucky Fried Chicken where I'd worked that summer and strapping it to the back of a chopper. They were nothing like the fibrous, lumpy-looking creatures now lurching around Weeley.

The event, we discovered, had been organised by the good burghers of the local Round Table, who normally laid on wholesome bank holiday fund-raisers – cake stalls, Bash the Rat, Guess the Weight of the Vicar, that sort of thing. But this year they were branching out. They'd booked half a dozen local acts, plus the chart-topping Mungo Jerry, from nearby Dorset, to perform 'In The Summertime' and other harmless jug-band fare, and were hoping to draw a capacity crowd of five thousand to their cheerless stubble-field. All was going according to plan until a projected fourth festival on the Isle of Wight was suddenly cancelled, leaving a vast and expectant roaming army in need of a new location on which to park their bony behinds, smoke their three-quid deals and watch Ken Pustelnik of The Groundhogs do a twenty-minute drum solo.

All hell, very gradually, broke loose. The more the tickets sold, the greater the number of artists offered by promoters and the more the Round Table rightly sensed a larger pot of gold for their charities. So, more acts were added and more tickets were bought and the taped-together infrastructure of the whole creaking caboodle must have started fraying at the edges. In the end so many bands were booked they had to play non-stop between midnight on the Friday and nine on the Sunday morning, with the result that anyone not hammered by drugs or maddened by the poorly synched sound-system was reduced to a whey-faced gibbering wreck simply through lack of sleep.

In the end more than a hundred thousand souls had descended on Weeley, clutching their two-pound weekend tickets, at which point, catching the powerful aroma of cash profit, the spirit of free enterprise raised its opportunistic head. Noting some of the more smoke-filled stragglers hadn't even brought a sleeping-bag, one nearby farmer started selling old fertiliser sacks for a monstrous ten pence a time off the back of a trailer, which, users balefully reported, had a double disadvantage: they were made of paper and they still had pellets of chemically charged fishmeal at the bottom. Add a pair of warm and fragrant feet to the mix and you produced a fizzing stench that tore the bark off trees. Local traders set up food stalls but found the competition tough. For a start, they were undercut by the hippie-hating East End mob, who'd secured the hot-dog concession and ran the vans making deep-fried doughnuts. Then seventeen cartloads of fruit were carried off by light-fingered flower-children. Next, sensing a humanitarian disaster, the Salvation Army arrived and, very sweetly, began handing out free food parcels, though a lot of the crowd were happily surviving on just herbal relaxants and the life-affirming rhythms of Mott The Hoople.

Anyway, exciting news had worked its way through the multitude regarding our safety and security.

'Heard what's going down, man?'

We hadn't, no.

'The Angels are in charge!'

'What . . . the *Hells* Angels? Wow, that's . . . that's cosmic!' We tried to look relaxed.

'The Hells Angels, yeah, they're looking after us. It's a beautiful thing, man. It's a thing that's beautiful.'

Hang about. The last time the Angels 'looked after' anyone was when the Stones played Altamont and it was a total bummer, right, and people got lamped with billiard cues and stabbed and stuff and it actually wasn't very beautiful at all.

'They're doing this in-charge thing in a really cool way, though, right?' I asked.

'*Totally* cool! They've got rid of the fuzz and they're running the whole show, man. They're using the old church as their HQ. Some guy called Johnny Nomad's in charge.'

Will held the fort while I wandered down to the ruined church to see what was occurring. The Angels were indeed in residence, a collection of grotesque, gap-toothed orcs squatting amid the rubble, barbecuing things over hot coals – wild animals, possibly, or Bolan fans – and looking nine times more terrifying than the Aldershot mob and worse, far worse, than the gang my mates had run into at the Isle of Wight Festival the year before, who were led by a character called Buttons. He might have been wearing a dead chicken as a necklace but at least he'd let them share some of his stew. You wouldn't get much stew out of Nomad. He made Buttons look cuddly.

What we hadn't fully grasped was that a grand total of *four* security forces were in fact jostling for pole position. The Hells Angels were indeed our self-appointed guardians but the police had turned up too, and in large numbers, and Clacton's understandably cautious Round Table had also hired a gang of local heavies in the event of a disturbance. Plus a collection of heat-seeking hippies calling themselves The Marquee now claimed to be in control.

It all kicked off by one of the food tents. I wandered over to watch – scary and a little bit exciting, and some distance from the peace-and-love propaganda of Barclay James Harvest who were onstage at the time, a thirty-piece orchestra sawing gently behind them. The hot-dog vendors had taken against the Angels, the Angels had a pop at The Marquee, the security swung a fist at both of them, and then the cops got involved. Girls in floral-print dresses dropped their chips and ran for cover. Stoned men in robes thought it was an authentic piece of street theatre. At one divinely comic moment, a division of bikers dived through the back flap of a catering tent, closely followed by the 'Filth', the canvas bulging like a *Tom and Jerry* cartoon, and some bruised-looking Angels popped out the other end, still pursued by police. The hot-dog gang duffed up some Harley-Davidsons with stake-hammers and set one on fire and, in the confusion, some of the cash from the turnstiles went missing.

Otherwise, great.

I raced back breathlessly to report to Will, the air pungent with the smell of stewed frankfurters and petrol. Chaos, anarchy, mob violence, rock and roll: excellent! There wasn't a lot of *this* on Fleet High Street. The perimeter fence had been overrun, he'd heard, and the festival declared free, but it was stumbling to a halt anyway. In the watery half-light, people were shuffling off, like tattered troops leaving a battle-field, out past the overloading toilets, which consisted of two lengths of scaffolding quivering above a turd-packed trench – you leant on the upper one and sat on the other, a brand of sanitation that would have been sub-standard even in The Black Hole Of Calcutta.

'One poor bloke took a tumble apparently,' Will said, packing his bags. 'Lost his footing and fell in.'

We paused for a moment of quiet contemplation, shivered, and carried on. Foot-rot, burrs, sheep ticks, fertiliser rash, the jarring pain that comes from sleeping on a tree root . . . none of it bothered me. A powerful alchemy was at work that made it all seem magnificent. Some uncritical force was in play that made anything involving loon pants and electric guitars acceptable. Until then, music had mostly accompanied mooching about in bedrooms, the mystic sound of albums and late-night radio beamed from another galaxy, earnest little avenues into some sort of self-discovery. Now it seemed like the soundtrack to a great, captivating juggernaut of a movie thundering into the unknown, a whole new world of fascination and thrills.

3

Pork Pies And *Pick Of The Pops*

I missed The Beatles when they played Aldershot. I was four miles away, eight years old and asleep. Very few people had heard of them outside Liverpool or Hamburg in December 1961 and only eighteen turned up on a perishing night at the Palais Ballroom in Queen's Road. At one of the set's many low points, their two guitarists left the stage, put on scarves and overcoats and waltzed round the dance-floor to the sound of just the bassist and Pete Best playing 'Till There Was You'. They scratched 'THE BEATLES WERE HERE' on the stage door and began the joyless 230-mile journey home in their knackered Commer van.

They'd made this eighteen-hour round-trip because Aldershot was forty miles from London and their manager had fondly imagined some A&R men from record labels might stroll on down to see them. If they had, I used to fantasise, then it could have been our godforsaken corner of fun-free Hampshire that put The Beatles on the map, and vice versa. The whole caper was so disastrous that it pushed them into signing with Brian Epstein, so perhaps the dependably dreary 'Home of the British Army' *did* play its small part in turning my world upside down.

That happened a year later, a moment in which, I like to think, birds flapped, tweeting, past the window and the sun leapt from behind a cloud, but that might be a little fanciful. All I know is my Ektachrome memories of life before The Beatles – of steam trains, prams and wooden toys, tins of pink Germolene, hand-cranked mincing machines and the smell of the coke-fired boiler – seemed wedded to the sound of two men. One was Roy Orbison and the other Bernard Cribbins.

Roy was spooky, cold and unsmiling, and always wore sunglasses. His mournful, operatic tones echoed from shop radios and from the jukebox in the little café on the High Street that sold frothy coffee and was full of towering teddy boys in drape jackets. Roy's records weren't encouraged in the Ellen house as he was part of a dark rock and roll under-world led by the jiving hell-raiser Elvis Presley. Cribbins, however, was all over the place. A worn copy of his magnifi-cent 'Right Said Fred' sat alongside Lonnie Donegan's two chartbusters, 'My Old Man's A Dustman' and 'Does Your Chewing Gum Lose Its Flavour (On The Bed Post Overnight?)'. (My sister Al had researched this and said it did.) Novelty singles were everywhere: throw a paper dart and you'd hit a person whistling one.

So, the first record I ever fell in love with – purchased by democratic vote and the pooling of pocket-money with all three of my sisters – was Bernard Cribbins' masterpiece 'The Hole In The Ground', a symphony of sparkling tunes and comedy rhythms. I stared at its shiny sleeve for hours, a picture of the great man in a crumpled hat pulling a doleful, rubbery face. In just one minute forty-five seconds, he mapped out a gripping class-war collision while playing two different parts, the hole-digging road-worker and an interfering toff in a bowler hat. We'd spend long, carefree afternoons clambering over the little wire fence by the railway line near our house, putting pennies on the track and nipping back to watch the London-bound locomotives thunder over them in a cloud of cinders, squashing the King or Queen's face into grotesque and amusing shapes – the more you put the same coin back, the thinner and wider it got. We'd do this while singing 'The Hole In The Ground' over and over again, swapping parts, marvelling at its rhymes and howling with delight at its murderous punchline.

But a whole new chapter was about to begin, a richly tinted episode starring pork pies, bicycles, crisp packets with little blue twists of salt, vacuum flasks of soup, the fug of wet dog in a Bedford Dormobile and a prime minister called Macmillan who had a funny moustache. And its soundtrack was provided by The Beatles. I bowled up to supper one evening to find an uncomfortable silence. Al had apparently squandered thirty-two shillings and sixpence on 'a long-playing record by this new pop group from Liverpool', and when the wisdom of this was questioned, she'd flounced from the kitchen, steamed upstairs and – amid hot tears and tantrums – slammed her bedroom door. The abominable, cash-sapping Beatles could now be heard at top volume through her cork lino, punctuated by soft parental sighs and the rattle of trains.

I crept up later and listened outside, eventually allowed in to sit on her bed, the value of a pro-Beatles ally outweighing the misery of a younger brother who liked the same music as she did. There she was, still flushed and furious, surrounded by pictures of four boys with astonishing haircuts, a fizzing, cymbal-filled backbeat crackling from her little record-player. And that was it. I'd liked Elvis and his 'Hound Dog' and Guy Mitchell's 'Singing The Blues' but they were Americans, mysterious beings with strange accents from another planet. The Beatles seemed real. They lived up north but at least they were in the same country. They'd been to Aldershot. We might run into them one day.

The Ellen household was the perfect launch-pad for a love affair with pop music – three elder sisters and parents who disapproved. The first gave me a wildly colourful view of it all, the clothes and the characters involved, the second a powerful urge to hear as much of the stuff as possible. Dad worked for the Church and took the train to London every day in a bowler hat. He played dull, wobbling opera on his radiogram by the fireplace, a great humming machine in a polished cabinet with carved wooden legs and a green luminous dial; spin its wheel and you'd hear foreign voices and ghostly music from out across the ether. Mum grew vegetables, fed the chickens, darned socks and spent hours hand-scrubbing laundry while humming along to Mozart on the wireless. Al was fifteen and had a Helen Shapiro bob, plastic earrings and her own transistor radio. Zacky was thirteen and played singles non-stop in her bedroom, the floor creaking as she danced along. Cath was eleven, sang loudly and had thick cord trousers and a duffel coat.

We didn't have a telly so information was thin on the ground. Apart from Alan 'Fluff' Freeman's *Pick Of The Pops* on the Light Programme – playing 'the uppers, downers and just hangin'-arounders' – I had to rely on the records and fill in the gaps myself. The sum total of my Beatles knowledge came from the back of their first album.

'George Harrison is the leader of the group,' I announced, after reading the sleeve notes.

'*John*'s the leader,' Al insisted.

'It's *Paul*!' Zacky reckoned.

'Well, it's certainly not Ringo,' said Cath.

They were wrong and I could prove it. The Beatles' names were listed on the cover with George Harrison first, presumably because he played the important-sounding 'lead guitar'. He was mysterious and had wonky teeth, and people said he wobbled his knee when he played in concerts. Next in the hierarchy was John Lennon, on the less significant 'rhythm guitar', who had bandy legs and mucked about and sometimes wore specs. Third from top was Paul McCartney, on the even lowlier 'bass guitar'; he winked at girls and was soppy and a bit pleased with himself but I thought he was the best. And last – fair enough as he had no guitar at all – was foghorn-voiced, wise-cracking teddy boy Ringo Starr. No one pointed out they were in alphabetical order. The girls had already bagged a Beatle each so I had to make do with the big-nosed drummer.

Boys at school argued about which one wrote which song and who smoked the most ciggies, but the girls'-eye view was different. Pop music was a whole package, a flurry of collarless jackets, winkle-pickers, sex appeal and sparkling asides. Point your mental kaleidoscope at all this, play the records, give it a twist and the whole thing came to life. The Beatles seemed to be the same person reproduced four times with four heads and eight arms, an invincible gang who charmed everyone, waved at crowds, ruffled the hair of small children and raised the sum of human happiness.

Other pop stars now rattled from the radio set and I'd peer at record sleeves in shop windows to get an idea of what they looked like. There were two Americans called the Everly Brothers, who seemed to have come straight off a Brylcreem poster in a barber's shop. There were some choreographed shop-window dummies called The Shadows who had creepy grins. There was beaming crooner Sam Cooke and his new craze The Twist, magically mastered by pretending to stub out a fag-end with your right toe while drying your back with a towel. There was an appalling creature with a guitar and a wimple called The Singing Nun, who Mum and Dad thought ought to be encouraged, and a cheeky, big-eyed poppet called Little Eva with a brand-new dance called The Locomotion that we'd do when the trains went by. And there was the rubber-lipped and lecherous Mick Jagger and his leering Rolling Stones, scourge of decent folk world over.

As singles were six shillings and eightpence, a lot of 'odd

jobs' were required before a trip to Clarke's Electrics on the High Street, opposite a butcher's with hares and woodcock hanging from its awning on strings. Clarke's was full of brand-new household gadgets – Hoovers, food-mixers, spin-dryers, two-bar fires – and had a thrilling scent of warm Bakelite. Occasionally assistants would give a demonstration and some machine would whirr into life to a chorus of appreciative sighs. At the far end was a little counter where a bloke in a button-down shirt, who looked like a member of Herman's Hermits, kept a wooden box of records, singles (or '45s') on one side in their paper sleeves, four-track EPs ('extended play') on the other with their shiny picture covers; if you wanted a long-player you had to go to Guildford. Back home we would sprint, with our new Beatles' 45 in its green wrapper, and watch it clatter down the spindle of the Dansette. I'd stare, mesmerised, at the needle, waiting for the huge, clamouring, slightly curdled chord at the beginning of 'A Hard Day's Night' to begin, and the crackling sound at the end – *doonk-sher, doonk-sher* – as it waited to be ejected.

Life was full of mysteries for my sisters and me. Where did Cilla Black get her belted plastic raincoats? Wouldn't it be great to live on a double-decker bus if it didn't have the smarmy Cliff Richard on board? Why were boys in Dusty Springfield songs always going off with other girls while poor dark-eyed Dusty – who looked like a lot of fun to me – hung about bravely hoping they'd come back to her? And, for that matter, why was French chanteuse Françoise Hardy, clearly possessed of head-wrecking pulchritude, wandering alone and unloved in her roll-neck sweater when everyone else was having a laugh and holding hands? What kind of a world would allow this to happen?

But there were no mysteries for my father. He didn't mind the girls – Cilla, Dusty, Pet Clark, Sandie Shaw – but he detested the rest of pop's noble frontline. The boorish and irksomely hirsute Beatles made a dismal racket but at least they'd been known to wear ties, and the unwashed Stones he'd managed to ignore as they were yet to urinate in a garage forecourt and, thus, infiltrate the pages of *The Times*. But The Kinks were the final straw, ghastly preening gadflies in silk shirts, sneering through their vulgar sunglasses. Worse, they couldn't even spell on their records – 'Kwyet Kinks', *Kinda Kinks*, *The Kink Kontroversy*. The fabric of society was coming apart at the seams.

Access to any of these people was hard to come by, especially if you were at a comical Molesworthian boarding-school in Dorset, stalked by eccentric pipe-smoking teachers, where radios were banned and the only time we were allowed to watch telly was for the state funeral of Winston Churchill. Four of us – tiny little boys with shorts and blue knees – would creep down to the aromatic boot-hole, where they kept all the gym shoes, on Sunday afternoons and gather in detection-dodging silence round Pete Gaskell's illegal transistor – Gaskell was the gang-leader as he had hair like Brian Jones and got *Beat Instrumental* magazine in the post. We'd worked out a system that seemed fair but brought a whole world of excruciating pain: we sat in a circle, each of us wedging the single white plastic earphone into our ear for two minutes, scrupulously timed, then handing it on to the boy on our right and waiting six tortuous minutes for it to come back round again. This was fine if your turn coincided with a favourite record – 'Just One Look' by The Hollies or 'House Of The Rising Sun' by The Animals – but a nightmare if you got a total stinker like 'Happiness' by Ken Dodd and then heard what appeared to be the excellent 'You're No Good' hissing from a nearby ear, miserably confirmed by the listener pointing, thumbs-up, to a picture of the Swinging Blue Jeans in the new edition of *Beat*.

★ ★ ★

But one night in the holidays Dad returned from London with cheering news: these new-fangled 'telly sets' were no longer sinister contraptions that scarred the vision and turned the brain to porridge. They were 'the window on the world', he declared, a marketing slogan he'd read in the *Evening Standard*. A TV duly arrived, with wood panels, and we could now see these groups in action, sometimes even hear them speak; thrilling for us, beguiling – often alarming – for our parents. Until then pop music had lived in the background, a distant noise, pictures on bedroom walls. Now its perpetrators were being piped directly into their living-room via the BBC's new programme *Top of the Pops*. Mum tried her best to be upbeat but Dad began to grasp the full extent of its awfulness. As each episode happened only once and was never repeated, you couldn't miss a moment. It was so precious I'd go to bed thinking I'd dreamt the things I'd seen and had to check with mates the next morning that I hadn't just imagined them.

So a fractious weekly drama played out in our and a million other households. After supper my parents usually busied themselves with the chickens or listening to Mendelssohn or putting tiny portions of uneaten food on saucers in the fridge – a spoonful of mash, a handful of peas – where they'd remain untouched for weeks, sprout luxuriant mould and be chucked in the bin, an old war-time habit they could never shake. But not on *Top of the Pops* night when they made infuriating appearances in the telly-room doorway, sometimes venturing in to turn down the volume.

'Who's this one? Shame she has to make that horrid noise as she's got *such* a pretty face.'

'It's *Lulu*, Mum! We're trying to watch!'

'Oh, look, it's that awful Jimmy Saviles! Must be almost *my* age!'

'He's funny, Mum, and a lovely man, and he likes the Dave Clark Five, which is *more than you do*!'

Dad was even less enthusiastic, the twin-generational agony ramped up most if The Kinks ever made an appearance. I adored The Kinks, way beyond the boundaries of reason. I was besotted with them. I could tell you which one liked steak and chips or girls who were 'sincere' or was kind to animals or was saving up for an E-Type Jag. I loved them so much I'd lie awake at nights picturing the tension if my father was to make one of his haunting cameos while they were on the telly. Which he always did. I could feel his loitering presence behind me.

'Dear, oh dear.'

The temperature seemed to have dropped.

'Oh dear, oh deary dear.'

The ceiling seemed a little lower.

'*Daaad!*'

'What on *earth* is that?'

'*That* is THE KINKS, Dad, and you hate them and you wouldn't understand anyway. Go AWAY!'

The camera would move in on singer Ray Davies, whose dangerously thin smile suggested some private joke from which we were all excluded. To me he was a living symbol of the magical world that lay beyond the suffocating confines of the southern counties. To my father he was a preposterous popinjay who'd barged into our home uninvited, and whatever he was up to, no good by the look of it, he was doing it both all day and all of the night. I'd hope – *pray* – the lens didn't pan left and alight upon the group's lead guitarist, by some margin the world's coolest man. But it did.

'Oh, my giddy aunt.' Dad again. 'What in TARNATION do we have here?' A vein stood out in his neck like a drainpipe.

We had the aggressively pretty *Dave* Davies, a tremendous fop given to knee-length boots and frock coats and wearing what could statistically be proved to be the longest male hair in the United Kingdom. In a dandyish centre-parting.

Please don't say, is it a boy or a girl?

'Is it a boy or a—'

'DAAAAAAD!'

To be fair, he had good reason to feel this way – not that, bless him, he ever expressed it, or that I'd have listened, cared or comprehended. Dave Davies was nearly nineteen, only slightly younger than my father had been when he was called up to fight. Days after Dad's twenty-fourth birthday he'd leapt from the jump-doors of a Dakota into the flak above enemy-occupied Normandy and spent three weeks camped in the woods, his paratroops as terrified of the owls and cracking twigs at night as they were of the gunfire. Leading an attack on some armoured cars, he'd been hit by a German mortar, rushed to a dug-out face-down on a stretcher, strapped to the bonnet of a truck, driven to the coast and shipped back to England to have his right leg removed above the knee. He'd worn a tin one ever since. Whatever future he'd imagined this noble struggle might secure, it hadn't included buffoons like Dave Davies of The Kinks turning the heads of the nation's youth.

By now another mysterious figure sparkled from our record-player. In his early pictures he looked like a farm labourer from the 1920s. I worked out some of his songs and played them on a guitar and a harmonica taped to a bent wire coat-hanger, but these soon acquired such a dark and mystifying edge that I barely knew what I was singing about. A 'hard rain' was going to fall. His minor-chord anthems now featured 'masters of war' with their guns and death-planes. Even his album sleeves were out of reach. On *The Freewheelin' Bob Dylan* he was arm in arm with the type of apple-cheeked girl in sturdy winter-wear you might meet in Mac Fisheries on Fleet High Street but he'd soon traded up: *Bringing It All Back Home* featured a brooding siren in a scarlet cocktail dress smoking a cigarette, a figure of such poise and sophistication it made my head hurt.

Another mind-bending moment was just around the curve. Al had heard a new single that contained important news for the future of the human race. Its message of doom was so distressing, she said, that the BBC might be taking it off the air, so she sat by the radio all day on red alert, ready to shout if she heard it.

'It's on! Quick, quick, before they ban it!'

I tore up to her bedroom, heart pounding, and we huddled round the speaker. She was right, things seemed very bleak indeed. According to the chart-bound 'Eve Of Destruction', the world was about to end. There was no Bob Dylan-style soft-sell poetry with *this* guy, no 'white doves' and 'cannon-balls'. Barry McGuire gave it to you straight. He painted a picture of apocalyptic chaos – bodies floating in the Jordan river, the eastern world exploding, H-bombs raining from the heavens. Escape was impossible, Barry said – 'if the button is pushed there's no running away'. With the world in a grave, 'there'll be no one to save'. I was haunted by it. I couldn't get it out of my head. I couldn't sleep, wrestling with images of eerie, smiling men in uniform, like Bond villains, launching rockets in the direction of Hampshire. The only thing between me and painful death was this sinister 'button' and some bony hand electing to push it. Was that just the low glow of streetlights in the night sky or was it . . . *a giant mushroom cloud rising from the charred remains of Church Crookham*? I lay there, toes curled in terror, imagining waves of radio-activity surging towards me, melting everything in their path – Mac Fisheries, Clarke's Electrics, my mate Will's house . . . What was the point of anything – holidays, life, maybe even breakfast? A hard rain indeed. We were in a right old pickle.

Other harsh realities were creeping into the pop charts, glimpses of strange adult worlds with their sobering complications. Songs like Georgie Fame's 'Yeh Yeh' or 'I Got You Babe' by Sonny and Cher gave the warm impression that boys met girls and this led to dancing, flowers in the spring, ring-wearing and some sort of romantic harmony. Positions improved, worlds expanded. But not any more. When I flipped the new Beatles' single 'Ticket To Ride', I found a great churning ballad called 'Yes It Is' and the agonised John Lennon tangled up with one girl while still haunted by another. And life for Ray Davies was now playing in reverse: on The Kinks' 'Sunny Afternoon' he'd lost all his money, his car, his yacht *and* his girlfriend, who'd returned, presumably weeping, to the bosom of her family 'telling tales of drunkenness and cruelty'. I worried about Ray and hoped he was all right, though Dad would have said he was a bad sort and it was no less than he deserved.

But nothing could have prepared the boot-hole gang for the sound of 'Eight Miles High' sizzling from the radio earphone. It was shocking and weird. I couldn't work out where it came from. The guitar solo was out of tune and just plain *wrong*. Two years later it would be the greatest record I'd ever heard but when it came out in '66, like various other things in life – sex, booze, Stilton cheese – it made absolutely no sense at all until my voice broke and my mental palette shifted to encompass its stinging discords and random self-expression. Pete Gaskell was ahead of the game: he shook his Brian Jones mop and declared it 'the tops', but the rest of us were baffled and a bit frightened. We stared silently at the picture of The Byrds in *Beat Instrumental*, fabulous creatures in fringed jackets and dark glasses who clearly knew something *we* didn't.

'Eight miles high on *drugs*, I reckon,' Gaskell whispered loftily.

'Drugs?' *This* was new.

'Been injecting pot by the sounds of things. Probably pot-*pushers*,' he added, 'pushing pot on themselves. And then injecting it.'

There was a lot to learn.

4

The Party Seven And The Dave Clark Five

A great divide was opening up in what 'Fluff' Freeman called the Hit Parade. Well-scrubbed pop acts like The Tremeloes, The Marmalade and Dave Dee, Dozy, Beaky, Mick & Tich carried on in one direction, and rascally, unvarnished singles-makers like the Small Faces and Steve Winwood were clearly off in another. Others, like Manfred Mann, hovered in the middle, frozen with indecision. The first lot produced sideburns and kipper ties, and hung around with dollybirds in miniskirts; the second began to melt into a stubbly underworld of donkey jackets, Afghan coats and thin girls with curtains of hair.

I could see this change in the box of long-players that had finally arrived at Clarke's Electrics. Not every disc had a cheese-scented promotional snap of the toothsome souls making the music on the cover. The new LP by John Mayall's Bluesbreakers had four unsmiling men on a slab of concrete in front of a graffiti-covered wall, one of them, the twenty-two-year-old Eric Clapton, reading *The Beano*. At precisely the moment I'd put away childish things, low-temperature heroes in thin trousers and Chelsea boots had facetiously re-adopted them. I studied this sleeve for hours in wonder and confusion.

Part of the reason music was so precious was that you very rarely got to hear any. It never played in shops or public places, only in pubs and cafés with a jukebox. You had to be at home with a turntable, or sitting by a radio all day hoping for a particular song. So the new toy now available in Clarke's was a revolution, the Philips battery-operated record-player, a breath-taking invention that allowed you to play whatever music you wanted to hear when and wherever you wanted to hear it. I remember carting this contraption to a field, taking its lid off – which separated into a pair of speakers – slapping on the Small Faces' 'Lazy Sunday', clicking back the arm to start the turntable, dropping the needle, lying with my head between the two plastic cabinets, the whooshing stereo panning between them, and trying to imagine how life could get any better.

Feeling the volcanic effects of a giant hormonal rush, I taped a picture of Julie Driscoll to my school folder. There were female pop stars but only two girls in British rock, the low-lidded Christine Perfect of shadowy blues-wailers Chicken Shack and the smouldering Driscoll with the whirling chart hit 'This Wheel's On Fire'. I went for Driscoll, a panda-eyed siren with a shaved head and polka dots. This was partly out of loyalty to what *Melody Maker* called our 'home-grown rock scene' and partly because American girls looked a bit scary. Janis Joplin was the sort of hard-living loon who'd put bourbon on her corn flakes. Grace Slick of Jefferson Airplane was pretty but looked like she might have some wind chimes. Joni Mitchell was adorable but might spend all day playing a dulcimer instead of going to the pub. But Julie seemed like a laugh and probably drank cider and smoked No. 6.

In this alternative universe there were a thousand new gangs you could join, all charging up the sides of Mount Exotic and planting flags on the top. The more other-worldly their record sleeves, the more I wanted to dive into them and live there forever. My two favourites were *The Doughnut In Granny's Greenhouse* on which spoof-thirties psychedelic jazz group The Bonzo Dog Band cavorted with their space suits, devils' horns, wolfhounds and eyeballs on springs, and *The*

Hangman's Beautiful Daughter where Celtic minstrels the Incredible String Band posed in leafy woodland surrounded by dogs, small children and blissed-out hippie maidens in sturdy, hand-stitched clothing.

Album covers were a key part of the package, magical windows through which you entered the music. I'd just scraped into the bottom form of a new school, Winchester College, a place mostly full of bright and eccentric boys whose small rock fraternity expressed their impeccable taste and individuality by carrying favourite records around like a form of ID, pretending they were on their way to play them somewhere. Only when I'd bought Chicken Shack's unimpeachably hip first album did I dare join this high-risk parlour game. I sprang optimistically onto the street with it under the arm of my duffel coat in the hope of bumping into some fellow 'groovers'. Sure enough, a gaggle of lads were comparing battered cardboard sleeves outside the science block.

Someone had *Steppenwolf* by Steppenwolf.

'Wow, amazing!' I ventured.

'*Maximum* heaviosity,' he confirmed.

Someone else had *Waiting For The Sun* by The Doors. 'Have a listen to "Five To One", the last track on side two,' he suggested. 'It's all about wanking.'

'Righty-ho!'

Out came Sly & the Family Stone's *Dance To The Music*.

'Nicely done. And some good shirts going on.'

Then *A Saucerful Of Secrets* by Pink Floyd, which was perfect as I'd memorised stuff about them from the music press.

'Amazing guys,' I said breezily. 'Syd has black hair and green eyes, apparently. Roger enjoys Beethoven and horse-riding. Rick plays the organ and is "exceedingly absent-minded". Nick would like to write movie scripts.'

'Syd's left,' they pointed out. '*Way* too much dope. Draggy scenes. They've got a new guy called Dave.'

I'd never heard of Dave. My reputation was starting to slip.

'What have *you* got, mate?'

I pulled out my Chicken Shack LP. The title alone was surely worth a few points, *40 Blue Fingers Freshly Packed And Ready To Serve*. To ram home this delicious spook-factor, it had a picture on the front of a supermarket food can whose label featured a bunch of repulsive, ready-to-eat human hands, like violet-coloured asparagus in a watery brine.

'Looks a gas,' one admitted. 'This is the band with Stan Webb, right, the nutter with the two-hundred-foot guitar lead who wanders into the audience playing solos?'

It was. I think I'd passed the audition.

Someone tipped off someone who told someone else who notified the brother of a bloke who played cricket with the guitarist of shambling school rock band Ian Bentley's Rectal Prolapse that Mark Ellen of E House had a Chicken Shack album and a bass guitar. A few days later I was stopped just before double maths by a tall, freckled individual called Socks Millar and asked if I'd like to attend a rehearsal. The best way to get into bands, I'd discovered, was to play the instrument nobody wanted to play as every other position had a queue. Schoolboy drummers tended to be Keith Moon-moulded, bug-eyed lunatics who drank Heineken and broke things. Guitarists were either mystic weavers in the style of Peter Green of Fleetwood Mac or trainee demigods like Eric Clapton. Keyboard players stood motionless in the background and wore exotic hats. Singers were would-be bird-magnets who tried to swing microphones like Paul Rodgers of Free. The bass-playing role-models were dull ex-jazzers, creepy old uncles like the Stones' Bill Wyman, or missable hippie drones plying their uneventful trade in the shadows, none of them glamorous. Own a bass and it was a shoo-in.

The rehearsal with Ian Bentley's Rectal Prolapse consisted of a thirty-minute stagger through a song by The Velvet Underground. Socks was on lead guitar, the shades-wearing team-leader Bentley played rhythm, the enigmatic Jon was on drums, and the lead vocalists were a pioneering twin-pronged double-act, the frenetic Piers and the camp, theatrical Adie. We set up our cut-price gear with its tinny speakers in a musty little lock-up by the classrooms and leant some old mattresses against the walls. Listening to records was thrilling enough but trying to reproduce them was overwhelming: my heart beat so fast my fingers shook. 'I'm Waiting For The Man' was mostly two chords and, if you all played roughly at the same time, it wasn't hard to sound a bit like the original. In fact as it lumbered on, with the odd guitar frill and some confident tub-thumping, it began to feel like an improvement.

'Hey, Lou Reed and your so-called Velvet Underground!' Bentley shouted, as we clambered to a rousing finish. 'Nice try, mate, but *that*'s the way you should have done it. *Listen and learn*!'

The Prolapse, as they called themselves, were pro-American. British music was a bit parochial compared to the strains of the vast, sun-drenched liberated continent of America. The best example of this great nation's work, Socks reckoned – a new killer card in any game of record-sleeve poker – was *Trout Mask Replica* by Captain Beefheart and His Magic Band, an art-statement apparently beamed from Mars. The back cover featured the most frazzled collection of maniacs imaginable, the brilliantly named Beefheart holding a lampshade. They weren't just 'heads', they were card-carrying, fully American 'freaks'. Heads were people who smoked dope but still had a foot in the real world; they did normal things, like buy sausages or hold down a job. Freaks were glassy-eyed counter-cultural activists who'd pan-fried their brains with something called 'acid' and were only capable of eating pulse foods, sprouting waist-length hair and campaigning against Lyndon B. Johnson while bashing a tambourine, or strolling on a hallucinogenic hillside in silk robes and sci-fi shades like the magnificent Magic Band.

Socks and I cackled with delight at their names and the instruments they claimed to play, and tried to imagine the conversation at the photo shoot.

'Have you brought your steel-appendage guitar for this free-form promotional happening, Antennae Jimmy Semens?'

'No, The Mascara Snake, just my flesh horn! My, how the autumn nights are drawing in.'

Every record was the background to some particular activity, a little ritual that naturally rolled into action. 'Whole Lotta Love' by the speaker-shredding Led Zeppelin involved Prolapse members gathered in earnest argument as to who could play more notes per minute, Jimmy Page of 'Zep' or Ten Years After's Alvin Lee. Inscrutable Dylan tracks were heard in total silence followed by intense debate about what he might mean by a 'geranium kiss' or a 'mercury mouth'. 'The Boxer' by the chiming and tuneful Simon and Garfunkel accompanied lone, bedroom-based contemplation of the friendless lives of others in the winters of New York City – two spins of this and I'd start scribbling reams of self-pitiful verse. All were heightened by testosterone, which filled the music with a great surge of teenage manic energy.

But the loosest, daftest, lumpiest and most graceless activity of the lot was dancing, a highly charged procedure that only worked with certain singles. As there was one school dance a year, this entertaining caper mostly played out in the holidays, in cramped living rooms lit by red light-bulbs or bale-filled farm buildings in dead-end places like Dogmersfield, Yateley and Lower Froyle. Tables, shunted to the walls, bore plates of white sliced bread layered with an apparently pre-digested vegetable paste called Sandwich Spread. Sausage rolls appeared in hundreds. And cubes of Cheddar on cocktail sticks stuck into half a grapefruit. And, if you were lucky, cup cakes. There'd be bottles of Strongbow cider and Babycham for the girls, and Watneys Red Barrel for the boys in giant Party Sevens that you pierced with a tin-opener; you could barely lift them when they were full and the warm, flat final serving was a murky stew of fag-ends and dead wasps.

For some reason, maybe a hangover from the fifties, dancing still involved two people. You only danced on your own if it was the last record or you were colossally pissed. Boys asked girls to dance but girls never asked boys, a nerve-shredding custom, my sisters told me, the pop equivalent of those dismal team selections on school playing-fields where the last ones to be picked had knobbly knees or glasses. I made a beeline for Penny Cotter, a plucky, moon-eyed type with a glossy mane of hair, a Che Guevara radical beret and a maxi-skirt. I'd had a massive crush on her since the day Ramblin' Will Thompson asked her to join our blues band and she'd turned up for the photo session in a top hat.

You got the same songs every time, played either by some-body's elder brother or a tragic old git of a DJ in slacks and a frilly shirt with a big collar, probably in his late twenties, who arrived in a Cortina and tried to slip on has-beens like Unit 4+2 or The Searchers. Things usually kicked off with 'Lady Madonna' by The Beatles, then 'I'm A Believer' by The Monkees, Sandie Shaw's 'Puppet On A String', 'Light My Fire' by The Doors, 'Mighty Quinn' by Manfred Mann, 'Mony Mony' by Tommy James and The Shondells, and then, hopefully, 'This Wheel's On Fire' by – be still my beating heart! – Julie Driscoll and Brian Auger's Trinity. Then there'd be a boot-stomping comedy moment with 'Glad All Over' by the Dave Clark Five for a bit of early-sixties nostalgia, then on came the fearful 'Judy In Disguise (With Glasses)' by John Fred and His Playboy Band when you'd duck out for another sausage roll. I wore my blue nylon shirt, denim flares and Hush Puppies and had two gangling routines I considered my signature moves: the first involved cementing my feet to the floor while performing a waist-up wig-out with a lot of creative head-shaking; the other was a loose approximation of the Twist – one heel dug in, elbows flapping, pot plants flying in all directions.

With half an hour to go, a little metal box would clank into action projecting blurred patterns on the wall that looked like strawberry jam. We'd get 'For Once In My Life' by Stevie Wonder, me sprocketing round the dance-floor playing an imaginary mouth-organ, the moon-eyed Cotter gamely swishing her maxi-skirt, arms flailing like branches in a gale. Then a full-scale freak-out for 'Honky Tonk Women' by the leering and rubbery Stones, the air thick with sausage rolls, and you prayed for 'Something Stupid' by Frank and Nancy Sinatra before the parental cars pulled up, a slim chance to steer Penny towards the hay bales in the hope of some energetic snogging.

The school dance, however, was a bit of a nightmare, always staged in the gym. No Penny Cotter, and knots of shy but shrieking sixteen-year-olds from the local girls' school with bell-bottoms, strings of plastic beads and big felt hats with scarves tied round them like number-one rock chick Anita Pallenberg. They looked terrifying and came wrapped in dizzying clouds of perfume.

But salvation was around the bend: one year the Prolapse got booked to provide the music, supporting the enviably popular blues trio Sleepyhead. Once onstage I'd be above this daunting scrum and could adopt a dazed, faraway look that implied my mind was on higher things, like the mysteries of rock, as opposed to getting on the good foot to 'All Right Now' by Free with a barely visible stranger in a headband lit by a stroboscope made by some geek in physics. As the Prolapse was an equal-opportunities democracy vaguely based on The Beatles, it was decided that each group member had to sing at least one number. The team-leading Ian Bentley got 'I'm Waiting For The Man', the freckle-faced Socks, in his Afghan jacket, got 'Johnny B. Goode'. The enigmatic Jon took care of 'Hallelujah I Love Her So' which we thought was a Humble Pie song but was actually by Ray Charles, and Piers and Adie sang the back-up vocals and the lead on 'Gloria' by Them, Neil Young's 'Southern Man' and 'Foxy Lady' by Jimi Hendrix.

I got 'Phoenix' by Wishbone Ash.

The Ash – to give them their full name – were firm favourites of the Prolapse, not least because their songs were only half as hard to play as they appeared to be. You could pull off the odd high-register trill while waving at your mates in the audience. We adored the Ash: whenever a new picture of them appeared in *Melody Maker*, we'd pore over it and play another much-loved parlour game, Name That Line-up.

'Andy Powell on the Flying V,' Socks would start, pointing. 'Ted Turner the other guitar . . .'

'Martin Turner – no relation! – on bass,' I'd chip in, 'and Steve Upton, of course, on drums.'

The voguish rock warriors were dipping a toe in the mystic waters of medieval folklore so their songs were awash with doomed knights on haunted battlefields – excellent! – though with a PA system worse than a fairground's, there wasn't much chance of anyone hearing our versions anyway. But on we went, trembling with excitement. The room smelt of carbolic soap and damp rubber shoes. Fractured sound was bouncing off the wall-bars. The shrieking white noise died down and a primitive spotlight picked out Piers and Adie.

'Good evening and thanks for coming out,' they said in stereo, our twin-vocal gimmick. 'We're Ian Bentley's Rectal Prolapse!'

The girls looked horrified. Some of them winced. Maybe it wasn't such a great name after all. Why hadn't we called ourselves Flowers or Driftwood or Seagull or something? Or one of those cool, goofball names like Mister Perkins and His Blue Hat? Just the Ian Bentley Band might have been better. We were off, whatever, crashing into 'Foxy Lady', a bass part so basic I had plenty of time to wonder why the hell I was wearing sandals and not John-Lennon-on-the-cover-of-*Abbey-Road*-style white plimsolls like Socks. By the time we got to 'Southern Man', there were brave scattered outbreaks of dancing and a powerful rock-star fantasy had its claws in me. I wasn't a sixteen-year-old in a school gym with bad shoes. Even standing at the back I'd started to think I was Neil Young, the lone wolf of the West Coast himself with a buckskin jacket and sideburns. I wasn't dodging the gaze of my maths teacher in the doorway but surveying the long march of American history from the rolling landscapes of the Deep South while radiating a kind of animal magnetism. I was older and wiser. And nearly ten times better-looking.

'Thangyew, yeah! Our bass player's going to entertain you now. This one's called "Phoenix" by Wishbone Ash!'

The Mark Ellen vocal showcase began with a tremendous drum flourish and a clattering dual-guitar overture in three-four time, impossible to dance to. Courageous fruggers gave it their best shot, then leant against the trampoline. Next some descending chords with Bentley's new wah-wah pedal to the fore. I sang something about a phoenix rising from the ashes and leaving the ruins of the fire behind it, and there was a tinkling of cymbals and some bracing top notes from

Socks while the rest of the band threw shapes. Knots of girls began shuffling about and talking. Why had we chosen a song that seemed to last a fortnight? Another line from me, this about how the spirits of the dead knights on the battlefield were only visible to myself and the titular bird.

Then the big finish.

'Phoenix, rise! Raise – your – head – to the *ski-i-i-es!*'

There was a frantic twin-guitar wig-out clambering to a quivery climax, some shimmering of cymbals and a clipped power-chord. And then silence.

'Goo'night, God bless!'

A band meeting was held in the changing rooms in which 'Phoenix' was voted out of the set-list. The Ash were never spoken of again.

5

Everything Is Green And Submarine

The first rock musician I ever saw walk onstage was in a band who were bottom of the bill at the Roundhouse. I was smitten. He was thin and lanky with long hair and a checked shirt, and I found out later he was called Nick Lowe. The poster outside said:

IMPLOSION!
Roundhouse, Chalk Farm, 3.30 – 11.30 p.m.
★★★
SOFT MACHINE
ANDY ROBERTS with EVERYONE
BRINSLEY SCHWARZ
DJ JEFF DEXTER (records from Musicland, 44 Berwick Street, W1)
LIGHTS by FIRST LIGHT
AMPLIFICATION by HI-WATT
FILMS + STALLS!

My friend Andy and I stared at it in wonder. We'd spent long nights endlessly playing *Third*, the latest challenging release by prog-rock jazzers Soft Machine – two discs with only four tracks, each occupying *the whole side of an album*: epic! We'd reached a moment in life where we didn't want music that moved or inspired us, we just wanted it to be more difficult than what anyone else was listening to so we could feel superior. We sat in smug, nodding contemplation, tapping along with their knotted rhythms. There was something hugely

41

satisfying about a complicated time-signature – especially if Andy hadn't worked out it was six-eight yet and I could tell him. It was like solving a maths equation.

It was nearly ten bob to get into the gig but we'd been saving up. In fact, it seemed a good deal as there were two other bands thrown in. We got a red double-decker to Camden Town where the Roundhouse turned out to be an old brick engine-shed with dingy little arches full of hippies in trench-coats smoking dope. Girls in long dresses sat on planks set up on some scaffolding and swung their legs, and the whole place smelt of mould and marijuana. Next to us was a huge guy with an Afro stuck full of glowing incense sticks doing some sketching. The DJ had round shades and a ponytail and Hi-Watt were doing a brilliant job of the sound, we reckoned. The lights by First Light weren't half bad either.

Hours passed while we simply stared at the amps. 'Underground' bands were never on the telly, so if you hadn't got their records or seen them in *Melody Maker* you never knew what they looked like. We sat there trying to picture the five members of Brinsley Schwarz, who sounded American but turned out to be hairy, country-rock frontiersmen from the southern counties in seedy greatcoats. Nick Lowe, the leader, strolled on first, bathed in an orange glow and waving a beer bottle, a cigarette burning in the machine-heads of his Fender bass, an image tattooed on my memory. We cheered loudly whenever the songs ended but no one else seemed to bother. We didn't think much of Andy Roberts and wandered off to look at the stalls – hash pipes, Rizlas, slim volumes of verse, CND propaganda sheets and badly printed T-shirts with a naked picture of John Lennon and the unsettling Yoko Ono. Wear one of those in Fleet, Hampshire, and you'd be banged up. Then Soft Machine wandered on, one of them clutching a bottle of wine – Blue Nun Liebfraumilch; we could see the label. I clambered to the front with my camera and took a trembling snap. They fiddled around with knobs and dials in a ghostly haze and made various honks and squeaks, and we realised the set had started. They played all four tracks on *Third* in one continuous ninety-minute stream without saying a word. My friend Andy was an old hand player of Name That Line-up.

'Mike Ratledge, keyboards,' he trotted out, squinting into the lights, 'Elton John on sax . . .'

'Elton *Dean*, I think you'll find,' I butted in. 'Big Bopper on bass. Dave Bopper. Dave Fender. Hugh Fender. Hugh Hefner . . .'

'Hugh Hopper on bass,' it was thirty–fifteen, 'and Robert Wyatt, of course, on the drums.'

I made mental notes on the way home – grow hair, buy trench-coat, fiddle with knobs and speak less onstage, smoke more fags, drink Blue Nun and ban any available bombs: onwards!

Going to gigs was a pastime mostly confined to the holidays. The stiff Victorian rectitude of boarding-schools didn't allow for the ruinous influence of live rock music, and anyone caught attending any of these corrupting events was likely to be expelled. So there was a fair amount of stealth and anxiety involved when Socks and I nipped out one Sunday in June, changed into our most exotic T-shirts and took a train to the Reading Festival to marvel at the prog-blues band Hookfoot, flaccid boogie-monsters Brewers Droop and a group called Medicine Head, the most basic unit imaginable – two monstrous hairies, one on guitar, the other sitting on a stool playing bass while operating a drum kit with his feet.

Back home I set out to see any rock act that came within a bus ride of my fun-free home town. One was Elton John at Guildford Civic Hall who turned out to be a podgy twenty-three-year-old with stack-heeled boots and plastic sunglasses.

I shuffled up the aisle on my arse to get a picture of him trying to do handstands on his keyboard but security weren't having it. Genesis didn't even have a stage when they played Farnborough Tech: they just set up their equipment on the refectory floor. The drummer Phil Collins had long, stringy hair and dungarees, and the singer Peter Gabriel spun about with a tambourine in a hoop-necked top and Penny Cotter said he was 'a pseud' but, on a happier note, their song 'The Return Of The Giant Hogweed' was nearly nine minutes long. George Harrison had popularised the sitar so we raced off to sit dutifully at the feet of Quintessence, a new 'raga-rock' act who burnt joss-sticks, played flutes, tapped finger-cymbals and had names like Shiva, Sambhu and Raja Ram despite appearing to be English and coming from Notting Hill Gate.

But the main activity, now the Soft Machine phase was over, was plumbing the fathomless depths of rock for clues to the meaning of life, a reflective rite of passage that involved a circle of schoolboys on giant foam-filled cushions, some cider, a packet of No. 6 and an orange light-bulb screwed into an Anglepoise. And the best accompaniment to this ritual was Pink Floyd. If you wanted things to be vast in every sense – which I did and badly – then the Floyd were the team to back. They had hugeness in spades. Whatever any band attempted, they did it bigger, longer and louder, and hung around with fabulous-looking girls called Jude and Ginger while they were about it. They even had the most equipment: there was a picture of it on the back of their *Ummagumma* album, all laid out in a huge fetishistic orgy of amps, guitars, battered tom-toms, Marshall Stacks and a xylophone. *Real* fans knew how many drumsticks Nick Mason had as you could count them on the sleeve.

In a basement room at the witching hour of midnight, Prolapse members would gather to play the new Floyd album *Meddle*, a message from beyond, a cryptic sonic code that only we could crack, a sorcerous tablet of vinyl that would bust wide the doors of perception – as long as Socks hadn't got any jam on the grooves or left it on a radiator. Talking was allowed while side one was on but the moment the disc was flipped and the twenty-three-minute 'Echoes' started, silence descended and the ceremony began, an intense quest for spiritual revelation and, hopefully, a complete personality change. We sat cross-legged, pretending to be on drugs. Great planks of shimmering noise filled the room dusted with mystic words and dreamlike sound effects while we scoured the cover for clues, a colour-saturated photo of a huge blue psychedelic ear. Eyes tight shut, Socks tweaked imaginary strings, Jon tapped invisible drums, I'd sing along and Adie and I would have the same fractious, scene-lowering debate about the lyrics, which we had no way of checking as they weren't printed on the sleeve. The vocal drifted in, a whispered verse about an albatross floating motionless above labyrinths of coral caves and how echoes of the past drift over glistening sands . . .

'. . . and everything is green and submarine . . .'

'It's *summery*,' Adie would say, 'not submarine.'

'*Submarine*,' I'd insist. 'Rhymes with green.'

'Summery. Submarine's not an adjective.'

'It is, fact. Marine's an adjective. Why can't 'submarine' be an adjective?'

'Submarine's a thing.'

'Adjective. How can it be summery under water?'

'Not an adjective.'

'Do you think the Pink Floyd sit around all day arguing about the correct use of bloody adjectives? No, they do not! Why? Cos they've got better things to do,' I said, stubbing out a ciggie. 'They're having a wild old time on a yacht somewhere *summery* with Jude and Ginger, for God's sake – and probably Lennon and Clapton and Beefheart and Julie

Driscoll – and they're thinking about cosmic stuff, mate, and planets and caves and albatrosses, and smoking something a lot stronger than No. 6!'

'Summery.'

'*SUBMARINE!*'

The four-hour communal listening experience was less competitive when it was just me and Penny Cotter. For some reason, the moon-eyed Cotter didn't seem to care how many cymbals the Pink Floyd had, and had loathed Soft Machine with a burning passion – 'Oh, the *Softs*,' she'd mock, with a hollow laugh.

Penny only cared about one musician. His second album had come out two years before and we'd played it so much that its grooves wore out and its sound became tinny and thin. Some of it was set in the Biblical east, other bits in cheap motel rooms or in the French Resistance of the Second World War. It was filled with ragged glamour and mystery, mordant soul-stretching poetry sung to an acoustic guitar, the most romantic thing imaginable. The front sleeve of *Songs From A Room* had a portrait of the singer bleached into black and white. The reverse had a grainy snap of a girl in a towel called Marianne sitting at a typewriter on the Greek island of Hydra. The message was clear: play the guitar and write deathless verse plumbing the depths of the human condition, and numbingly attractive women might climb out of your bath and offer to type it for you. Being a rock star was an aphrodisiac in itself but these new singer-songwriters were alchemists of an even more powerful kind.

You either 'got' Leonard Cohen or you didn't. Penny and I got him and it filled us with righteous energy. We felt deep and meaningful and hot-wired to the great verities of consciousness. Anyone who dismissed 'Laughing Len' as a one-note, suicidal bore might as well wear a lapel badge saying 'Superficial Wanker' and get back to their pop singles by gormless puppets like Clodagh Rodgers, or top-drawer donkeys like Gary Puckett & The Union Gap. Relationships could founder upon Cohen's absence from a record collection – no Len, no friend.

Hours, days, weeks, months passed in the upstairs room at Penny's house, the heavy drapes wrenched shut to block out the sunlight, felt hats and lipsticks scattered on the carpet, a silk scarf on the bedside light, gauche poetry on scraps of paper, smoke floating from a bouquet of joss-sticks and *Songs From A Room* wheezing mournfully from her little Dansette in the corner. Occasionally her mum would bang on the door and suggest we 'get some fresh air' or ask if we wanted any Jaffa Cakes, but we had our own little world and everything else seemed shallow and two-dimensional. Had anyone apart from us ever really grasped the towering complexity of life as mapped out by this record? Had anyone explored such rich and sunless corners of the imagination, or felt its fluttery rushes of guilt and joy? Only three people on the planet had ever reached such intense emotional altitude, I reckoned – me, Penny and Leonard Cohen. And maybe the towel-clad Marianne. And Nancy and Suzanne and all the other girls in his songs. If I hear a split-second of that album today, I'm transported back to the fug of that scented room and the funny old business of falling in love.

Wandering home from Penny's one afternoon, knocking ash and crumbs from my denim jacket, I found my father by his radiogram. It was Saturday. In one hand he held the notes for the sermon he was going to preach at the local church the next morning – he was an Anglican lay-reader – and, in the other, my copy of *Hot Rats* by lecherous rock agitator Frank Zappa. He wasn't annoyed or angry: he wore the resigned look of someone having to accept that the world had snowballed way beyond his control and understanding and there wasn't an awful lot he could do about it.

The cover featured a tinted snap of a creepy, androgynous weirdo with an explosion of hair crawling from a mould-filled empty swimming-pool. Through Dad's eyes, this was the stuff of nightmares. The reverse pictured the absurdly named Zappa with his rebarbative colleagues, the Mothers of Invention. He turned it over with a jolt of pain. The bowler hat was the trademark of hard-working pillars of society who carried a rolled umbrella on their daily commute to London. Here it was, this symbol of decency, perched sarcastically upon the stringy, soap-free locks of a sinister, chain-smoking hippie with a preposterous moustache. I sensed this was the final straw.

'You can't really play this stuff on the radiogram, old boy,' he said softly.

'Why not?'

'Damages the stylus.'

'How can it damage the stylus?'

'Cheap recording. Poor quality. Not good for the deck. They cost money, these needles, you know.'

'For your information, Dad, Frank' – I couldn't quite add Zappa – 'is not only doing brilliant stuff at the cutting edge of modern music but uses production values of the very highest standard.'

Straight out of Melody Maker. *Sounded good. No idea what it meant.*

'I'll have you know,' I added, 'it cost Frank a packet to make this record! And this,' I snatched up Pink Floyd's *Atom Heart Mother*, 'this actually has an *orchestra* on it. Ha!'

'The EMI *Pops'* Orchestra,' he pointed out, peering at the credits. 'It's hardly the Berlin Philharmonic – which you could do worse than listen to, incidentally. Cheap,' he said. 'Low quality. Bad for the stylus.'

'Dad!'

The problem was that rock music invited you to rebel even if you were a public schoolboy without much to rebel against. I came from the kind of family whose idea of a major row was whether to watch *Dixon Of Dock Green* or *The Stanley Baxter Show* (they tuck you up, your mum and dad). Infuriating though he could be, Dad's attempts to steer me from the degenerate path of pop now seemed rather touching. He'd lost the battle and accepted it. This 'stylus' ruse wouldn't cut any ice and he knew it. If he'd failed to steer his ten-year-old son from the horrors of The Kinks, then could the creepy-looking Zappa be far behind in his sacrilegious hat?

Friends in London were spoilt for choice, with their clubs and import shops, but I was so pathetically grateful for any crumbs of entertainment thrown my way that I broadly loved everything – the prog sorcerers, the frowning poets, the singer-songwriters, the breast-beating troubadours, the amped-up blues-wailers, the budget art-rockers. There seemed to be no earthly reason to chuck beer cans at any of them. The only obstacle in *my* path was the mind-numbing middle-class tedium of this deadbeat southern county where bugger-all ever seemed to happen. Our suffocating slice of suburbia seemed ever more clipped and ridiculous. There was a party going on somewhere and this wasn't the centre of it. I wanted to belong to something. I was desperate for a sense of involvement.

Part of Dad's identity had been forged for him: he'd survived a war and was now perfectly happy to smoke his pipe, feed his chickens, prod his bonfires, preach his sermons and marvel at the fact that he was still alive.

His generation had adventures thrust upon them. We had to cook up some of our own.

6

To A Hippie Commune, Via Budgie And Slade

Our final ride to the Great Western Festival was from an Old Person. I can see her now – late thirties, maybe forty – driving an Austin Cambridge with an anorak and a look of anxiety. She'd seen us hitching in the drizzle and given us a lift to an ugly great corrugated-iron fence in the middle of a field in Lincolnshire. Damp hippies filed into its throbbing interior through turnstiles. You could hear the muffled thump of music. She turned off the engine, stared through the rain-speckled windscreen and shivered.

'My daughter's in there,' she said.

Festivals in 1972 weren't thought to be good places for daughters to be. You might as well send them straight to the sacrificial altar. Local press gave the impression of vast orgies where teenage girls would be force-fed LSD and hurl themselves, saucer-eyed, into riotous sexual abandon with men who hadn't had a bath since Christmas. Ten minutes' exposure to the sinister pulse of evil dream-weavers Hawkwind and your virgin child would be brainwashed and spend the rest of her life on a houseboat full of dogs and babies stirring vats of vegetable curry while someone played 'Silver Machine' on a guitar with only three strings.

'She's seventeen,' she said weakly. 'I hope she's all right.' She turned to us in the back seat with maternal concern. 'I hope you two boys will be all right too.'

We laughed a merry laugh as we waved her off – daft old bat, what a straight, of *course* we'll be all right! I was an old-hand at this festival lark; I'd done Weeley *and* Reading. I had twenty Bensons and an army coat with brass buttons, my mate Nick had a blue velvet jacket and we were both wearing cowboy boots. In our heads we looked like members of Traffic or Blodwyn Pig in their breeze-ruffled snaps in the music papers. We'd left school, got places at colleges and I was working in a tractor factory to earn enough cash to visit far-flung places like France. Apart from mourning the tragic end of the Cotter-Ellen alliance, I couldn't have been *more* all right, thanks all the same.

We picked our way through a scene that would have looked like *The Wreck Of The Hesperus* if The Hesperus had been carrying a cargo of cheeseburgers and Double Diamond – glass beer bottles, chip wrappers, trampled programmes, moist pages of *New Musical Express* and flailing wackos vibrating freely to the motivating funk of the Average White Band, all of it with the stench of fried onions. In breaks in the rain, people shuffled out of bunkers they'd built out of hay bales and bits of the perimeter fence and looned about with a foam machine. We charged off to the 'Giants of Tomorrow Tent' to see raucous Welsh noise-mongers Budgie, who Nick declared 'a total drag'. Atomic Rooster, Status Quo, Walrus, Roxy Music, he had no interest in any of them. He'd only come to see exotic Americans like Buddy Miles and the Beach Boys, but he cheered up enormously at the sound of a familiar voice coming from the wall of speakers, trying thoughtfully to reconnect some hopeless old stoner with his stash.

'Could Rainbow Lady come to the pink and white tent by the lighting tower as soon as possible as Bongo needs his insulin?'

We adored John Peel, a permanent fixture at festivals, towering above us on the scaffolding in his tie-dyed T-shirt spinning otherworldly records between the bands in his DJ booth, an ageless beacon of poise and sagacity. He'd done the moonlight shift on Radio London's pirate ship and been coaxed over to create the same kind of 'vibe' with his *Top Gear* show on Radio 1. We'd memorise his on-air comments and quote them endlessly. 'There's a sign on the Underground that says "Obstructing The Doors Causes Delay And Can Be Dangerous" – I think that says it all,' he announced before playing the nation 'Break On Through (To The Other Side)'. He once described Emerson, Lake & Palmer as 'a waste of talent and electricity'. We could even quote a poem he'd read on a Tyrannosaurus Rex album about a lark with a many-coloured zodiac coat and a mole in a pig's bladder balloon. He was our absolute hero, the shambling hippie potentate who seemed to live in some parallel universe full of commune-dwelling 'gentle cats' who strummed guitars, tended herb gardens and had a rare old time. That some-body was paying him to flap about in loose-fitting clothes playing American imports on national radio seemed a posi-tion of unimaginable delight. Everything he said came wrapped in a shrugging, self-puncturing tone suggesting fallibility and ineptitude, which seemed to make him even greater.

'I slept alone again last night,' he told the Lincoln crowd morosely, 'so if any of you ladies in the audience would like to avail yourselves of my lithe and athletic young body, report backstage to my caravan any time after Stone The Crows.'

During a fierce East Midlands squall, we ran into two elfin creatures in big hats sheltering under a tarpaulin, impossibly pretty. They were seventeen and had the soft scent of patch-ouli oil. One was wearing her gran's old fur coat which smelt of cupboards. They gave us some sandwiches they were embarrassed to admit their mums had made and we drifted along together like the male and female of the same species, four little teenage hippies, inseparable for the next two days.

Nobody tried to cop off with anyone. I don't think we even held hands. We barely spoke, as conversation was massively uncool, just swapped cigarettes and rapturous smiles and marvelled at the adult world around us.

In a rare burst of steaming sunshine, Slade arrived with their barrelling terrace anthems, the singer clumping round the planks on giant 'platties' in a battered hat with a sign on it saying, 'The Pope Smokes Dope'. Nick and I played Name That Line-up while the girls sighed good-naturedly and gazed into the distance.

'Noddy Holder . . .' I yelled above the noise.

'The Nod!' he said, even though he hated them. 'And on guitar . . . don't rush me. Bloke who looks like a monkey dressed in tinfoil. World's worst haircut. Dave somebody . . .'

'Dave Hill.'

'Jim Lea on bass and Old Matey at the back . . .'

'. . . Don Powell, of course, on drums!'

At one point, immensely thrilling, the great farting brass-filled sound of 'The Liberty Bell' announced the appearance of Monty Python's Flying Circus, so firmly a part of the counter-culture they seemed perfectly at home following the Dutch prog-makers Focus. Now and again they nipped into the wings and reappeared with bowler hats or Gumby-styled knotted hankies and braces. Acres of wet long-hairs joined in lustily as if the sketches were songs and the catch-phrase the chorus – 'He's not dead, he's just PINING FOR THE FJORDS!' Eventually the Beach Boys wandered out beneath angry purple skies, a scene about as far from Nick's dazzling visions of the American West Coast as it was possible to imagine. We crowded onto a patch of high ground and watched above a soup of puréed mud and beer cans while they conjured up a world of sand and surf and high-school hops and good vibrations and girls called Barbara Ann and the chrome peeling on the sun-baked bumpers of Cadillacs.

I'd read about their tortured genius Brian Wilson and tried to fascinate the girls with stories of his great shimmering symphonies of sound, shouting above the wind and rain, even pointing him out playing bass, until a bloke on the next hay bale told us that *Melody Maker* said he'd left the touring group and now just mucked about in a studio in Los Angeles, and we chewed our food for a bit in silence.

We had no tents or even sleeping-bags so the four of us slept both nights on mounds of straw under a plastic sheet in a great warm nest of fur and smoke and tangled hair, like puppies in a basket, and I couldn't remember when I'd ever been happier. I'd wake occasionally to hear the comforting rumble of a band and the roar of the crowd and drift off again. Music seemed like a refuge from whatever the outside world chose to throw my way. The heavens stayed open, rain pattering on our little roof, the festival stumbled to an end, and the girls headed off through the mist to meet their mothers, who I pictured waiting anxiously in their cars – one in the Austin Cambridge probably – praying they'd had a good time and eaten all their sandwiches and hadn't had sex with anyone.

Thumbing back south, I felt hopelessly in love with it all. Nick and I watched the trucks splash past from the side of the road and wiled away the hours impersonating John Peel and talking about these new-fangled communes he so warmly recommended. The Grateful Dead were living on a ranch, apparently, where everyone arsed about in hammocks picking a banjo. The Incredible String Band had a place in the Scottish lowlands where they cooked pies and played fiddles, and one had a girlfriend called Licorice. Led Zeppelin had written some of their third album in a cottage in Snowdonia called Bron-Yr-Aur – 'Hill of Gold!' – which had no lights or electricity; *NME* said they'd squeezed precious extra life from their tape-recorder batteries by standing them near the log

54

fire. And Traffic had decamped to a farmhouse on the Berkshire Downs where they rambled on hillsides, tinkered with keyboards and generally 'got it together in the country'. One of them had been spotted wandering round Aston Tirrold in boots that were painted purple.

All of this sounded sensible and unbelievably attractive. In my overcooked imagination, I thought I should be in a commune too.

And four months later I managed it, though this strange social experiment brought a humbling new sensation, the feeling that all of my record collection was redundant.

I'd found a job picking grapes in the South of France and hitched down there magnificently dressed in a Donovan-style peaked cap and a US-import denim shirt with three pearl cuff-studs as worn by 'Pigpen' McKernan on the inner sleeve of the Dead's *Skull And Roses* album. I'd seen a card later in a hostel in Lyon saying a pair of pioneering souls had bought a sixteenth-century village called Bardou in Languedoc and let people stay for free if they helped with its restoration, and I felt compulsively drawn to the place. An extraordinary collection of people had assembled in this remote stone ruin up a winding track in the Pyrenees – poets, musicians, college graduates writing self-seeking 'journals', back-to-nature idealists with dogs and small children, draft-dodgers, Vietnam War deserters and wide-eyed gap-year kids like me looking for something to give their earth's axis an almighty tweak. I was the youngest there and overawed by some of those wizened road-warriors but signed up and moved into the bunkhouse with a view of a chestnut forest. There were no phones so I sent a postcard home once a week from the bottom of the mountain; Mum and Dad heard nothing at all for a month until four arrived on the same day.

There were no record-players and the only power came from a generator, so the long winter nights of '72 were spent splitting logs, hanging pots of stew from chains in the chimney stack, drinking cheap wine and listening to the all-American workforce playing their folk, blues and ragtime in the flickering firelight. My whole world-view went into a wind-tunnel. When the deserter talked eerily about the raids on Saigon, and about napalm and B-52s with nuclear weapons threatening Soviet airspace, I was gripped by the suspicion that I didn't know very much about life at all. The same went for the music they played. The singer-songwriters these people knew seemed wise beyond their years: the forlorn, self-loathing 'Motel Blues' by Loudon Wainwright was about trying to pick up girls and bring them back to dismal rooms with 'Styrofoam ice buckets', lust and loneliness masquerading as love. They'd learnt every creaky old blues anthem from the Deep South, mournful tunes as grizzled as time itself about a fate-filled life you couldn't adjust – 'this old world is almost done' ran the chorus of a Blind Willie Johnson tune. Hear a ponytailed war survivor playing 'Death Don't Have No Mercy In This Land' by Reverend Gary Davis – the wine, the wind in the trees, the moon on the mountains, the smell of woodsmoke – and you keep very quiet about your Jethro Tull albums. I'd never felt so provincial in all my nineteen years. I came from a cultureless town full of dogs and dishwashers; these people felt like they'd been born on the prairies or hewn from the living rock. Compared to the soul-mining laments of Leadbelly and Mississippi John Hurt, the universe of Slade and Budgie now seemed grotesquely embarrassing. Even the shiny futuristic visions of David Bowie seemed shallow and artificial. What *in God's name* had I been doing watching him and Mick Ronson capering about on *Top of the Pops* in space suits when I could have been probing the fathomless depths of Howlin' Wolf?

I used to collect blues 78s in junk shops with Ramblin' Will Thompson. What had derailed me from this noble mission to gawp at Quintessence?

7

Playing Reggae To The Chickens

At some stage the middle-class teenage commune-dweller has to make a decision: is he going to spend the rest of his life building some free-range Shangri-La in a place with no gas or running water, or is he going to come back down his mountain and attend the nice, centrally-heated university that's been kind enough to offer him a place?

Oxford in 1973 looked something like this. My college, Pembroke, was made up of four main student types. There were the science and maths intellectuals who spent most of the day in the library. There were the roaring public-school toffs in blazers who did rowing and went out with girls called Antonia. There were the friendly, conscientious types in jerseys who joined a lot of clubs and went on demonstrations. And there was us, the pretentious arts brigade, who wore flares and gave thanks daily that the government was paying us to loaf about on lawns all day reading the collected works of Shelley.

A sub-section of the arts wing were glam-rockers, who had feather-cuts and wore knotted scarves, high-waisted baggies and either clomping great platties or clattering wooden clogs. They invited me over to their rooms to eat biscuits, drink instant coffee and listen to *Aladdin Sane*, where I tapped a respectful toe but didn't have the nerve to say I'd grown out of David Bowie and thought he was rubbish. Then again they didn't much care for American rock, like the Allman Brothers and The Ozark Mountain Daredevils, but were too polite to say anything either. Rock fans *needed* each other, safety in numbers. There was no point in falling out. They expressed their allegiance to Bowie and Mott The Hoople via the extravagance of their clothes – the more colour, the more scarves, the more eyeliner, the more committed they appeared to be. For us it was about the length of our hair, every inch of which was crucial. The longer your hair, the deeper your dedication to raising the flag of the counter-culture in the face of its capitalist oppressors – apart from the ones who organised student grants. One bloke in the third year had a mane almost a yard long and a riotous bushy beard; we nodded respectfully whenever he passed and gave a silent thumbs-up.

Life looked up a notch when I went to the Duke Of Cambridge one night in Little Clarendon Street and saw a girl standing on a bar-stool by the jukebox singing along to 'California Dreamin'' by The Mamas & The Papas. She had a beer bottle for a microphone. When this got a round of applause, she stuck another coin in and encored with a belting version of 'The Night Has A Thousand Eyes' by Brylcreemed sixties pin-up Bobby Vee – bells, whistles, the works. She had long, centre-parted hair and some Marlboro Lights and called everybody 'darling'. She was Anji Hunter, people told me, and she looked like an awful lot of fun.

We knocked around together for a few days and discovered we were 'going out'. We rented a house in Chilswell Road and piled in with six others, a seedy residence I tried to turn into another commune by buying sacks of cut-price vegetables and installing some bone-idle chickens in the back garden. Rival college households had laughable rotas pinned to their kitchen walls to co-ordinate domestic chores – 'Mondays: Boo and Jim. Tuesdays: Jezzer and Kate. Wednesdays: Acid Al and Vanda . . .' There'd be none of that bollocks at our place. Being radical free-thinkers not scene-crushing *drags*, we hammered out a series of brave new rules, to wit:

* No buying or cooking of food unless you feel like it.
* Ditto washing-up.
* We must find a stray dog and invite it to live with us.
* An extension speaker will be set up by the hen-house playing reggae to encourage egg-production.
* No more than five people per night can crash in the sitting-room.
* *Twelve Dreams Of Dr Sardonicus* by Spirit must be played at least three times a day as it's 'a statement of unparalleled genius'.

The main architect of these doomed philosophies was me. Within days this system had sunk into chaos and I couldn't bear to admit it. Some self-serving gene in humankind seemed to make it unworkable, its death-knell sounded by the arrival of a note in the fridge saying, 'Pete's Cheese: Hands Off!' Another deadly blow was dealt to my fresh-faced pride a few days later when a door-to-door salesman pressed the bell. The entire household was downstairs in a scented haze of smoke and unwashed crockery. I stood manfully in the doorway – with my tangled ringlets and all-weather trench-coat – and he looked me up and down.

"Allo, sweetheart,' he said. 'Is Mummy in?'

I leant back gently to close the living-room door but the damage was done. Great howls of deathless mirth filled the air. There were worse things in life than being mistaken for a tall, fat-faced girl without a hairbrush but for quite a while I couldn't think of any.

Music was the soundtrack to everything at Chilswell Road, every moment, every action, every conversation. It telegraphed the mood, it governed every second of the day and night. I woke up, padded down to the living room, stepped over someone asleep with their head in an ashtray, lifted the stylus from last night's un-ejected album – *doonk-sher, doonk-sher* – and dropped it back at the beginning, inhaling the rich aroma of warm vinyl and overheated valves. The day couldn't start unless there was a record playing. It was like oxygen. We couldn't function without it. There'd be barn-storming singles by Free and Tina Turner to nudge the house into motion; at night there'd be Stevie Wonder, the Steve Miller Band, Bob Marley and, in the soft hours of dawn, you'd hear the faint strains of a singer-songwriter from other rooms – Nick Drake or Joni Mitchell or J. J. Cale or, if someone's boyfriend was away, Al Stewart or Cat Stevens. I'd lie awake listening to car tyres on the wet road outside and the eerie murmur of 'Days Of Pearly Spencer' by David McWilliams playing in some distant corner of the house, a haunting single we all adored about a shoeless child in a broken tenement which had brooding strings and a chorus that sounded like it was sung through a megaphone.

But living together brought a whole new dimension to the musical experience: compromise. I was twenty years old and I'd never met this before. I'd always played whatever I wanted whenever I fancied hearing it, but now our albums were racked side by side on planks and bricks in our bedroom it was a very different story. Anji was nineteen and thought music was designed for singing, jubilation and annoying the neighbours. It *wasn't* designed for chin-stroking scrutiny and earnest contemplation. If it didn't have a practical purpose, forget it. It had never crossed my mind until I met her that Frank Zappa was anything other than a cryptic genius working at the coalface of the avant-garde, rather than a hideous dullard who upended groupies and wrote lewd songs about it. Captain Beefheart was not, apparently, a brave sonic explorer patrolling the outer limits of self-expression but a crashing bore whose death-rattle vocal could curdle milk and whose music knotted the knees and brought dance-floors to a shuddering halt. Roy Harper wasn't popular either, another hero of mine. For weeks on end I listened to no one else, but if she wandered back to find me alone in our bedroom immersed in his epic *Stormcock* or *Flat Baroque and Berserk*, it got very short shrift indeed – 'Darling, the man's a *buffoon*.' Why waste precious time on the 'so-called baroque poetic visions' of a powerfully dull hippie string-twanger when I could be down the pub or at a party?

The girls, led by Anji, soon began to rule the roost. The boys' records were often gonged off amid peals of laughter and the eye-watering sound of a needle being dragged across the grooves by a hurried female hand, the offending disc banished to a cupboard never to see the light of day again. *Nantucket Sleighride* by Mountain lasted less than ten seconds before Anj pointed out they were directionless dolts and nearly all weighed eighteen stone. The girls didn't care if a single got scratched or covered with Marmite as long as you could still dance to it; the boys rarely hoovered or did any tidying up, yet howled with physical pain if so much as a *thumbprint* appeared on our copy of *Can't Buy A Thrill* by Steely Dan.

It pained me to admit it but there was something to be said for her firmly enforced policies. Which, in all honesty, was more fun: four guys nodding intently to a Nick Drake album while arguing about where he'd bought the velvet jacket on the cover, or the living room after the girls had slapped on 'Who's That Lady' by the Isley Brothers and everyone was leaping all over the furniture and trying to punch holes in the ceiling? I began to think she had a point – whatever, it was all clearly part of the general barter of domestic life. There had to be give and take on both sides. One midnight I suggested four of us charged off to Stonehenge to see the summer solstice and she cheerfully agreed. She even did all the driving and sat, with breath-taking patience, on a lump of Neolithic rock while people dressed as druids waved candles and a group called Zorch crunched away gamely on a flatbed truck. I owed her one and I knew it. The next day Quicksilver Messenger Service were hoicked off the turntable with alarming hand-eye co-ordination.

'Darlings, what *is* this nonsense? Boooo*ring*!' she scoffed. 'On and on and on and on. It's just a noise! Golden Earring are playing on Saturday. Who's up for some proper music? *You* for starters,' looking at me.

This monstrous collection of twerps were a laughing-stock for anyone who called themselves a rock connoisseur. First off, they were Dutch and not from somewhere cool like San Francisco. Second, they were vendors of gauche, bantam-weight boogie and one of their number played a twin-necked guitar, an absurd affectation and the reason I'd dropped Led Zeppelin like a hot brick. Third, they were called Golden Earring, for crying out loud, not something amusing like Crabby Appleton or Commander Cody and His Lost Planet Airmen. And fourth – and this hurt – their lead singer looked a lot like finely chiselled godhead Jim Morrison of The Doors and wore shrink-to-fit leather strides, the better to advertise his legendary arse.

'Saturday?' I stammered. 'I've got this essay on Wordsworth and I—'

'Don't be ridiculous, darling, you're coming. The rest of you boys can board the old Mogadon Express with the Ozark Riders of the Purple bloody Mountain or whatever cos Mark and I are off to the New Theatre. To see a man who looks like Jim Morrison in slightly tighter trousers,' she added brightly. 'A man, in fact, who has *the sexiest bum on the planet*!'

Time hangs heavy when Golden Earring await. The days dragged by. It was like looking into a long tunnel with the celebrated rear-end of Barry Hay at the far end of it (*Barry*, for God's sake: what kind of rock name is that?). And word had spread. Men I didn't even know stopped me on the street to laugh or commiserate. This, I was reminded, was an abandonment of principles and a shameful lowering of standards. It was a betrayal of all that was noble in the right-thinking world. It would be ninety minutes of unadulterated torture, probably in a hail of underwear.

There were about five other blokes in the whole place. One was wearing a duffel coat and punched the air now and again in a pathetic attempt to impress his date, but I felt an instant bond with the others. We all wore the hangdog look of a man whose girlfriend was standing on the armrests of her seat screaming at a sex god, a look that said, 'I know, total nightmare, and they can't even play their instruments.' But Anji had driven me to Stonehenge, bless her heart. She'd seen druids. She'd put up with Zorch at four in the morning and it had rained. She'd even come to see Captain Beefheart with me while I jabbered on about how one of his Magic Band played a trombone called 'an air-bass'. I *had* to rise above it, I owed it to her. But I *couldn't*. I'd lost the will to live.

Barry grabbed the microphone and announced their one and only hopeless hit, 'Radar Love'. He'd been driving all night, he sang, his hands wet on the wheel. And it was half past four and he was shifting gear. Barry Hay. Of Golden Earring. In those trousers. Doing 'Radar Love'. This was fucking dreadful.

'We've got a thing that's called "Radar Love",' he said.
Kill me now.

'Oh, look, darling, you'll like this,' Anji shouted sweetly. She jumped down and gave me a nudge. 'Bass solo!'

Some utter clown began a thumb-whacking excursion that seemed to last three weeks while the rest of the band lit ciggies and sat on the drum-riser.

'Good, eh?' She beamed encouragingly. 'And when the

bass guy does his thing then, fingers crossed, the drum chap might have a bash too!'

He did. And in my head he's still doing it.

The other main communal activity was watching *The Old Grey Whistle Test* on our knackered TV set. We'd hold hands and pray while one of us knelt on the carpet wrestling with the wire coat-hanger jammed in the back as an aerial. There'd be a series of bleeps and whistles, and the smiling, bearded figure of the presenter Bob Harris would crackle into life, sitting on a bar stool in adventurous knitwear. Our telly was black and white so we could never tell what colour it was – bright, we reckoned – and its horizontal hold was shot: if I ever met him, I imagined he might have a head like a wedge of cheese and legs three feet to the left of his tank-top. We'd leap round the room when it started, kicking imaginary planets like the jerky little star-man in the title sequence.

'Whispering Bob' sat alone in a cavernous studio that seemed to be made out of plywood. His earnest introductions were barely audible but we loved his sense of commitment. Even if we didn't like the bands he was introducing, we never got to see them anywhere else, and at least he was taking them seriously. We polished up our fond impersonations of him – rhythms sections were always 'tight', bands did 'two cuts from their latest long-player' – and thought he had the best job in the world, sitting there in his gaudy jumpers smoking filter-tips while a peculiar mixture of rock acts filed in to perform for him – Montrose, Lynyrd Skynyrd, the magical Tim Buckley. One night, to raucous male cheering, Captain Beefheart appeared, growling delightfully, and I wrestled frantically with the controls to try to reconnect his polka-dot shirt with his trousers. The girls were less engaged by 'Whispering Bob' and dived, shrieking, behind the sofa when spooky albino blues-monger Johnny Winter loomed into vision, shaken by his ghostly pallor, his beak-like nose and the strange, trailing sleeves of his voluminous silk shirt.

I couldn't help thinking it would be fun to be on *The Old Grey Whistle Test*. And the only way to do that was to get back in a rock band.

8

A Hard Act To Follow

There were three main bands at Oxford in 1974. There was Bluebird, who were studious types playing Steely Dan songs and may have been 'classically trained', and two vaguely political units known as Flying Wedge and Frothy Green Stools. Attend any left-leaning party or banner-filled occupation of a university building and squalls of feedback announced that the Wedge or the unappetising Stools were about to entertain.

All of them had a few numbers they'd written themselves, so I had a crack at this caper and discovered it was harder than I'd imagined. In a fortnight my lustrous song catalogue had only three entries – a weak, twinkly thing called 'The Invisible Girl', a challenging rant called 'Sombrero Fallout' and a fey and ineffectual dirge called 'I'm Flying (And You Are The Sky)' – note the brackets – that goofed about on a chord sequence stolen from Nick Drake. For one sparkling moment I thought they were classics and saw myself performing them in a halo of soft lighting, like John Martyn, but when I tried one out on the Chilswell Road commune they suggested I stick to the bass.

But the best possible thing happened: an old school friend called Adam dropped by to say he'd formed a band that wanted to play covers and they hadn't got a bass guitarist. He had a beard and a mop of blond, shaggy hair and something shy and shrugging about him.

'What are you called?' I wondered.

'Ugly Rumours,' he shrugged.

'Why?'

'Because . . .' and he gave me a quizzical look as if my knowledge of rock's outer reaches fell shamefully short of the mark '. . . because *if* you hold the cover of the Grateful Dead's *From The Mars Hotel* album upside-down in a mirror, the shapes in the stars spell the words "Ugly Rumors". So we're Ugly Rumors,' he shrugged, 'but in English.'

Loose band rehearsals took place in somebody's flat in Jericho, which had an Aubrey Beardsley print on the wall of a man floating above a lily pond holding a woman's head with hair that seemed to be made out of snakes, and the ubiquitous poster of Frank Zappa sitting on a toilet known as 'Zappa On The Crapper'. Adam played rhythm guitar and brought along some Harp lager. Jim played the drums and had a fur coat and a chipped front tooth and never surfaced till 'Cool O'clock'. Al was the frontman, a proper lead guitarist with a knotted scarf, studded biker jacket and a flailing curtain of hennaed hair. He lived in Alma Place off the Cowley Road, which he referred to as Astral Space. We all had Cuban-heeled cowboy boots and spent a rackety afternoon trying to master 'Long Train Running' by Californian weed-enthusiasts the Doobie Brothers and 'Live With Me' by The Rolling Stones.

Within a month we'd cobbled together a set and played a couple of parties but nobody fancied singing. We took it in turns but this demanding activity interfered with the main point of being in *any* group which was posing expansively, waving at girls and wedging lighted ciggies under the top of your guitar strings like Keith Richards. A crisis meeting was held and a decision reached: Ugly Rumours needed someone out front. Anji had an old mate from Edinburgh at St John's College called Tony Blair, who'd managed a band and appeared in revue shows, so we asked him if he'd like to audition.

'Audition' was pitching it a bit high and the moment he arrived, wearing exactly the same boots as we had, he'd effectively got the job anyway. He had a folk-rock look about him – long hair with a fringe – and was keen, organised, quite posh, very funny and started a lot of sentences with the word 'guys'. We'd sent him the set-list so he'd been up half the night with his ear pressed to a speaker transcribing the words and breezed in waving sheaves of handwritten lyrics.

'Guys,' he said, 'great selection! Where's the name from, Ugly Rumours?'

Docked four points: *imagine not knowing that*. There was some tutting and a few raised eyebrows and Adam had to fill him in.

'Any chance of doing "I Don't Want To Talk About It" by Crazy Horse?' Tony wondered. He might have disgraced himself on the upside-down albums front but this was impressive: only the most insanely confident singer of a college rock band would dare suggest a ballad, let alone an obscure one. The audition got under way, two acoustic guitars, an unamplified bass, an upturned wastepaper basket and Tony emoting hard into a microphone that wasn't plugged in. We gave 'Live With Me' a whirl and, as we'd never worked out the words before and made most of them up, I was amazed to discover it was a lascivious tale about well-matured meat and debauchery among the goose-owning upper classes, now delivered in Tony's high, fruity tones with the odd Jagger move thrown in. We signed him up and charged off to The Bear in Alfred Street to drink to our glorious future.

The new five-piece Ugly Rumours began appearing on the party circuit, Al perfecting his gale-force solos and Tony adopting a courageous hoop-necked top that revealed several square inches of bare torso. The only tensions were the endless do-you-tuck-your-flares-into-your-cowboy-boots debates that panicked the ranks seconds before showtime, and the irritating sight of pretty girls in print dresses gathered round the central mike-stand. The set-list usually went like this:

- 'Honky Tonk Women' by the Stones
- The inescapable 'Johnny B. Goode'
- 'Long Train Running' and 'China Grove' by the Doobie Brothers
- 'Take It Easy' by Jackson Browne
- 'I Don't Want To Talk About It', Crazy Horse
- 'Wishing Well' by Free
- 'Live With Me' and 'Brown Sugar' by the Stones

'Guys, guys.' Tony called us together after one show. 'We're OK and everything but we could be *so* much better if we rehearsed!'

His level of enthusiasm was high even by my standards, and this was exceptionally keen, but as we'd been booked to support the well-oiled Bluebird at a benefit for the satirical *Strumpet* magazine, we began bundling our gear onto a little trolley we borrowed from a theatre and pushing it back up to Jericho. Posters featuring a dancing suffragette watched by morose, moustachioed rozzers were run off on a hand-cranked Roneo printer and pinned to trees.

Come to the Strumpet POLICE BALL
sat 8th march
east oxford community centre, cowley rd.
8pm-12 – 35p
featuring bluebird and ugly rumours

Nobody threw anything on the night, radical folk in suede shoes and military jackets clapped quite loudly and this whole Police Ball business clearly got to Tony.

'Listen, guys, you know these college balls that are twenty

guineas a pop and have dodgems and funfairs and slightly second-rate groups like Caravan, right? Why don't we do an *alternative* one? Pints of beer, quid to get in, Ugly Rumours top of the bill?'

The Corpus Christi Alternative College Ball was held on a cloudless June evening on a scented lawn with a rose garden. Anji wore a billowy blue frock and a felt hat. The ticket price included three bands, tins of lager, wine from bottles with plastic stoppers and saucers of Twiglets and Smarties. In a freewheeling attempt to be 'far out' we'd booked a string quartet to open the show – they looked a bit like Van Morrison's Caledonia Soul Orchestra, long-haired girls in flowing dresses – followed by a trad jazz band of old duffers in their forties wearing straw hats and striped blazers, rich irony in the grand carnival tradition of the Rolling Stones' *Rock And Roll Circus*. The idea was you could watch this cheesy, toe-tapping fare from the terrace while gearing up for the white heat of Ugly Rumours.

The crowd thought differently. A few top notes from a trumpet and they poured excitedly onto the grass, flooring cans of Heineken. Two minutes' exposure to these brass-edged stompers and they were hurling themselves about in riotous abandon, blokes in Indian shirts jiving uncontrollably and girls cantering down the little paths among the flower-beds. They were going to be a hard act to follow.

My heart was pounding as we stood and watched. I looked at the five of us, a great heap of split-ends and fag ash in our skinny T-shirts and giant trousers. Apart from Jim, we all had bare feet. We padded out nervously into the setting sun, squashing burning Marlboros into our guitar necks and placing bottles of warm Blue Nun on the top of our amps. The cowbell started up for 'Honky Tonk Women'. We cranked up the riff and gave Tony the nod and he burst from behind a hedge doing his now fairly polished Jagger impression – low-slung flares, bare midriff, one hand on a hip, the other wagging a cautionary finger, elbows flapping like a chicken. A couple of camp handclaps above his head and he pulled the microphone from its stand.

'Well awwwrright Corpus Christi Alternative College Ball, how *are* ya?'

They were fine, thanks, but a bit danced-out by the jazz band.

'Are ya ready for some rock and roll?'

Possibly, but they had to get their breath back first. And that beer wasn't going to drink itself.

We gave it our best shot – 'Wishing Well', 'Long Train Running', 'Johnny B. Goode' – but the moment had passed. No matter how much Al threw his hair about, or Tony said 'Awwwrright!', or Jim whacked his cowbell while looking cool and distant, or Adam grinned bashfully and stamped on his effects pedals, we couldn't fill the lawn like the boater-sporting jazzers. Tony knew it too, and made an announcement I don't remember discussing in the pre-gig huddle.

'Guys, we're going to try something different, OK?'

The crowd lowered their lager cans.

'We're going to bring on the string quartet for a jam . . .'

Scattered applause.

'. . . and let's have a big hand for our brilliant jazz band too. Come on back up, guys!'

Mass jubilant shrieks of delight.

What the hell was *this*? In the interests of creating an 'alternative happening', we were now lumbered with six pensionable goons in cricket blazers who were far better musicians than *we* were. They took up positions next to their opposite number and clearly thought 'game on'. It wasn't easy to look like a rock and roll renegade, the kind of groove-filled maverick who takes his lovin' on the run, when some grinning, moon-faced berk with a ridiculous hat and sideburns was challenging you to a 'bass-off' on 'Brown Sugar'.

It's after events like that, in the long sleepless hours of dawn, that even the most deluded axe-slinger in a college covers act tends to take a long, hard look at himself and ask some tough but quite reasonable questions. Such as this: if I was the least talented member of the fourth best covers group *at a university*, and unlikely to write a better song than 'Sombrero Fallout', how was I ever going to make it as a musician? Whatever uncertain paths lay ahead of the five of us, they wouldn't involve being in rock bands. *The Old Grey Whistle Test* was never going to happen.

But another thought soon crossed my mind. Every year the household trooped off to Knebworth Park in the grounds of an old stately home near Stevenage to see the big summer shows. On our third trip, the Stones were headlining and I wandered down to watch their stage-set being prepared, petrol-driven pumps inflating some lips and a tongue so they could play inside a giant rubber effigy of Mick Jagger's mouth. Nearby was a spacious, fenced-off area where roguish characters in leather jackets were enjoying some cold drinks and forking smoked salmon off paper plates. They had plenty of space and a great view and all wore stickers saying 'PRESS', and I got the strong suspicion it wasn't costing them anything. They probably hadn't paid to get in either or done much queuing. And they weren't going to trudge two miles to the car park or sleep in a hedge.

Allan Jones was in there, I reckoned. I followed his stuff in *Melody Maker*. He was always being bundled onto aircraft with members of Mott The Hoople and seemed to live a charmed life. Everywhere he went, much of it America, world-conquering rock musicians would bare their souls while filling him to the brim with steak and vodka. And he'd be on a wage for this, and expenses too. In one of his recent articles he was being ferried from a festival beer tent to one of these delightful press enclosures in an electric buggy. As it trundled past acres of the great unwashed – people like me, crammed in a field – it bumped over a tiresome tussock and spilt his gin and tonic. Mercifully this landed in the pint of beer the excellent Jones was holding in his other hand.

Surely this was the dream ticket. You wrote about music you liked. You met the people who made it. You could evangelise about the Mott The Hooples of tomorrow and would, I imagined, be showered with free records and carried shoulder-high above life's irksome hurly-burly on a sedan chair made of banknotes.

I wanted, badly, to be on that side of the fence.

Somewhere, somehow, someday soon, I was going to bust into that world.

9

Punk Rock Meets The Green Velvet Jacket

Were a passing pigeon to have flown over Abercrombie Street in the autumn of '77, over its smashed roof tiles, crumbling chimneys and weed-choked gardens, and directed its gaze at the upper window of number 72, it would have seen the author of this book bashing at a portable typewriter.

The residence of choice for the cash-strapped, post-campus bums of Battersea was this moss-covered stretch of Victorian terrace behind the Latchmere Theatre. The council tenants were slowly being re-accommodated so the whole road could be sold to the private sector. One by one the places became empty and were occupied by squatters. When your name reached the top of the 'alternative housing list', you grabbed a crowbar, nipped down the railway line, prised open a back window and changed the locks.

'Applecrumble Street', as it was known, was rapidly filling with low-earning fantasists like me, mostly musicians, writers and half-arsed 'resting actors', all working in bars and planning our romantic world-beating trajectories, in my case scaling the walls of the music press. A peculiar fragrance hung in the air at my house, thick and heady – mould, cabbage and woodsmoke, with top notes of dry rot and drains. Stagnant water pooled on its rotting lino floor and bacteria jostled for position on every surface. The meter was rigged so there weren't any bills and someone had nicked all the lead plumbing and replaced it with dripping hosepipe. At the end of our back yard was a signal-box. I'd lie awake listening to the clanking of its levers and the nostalgic sound of the trains rumbling past in the night. The outside loo had no door so I'd be engrossed in reading some thunderous editorial in *ZigZag* and look up to find carriages squeaking slowly by, their windows full of happy people all pointing and laughing.

Apart from *ZigZag*, there were four other main music papers, all weekly, and I kept them in piles on my bedroom floor. There was *Record Mirror*, a forlorn-looking rag with weird-smelling ink that came off on your fingers. It had never quite made the shift from singles to albums and read like it wished it was back in 1965 at a Hollies reception, or asking Sandie Shaw why she never wore any shoes. There was the lager-chewing *Sounds*, which flew the flag for heavy metal and tattooed punk urchins, and was soon to be championing mod revivers in skinny ties and the leaders of their latest invention, the Oi Movement, part-terrace brawlers and part-skinhead herberts like the fragrant Stinky Turner of the Cockney Rejects. There was *Melody Maker*, home of Allan Jones, which had shaken off its gauche mid-seventies news agenda – 'Bay City Bonkers!', 'Wings Metal Fatigue!' – and relaxed the house rule that its writers all had to be musicians or they weren't qualified to be critics. It now offered high-octane analysis by college graduates unafraid of a seven-eight time-signature. And, of course, there was *New Musical Express*, mass-market political soapbox for pop-cultural activists trying to take more speed than Joe Strummer.

NME was at the top of its game. It pulled off the sublime trick of ploughing brave new furrows in language and self-expression while, at the same time, cementing public opinion. Its power and influence were phenomenal. If the *NME* called Bryan Ferry of Roxy Music a posturing, sports-car-steering, *faux*-poetic lounge-lizard – which they did, nicknaming him 'Byron Ferrari' – then he was guilty until proved innocent. In the same way, if they declared The Slits or the Tom Robinson

Band to be the noble saviours of Planet Rock, then huge swathes of the populace would believe them. It sold a quarter of a million copies a week and each had three or four readers.

NME, then, was the place to be but if you rang them up and actually got through to anyone, they'd never commission you as they hadn't the faintest idea who you were. The only way forward, I figured, was to wear them down with my enthusiasm and availability. If I bombarded them with reviews of new acts every day then eventually I'd stumble on a band they liked and they might just print it. I washed dishes in a King's Road bar in the daytime and each night bought tickets to see anyone that sounded interesting – mod-warriors The Jolt or the 'dub-rock-shaped' Local Operator – and charged back to the squat to rattle off reams of florid prose. I'd feed a sheet into the little Remington and tap out a few lines with a flourish . . .

> 'The Saints have sprouted horns! Yes, the hard-gigging Ozzie six-piece blew the lid off the Marquee in support of their long-awaited debut album – devilish punk meets pop-soul with buzz-saw guitars. They're like The Members plus brass and some Stax-esque B-sides – in a blender. Move over, Boomtown Rats, your time is up!'

I'd read this back and picture it printed in *NME*. There it was with my name at the bottom. I could see myself in the office, another pin-sharp contrarian changing the face of rock scholarship! Maybe I'd get to meet Ian Dury and The Blockheads, like they all seemed to, or travel on The Stranglers' tour bus. Then I'd chuck another lump of skip-sourced wood on the fire, give the page a second glance and it would seem like gibberish. I'd tear it from the machine, ball it up and hurl it on the flames. Eventually I'd finish it, type up two copies, hand one in at *NME* the next morning and the other, for good measure, at *Record Mirror* where the girls on Reception gave me the kindly, pitying look they reserved for anyone who'd just moved to London and had a green velvet jacket and eighteen inches of unconditioned hair at the height of punk rock, and promised to pass it to the reviews desk.

One day, surely, the dam would break. And it did, though not quite in the way I'd imagined. After ten days of keen copy delivery, I summoned the courage to ring *Record Mirror* and a muffled conference took place. An anxious voice asked if I could review Elvis Costello and The Attractions at the Nashville Rooms in four hours' time.

'No problem!' I was flabbergasted. 'Am I on the guest list?' I squeaked, trying to sound professional.

'Should be, mate. Five hundred words by first thing, all right? Or maybe *second* thing if it all gets a bit out of order,' he added, with a knowing chuckle.

Second thing. Out of order. Costello presumably adored *Record Mirror* and the great man and I would be carousing all night. I might even get an interview. But one thing puzzled me: The Attractions were the biggest story on the block so why were they sending someone they'd never met? Rock journalism, I assumed, was so exotic they were all out of town – in California with Jefferson Starship or on the M1 with X-Ray Spex – and couldn't even rustle up an office junior for London's event of the week. And this was *enormous*. Costello's first album had arrived in a great whirlwind of publicity. Stiff Records made their fast-rising star seem dark and dangerous, and his shadowy manager, Jake Riviera, was universally reckoned to be terrifying. I bought a spiral-bound notebook to look the part and steamed off to West Kensington on my first commission.

A long queue spilt from the venue onto the Talgarth Road. It had sold out weeks ago but they were hoping for returns.

Strangely my name wasn't on the door and any mention of *Record Mirror* seemed to make things worse, my big break and not the ghost of a chance of even getting in. I wandered back outside to find a teenager in a leather jacket gazing fondly up at a giant poster of Costello taped to the pub window.

'My brother-in-law,' he said proudly.

'You're related to Elvis?' This was quite some claim to fame.

'He's married to my sister, Mary. See this?' He held up a finger with a signet ring. 'Family crest.' He pointed at the picture, the knock-kneed Buddy Holly pose of the album cover. Sure enough, Elvis was wearing the same ring. I saw my chance.

'Mark Ellen from *Record Mirror*!' I shook his hand warmly. '*The* Mark Ellen, yes, indeed! Look, mate, seems to have been a bit of a mix-up in the old ticket department, holding the front page and all that. Don't suppose you could ask your brother-in-law to stick me on the door, could you?'

He dived obligingly into the venue and reappeared seconds later with a familiar wiry figure in glasses and a black trilby. The crowd surged around him, panting for autographs.

'Press?' Elvis eyed me suspiciously. 'Follow me.' I was whisked inside, thrilled to the point of explosion. I spent two hours filling my notebook with everything from the quality of the bar snacks to the finer details of the keyboard sound, then bowled along to the backstage area where I assumed I should get some quotes from the band. The dressing room, smoke-stained and tiny, contained a steaming Elvis, his Attractions, a couple of Ian Dury's unsettling Blockheads, Graham Parker and two of the Rumour: the most terrifying collection of individuals I'd ever seen in my life. A man fitting the description of Jake Riviera was holding court by the entrance – drape coat, boot-lace bow-tie, silver tips on his shirt collar. His hair was gassed back like a rockabilly and he had very sharp boots. Someone was asking him what he'd thought of the support act, the Soft Boys, some rarefied dream-weavers from Cambridge University.

'I smell A-levels,' Jake scoffed, tapping his nose, and the whole place fell about. He looked up, saw me and shot an arm across the door frame. 'What you want?'

'I'm from the press,' I stammered, 'so I just, you know, wanted to check a couple of facts about the set, which I thought *totally amazing* incidentally, and—'

'Press?' His eyes narrowed. 'Which bit of the press?'

'*Record Mirror*.' I licked the tip of my pencil.

The notebook hit the deck and a sharp pain suggested the back of my head had made contact with the wall. I'm pretty sure my feet were off the floor. The room spun noisily, then stopped in a chilling silence. Jake had me pinned by the lapels and was banging me rhythmically against the brickwork while bawling like a drill sergeant.

'We HATE' *bang!* '*RECORD* fucking *MIRROR*!' *Bang! Bang!*

'Fair enough,' I spluttered.

'And do you know what else we hate?'

I didn't, no, and the banging continued.

'We HATE fucking HIPPIES' *bang!* 'with LONG HAIR and GREEN VELVET fucking JACKEEEETS!'

And I was out, kicked out of the door and stumbling down the North End Road.

As I wobbled towards Battersea Bridge, various thoughts battled for supremacy in my overheated head:

1. I owed Elvis's brother-in-law several drinks: anyone sent to review a concert they fail to attend is unlikely to make much professional headway.

2. There must be less life-threatening outposts of the
   music press than *Record Mirror*.
3. Perhaps velvet jackets *were* a bit 'Byron Ferrari'
   circa '74.
4. This whole writing caper was a far cry from the
   soft-pencil, sleeve-gartered notions of journalism I'd
   picked up from watching Jack Lemmon in *The Front Page*.
5. Maybe *this* was what they'd meant by 'a bit out of
   order'.

Shell-shocked, quivering and looking for something to blame,
I ripped off the offending jacket, hurled it into a bin and
walked four miles in the freezing cold back to Applecrumble
Street. I had my hair radically shorn first thing in the morning
and, second thing, delivered my glowing review to the
newspaper's Long Acre bunker where, for once, I was allowed
past Reception.

'Hallo, friend. How'd it go?' Quite a crowd had gathered,
eyeing me with interest.

'Brilliant!' I announced. 'To these ears, Costello's hard-
working four-piece gave a good account of themselves, even
foisting a brace of crack new tunes upon the unsuspecting
public. Never in the history of rock's rich tapestry . . .'

'Any trouble?' someone cut in cautiously.

Assuming trouble was par for the course, I gave them the
whole nine yards, the head-bashing sequence already at that
transitional stage between soul-scarring trauma and passable
pub anecdote. Was there, I wondered, any particular reason
for last night's violence or was it just the rock equivalent of
a warm handshake?

They stared at their feet and did some shuffling. There
was, they admitted. Following their snivelling dismissal of
Costello's *My Aim Is True*, they'd been rung by Riviera,
incandescent with rage. He'd told them he would 'personally

murder' anyone from *Record Mirror* if they dared set foot in the Nashville.

'Good work, mate,' one of them said, patting me on the back. 'You should do more stuff for us.'

A Storm In A T-Shirt

The Costello review appeared on 28 December 1977. I ran
all the way home from the newsagent's. I must have read
it a hundred times. I scoured the listings and showered
Record Mirror with more suggestions which I scribbled in
my diary . . .

- Thursday: Cado Belle (Dingwalls) or Earthquake?
- Friday: Medium Wave Band (Dingwalls) or Advertising
  at the Pegasus?
- Saturday: Deke Leonard's Iceberg (Chelsea Coll)
- Sunday: Pekoe Orange (Rock Garden)
- Monday: Dead Fingers Talk (Music Machine)
- Tuesday: Boyfriends (Dingwalls) or Siouxsie and The
  Banshees?

My fizzing reports of the week's hot properties like Staa Marx
and the Fabulous Poodles began appearing – one credited to
'Mark Ellan' – along with an eight-pound cheque for each
but, two months later, *NME* printed one of my reviews too,
a piece about some R&B stooges called Supercharge I'd
dropped off weeks before. The opening line wasn't my finest
– 'Supercharge are at large once again in Blighty and on the
evidence of tonight's show at the Music Machine they ought
to be a whole lot larger!' – but it was in and I boiled over
with joy. Editor Nick Logan, I later discovered, had been
laying out the last pages and had found my purple prose
among some sheets of A4 being trodden into the carpet and

thought it might fill a hole. Such were the random mechanics of the rock press: no work experience, written references or dissertations on Syd Barrett required, the boss simply peeled your copy off somebody's shoe. Whatever, the door was ajar now and they sometimes took my calls.

Getting to *NME*'s Carnaby Street compound in the spring of '78 involved a warring cacophony of sound and a parade of poor-quality clothing. The punk shops sold tartan bum flaps, gashed jeans with zips and safety pins, plastic jackets, crêpe-soled shoes and hole-filled mohair jumpers in luminous greens and pinks. The Clash, The Damned, The Pistols and The Banshees poured from their tinny speakers, and geezers with spiked hair and studs in their noses offered you blurred posters of the doomed Sid Vicious and his girlfriend Nancy Spungen. Across the way the mod outlets fought back with their Jam singles, mixed with a dash of The Who, and draped their window-dummies in Harrington jackets and shiny three-button suits. Beside these were boutiques full of stretchable boob-tubes and nylon miniskirts, which played Boney M, Chic, 10cc and the Bee Gees' 'Stayin' Alive' on a loop, and 'Wuthering Heights' by Kate Bush. I sprang through this symphony up the pungent stairwell of number 5–7 Carnaby Street and into Reception where the twenty-year-old Danny Baker was manning the console, a handsome, cheery soul in a big-collared shirt and waistcoat.

'City morgue!' he'd hoot, snatching a ringing phone. 'You stab 'em, we slab 'em!', an echo of The Doors' Jim Morrison when anyone rang his parents in California ('Morrison's Mortuary – you kill 'em, we chill 'em!'). I pictured the mystified manager of Bachman-Turner Overdrive on the other end somewhere in Marin County, scratching his head and wondering if he'd got the right number. I strolled past nervously to drop off my copy, thrilled and terrified by life on the inside. The whole place smelt of smoke, sweat and instant coffee, and everyone seemed monumentally cool because they worked for *NME*. The mess was overwhelming, even if you lived in a squat – piles of detritus, cups, overflowing ashtrays, empty beer cans, torn Jiffy-bags, half-eaten sandwiches in paper wrappers, and mounds of vinyl posted by optimistic press officers. Music crackled from every corner, people yelling above the din, a clattering of typewriters, a forlorn bleating of unanswered phones.

Various luminaries floated about. The expansive Vivien Goldman would dispense tales from the reggae battlefield with the wry and entertaining Chris Salewicz, both flown by record companies to Kingston, Jamaica, for weeks on end to point a microphone at Bob Marley, nice work if you could get it. Another dub evangelist, new editor Neil Spencer, wandered occasionally from his inner sanctrum speaking in a strange white-rasta patois – he left one lunchtime with the immortal words 'I an' I step out feh sandwich.' Punk rock hadn't quite erased his hippie roots – when someone asked him what he thought of Ireland he said it had 'a lot of happy cows'. Photographer Pennie Smith drifted about silently, dark-eyed and mysterious, and in the corner was the rough-hewn figure of Monty Smith who was loudly opposed to 'pretentious bollocks' and counting the days to the next Ian Dury album. The star new recruits were Ian Penman and Paul Morley, both engaged in a fierce competition to stick the English language in a tumble dryer. 'Pinmoon' looked like a young W. C. Fields and once ended a piece about the echoing world of dub reggae with the deathless phrase 'tomorrow-morrow-orrow-rrow-ow-w'. Morley penned gigantic tracts that analysed himself almost as much as the music. Delightfully energised, drunk on the size of his readership, half in love with the bands he wrote about, he was dispatched one week to Los Angeles and filed eight thousand words of charged and insomniac prose about this hollow, concrete Babylon and its bastard offspring, the art-rockers Devo. Those trying to scrape a three-hundred-word assignment for The Mekons at the Half Moon in Putney could only gawp with envy.

Occasionally someone poked their head from the windowless 'reviews room' in the middle of the office with an observation about a new Cure single and some lofty exchanges took place.

'The Cure? Derivative cod-glam disposable shite,' they'd declare, a herb-scented fog billowing behind them.

'Dream-like soundscapes, a haunting return to form,' a second would counter.

'The Skids on bad acid,' came a third.

It was like university with louder music, an intellectual snobbery where everyone announced their musical taste as a statement rather than an opinion to be debated, bull elephants battling it out in the pampas grass. I was too nervous to join these debates for fear of shooting down a sacred cow like Joy Division or gushing unguardedly about some hopeless old has-beens, like Slade, and being tagged 'distinctly uncool'.

There was always a crackle of electricity when any of the Big Four dropped by. One was former *Oz* magazine wonk and underground press legend Charles Shaar Murray, possessed of a giant afro and making gnomic pronouncements through a haze of filter-tips. A master of the comic one-liner, he once noted the lugubrious features of The Who's Pete Townshend looked like 'your own face reflected in the back of a spoon'. Charlie wore the full rock-scribe fig – denim and studded leather with big boots and a permanent pair of shades. It was like a uniform, as if he was on-call twenty-four hours a day and might get tapped up any minute to head off to Heathrow with the Pretenders. I imagined he dressed like that all the time, even when he went to the shops for a pint of milk.

Occasionally he'd allow the shiny-faced juniors to follow him to a greasy spoon where he'd regale us with hair-curling stories of Stones tours and towering theories about the rise of punk rock.

Another luminary came tottering in on black stilettos, petite and spindly with a voice to match, delivering barbed maxims in a West Country accent through a slash of lipstick. Everything Julie Burchill said was combative and scarily principled. She was eighteen and seemed to be on a mission to expose fraud and deceit, reserving large amounts of ammunition for punk sloganeers Sham 69 whose singer claimed to be a Cockney despite hailing from the village of Hersham. 'It must have been a bloody strong wind that blew the sound of Bow bells to Surrey,' she once told the office. Julie thought expenses and free gifts threatened her integrity as a writer, and meeting rock stars in the flesh compromised her opinions. 'Most readers only know bands through records and the radio,' she told me while we waited for the kettle to boil. 'We should be the same.' I rather liked the idea of 'ligs' and 'freebies' and getting pissed with musicians while record companies paid for it so I wasn't expecting this sort of self-sacrifice, but if you mentioned it to the others they'd point up her penchant for speed. 'Been on the old Berwick-on-Tweed again,' they'd say, tapping a nostril. Her boyfriend, however, was less ideological. Six years older, gruff, tough and intimidating, Tony Parsons pinballed round the place in a James Dean T-shirt recounting fresh adventures on the road with the Pistols, again fuelled by thick lines of 'Berwick'.

The fourth big star was the magnificent Nick Kent, whose arrival was preceded by great waves of expectation, especially among the girls. Would he be wearing his ripped leather trousers and, if so, any pants beneath them? He'd finally levered himself off heroin but was so enfeebled by his methadone habit that the fine details of his physical appearance weren't a high priority. His legendary lack of undergarments wasn't a fashion statement: he'd either forgotten to attach any or didn't own a pair in the first place. Kent would wobble through reception in a stained hat, an off-white scarf that could have done with a wash, a Johnny Thunders T-shirt, jangling biker boots and severely torn trousers, a brace of swinging testicles visible from round the back. He had the crepuscular pallor of a nine-pint blood donor and legs like a wading bird's, so stick-thin and rickety you thought his knees might bend the wrong way. One hand brandished a glowing butt, the other several sheets of cardboard from cereal packets with his latest *meisterwerk* on them in spidery scrawl. His overstretched pockets carried two tins of cling peaches, the only solids apart from corn flakes the drug-addicted scribe could stomach.

Kent was 'under heavy manners'. The editors had declared he could no longer submit hand-written copy so, wounded and complaining, he'd pay me a fiver to hammer out his scripts on a manual typewriter while he spooned his peaches straight from the can and loosed off colourful yarns about naked girls on fur rugs ignited when Keith Richards dropped a candelabra, or withering asides about some halfwit from the current rock circus who'd incurred his displeasure, usually Billy Idol of Generation X. I loved his elegant prose and his vast embroidered sentence constructions that rose to a multisyllabic flourish – any quote from Iggy ended 'declares the indefatigable Pop'. My toes curled with enchantment at his Kentian clichés – rock stars were inevitably 'in an advanced state of chemical refreshment' or, if they'd fought the law and lost, 'languishing disconsolately at Her Majesty's Pleasure'.

It was hard to catch up. In most of the places I'd worked, people showered regularly, wore underwear and had no clinical need for tinned fruit. And they weren't obsessed with

Aged 11 in 1965, imagining I'm 'the new Donovan'.

The Ellen family camping on the Isle Of Skye in '63, energised by an invisible keyboard – (from left) Mum, Zacky, Dad, Cath and me with a canvas bucket on my head.

The full line-up, taken with Dad's spiffy new self-timing camera, with eldest sister Al far left.

A quivering snap of my first rock
concert, Soft Machine at the Chalk Farm
Roundhouse, bassist Hugh Hopper (far left)
drinking warm Liebfraumilch from
the bottle: there was *so* much to learn.

Hampshire's skiffle-blues revival of
1970 was surprisingly short-lived
– (from left) Dave Willcox, Penny
Cotter, 'Mississippi' Mark Ellen,
Ramblin' Will Thompson.

Windswept world-changing hippies at
Oxford in '74, Anji Hunter and I at the top, a
rare moment when we're not all listening to
Twelve Dreams Of Dr. Sardonicus by Spirit.

Knebworth Festival, 1975: Captain Beefheart and his Magic Band move Anji to polite applause.

With Mary, fellow inmate of Chilswell Road. Note key fashion statements of the time – roll-up, ironic silk tie, dog on lead.

The male members of the 'commune' express their individuality through clothing, 1975. In our heads we're the Allman Brothers Band. Reggae-loving chickens not pictured.

(Above) Poster advertising Ugly Rumours at a benefit for the left-leaning Strumpet Magazine, and (clockwise from top left) the four other members of this unfearsome rock unit – lead-player Al, drummer Jim, rhythm guitarist Adam and singer Tony.

Still at college in '76 wrestling with existential woe: inspired by the cover of Syd Barrett's The Madcap Laughs, I've painted my floorboards. And I've painted my shoes blue, possibly a step too far.

Some romantic notion of rock journalism made me take this snap of my desk in the Applecrumble Street squat in December '77, the day my first piece appeared in *Record Mirror*.

The typewriter moves to the Roach Motel where I'm failing miserably to be the *NME*'s new Nick Kent, visited by old pal Mary. You can see the garden where many a Dr. Hook 12-inch died in the 'clay pigeon shoot'.

(Above) The only shot of Anton Corbijn and I in the late '70s: I'm wearing his clothes (right) in the picture he took for our piece about how 'air synthesiser' might replace 'air guitar'.

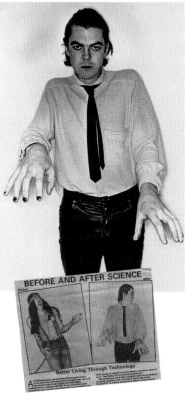

BEFORE AND AFTER SCIENCE

Better Living Through Technology

Pretending to play sax in a Nona Hendryx video. Her promotional picture doesn't do us justice: she's got a monstrous yellow top on and silk jodhpurs and I'm in a powder-blue zoot suit.

ROCK BIZ PIX   NONA HENDRYX

Enjoying the hospitality in the Knebworth press enclosure in '78 and heading for the shameful Slept-Through-Jefferson-Starship live review incident.

Sparkling Cider O'Clock!: no expense spent for a sales-celebrating *Smash Hits* news picture in '83. Ian 'Amanalone' Birch is far left, Lisa Anthony of the Saturday Girls below him with Sam 'On Target' Archer, and Neil Tennant in the middle. You can see the *NME* office the other side of Carnaby Street through the window.

The editor at his desk, a 'Lulu' promotional coffee mug close at hand.

Clare and I with the *Smash Hits* staff at our wedding in '82, Dave Hepworth (far left) leading an outbreak of the Madness' Nutty Train. There's a touch of Noel Coward about Neil and his tea cup.

rubbishing the past before they could build a better future. *NME*'s contempt for the mid-seventies was contagious. Fearful FM-radio wibble I'd loved like the Steve Miller Band now seemed like a howling embarrassment. The paper poured as much energy into tearing up the old world as trumpeting the new one, as if ashamed it ever liked it originally, a practice Charlie Murray called 'barbecuing the dinosaurs'. The same writers who'd adored the prog giants and rock monsters now hitched their carts to the punk bandwagon and were drawing a bead on the old regime as if they were eighteenth-century French aristocracy, milk-fed pompous nincom poops destined for a painful execution. Only a handful were spared, earth-wires like David Bowie, Iggy Pop and Lou Reed. Everyone else was a war criminal – Rod Stewart, Eric Clapton, 'Byron Ferrari', Paul McCartney. You might as well have pinned their faces on a 'Wanted' poster and filled it full of lead. If *NME* chewed upon its goose quill and declared *Marquee Moon* by Television 'a masterpiece', people thought it had a point. If it leant from its ivory tower to tip chamberpots upon The Eagles, Thin Lizzy and Blue Oyster Cult, maybe it was time to follow suit.

But I hadn't expected the office politics. I'd imagined the place would be some kind of Algonquin Round Table of convivial debate where cheerful fellow enthusiasts sought out new music for the common good. This was miles off-track. It was mostly blokes whose personalities were still under construction – as mine was – trying to figure out which sub-section they belonged to. There were arts ghettos, 'new pop' divisions, political chapels, weed-scented reggae factions, Kraut-rock contingents, Mancunian funk zones, pub-rock strongholds, none of them remotely interested in the other's point of view. There was even a 'Beer Crew' energetically fronted by Monty Smith who'd troop off at lunchtimes to any pub with a landlord he hadn't fallen out with to talk about football and Dr Feelgood, their thirsty leader often 'doing the gallon'. Others awaited the monthly arrival of a freelance who lived in the country and had a flourishing herb garden; he'd stroll among the desks delivering 'baggies' of a particular crop. To the outside world it was a glamorous 'forum for debate' but inside it was fractious and a bit exhausting, a gaggle of eccentrics with the best job in the world locked in low-level warfare. Occasionally there were fist-fights and typewriters chucked out of windows. Even the Beer Crew had their mournful moments. Danny Baker's dad once bowled up to the Sun and 13 Cantons in Beak Street to find his boy and the rest of the gang nursing their pints in silence, knackered by the grinding altercations of the office. He looked a bit baffled returning from the bar with a round.

'Doesn't produce much fucking conversation your line of work, does it?'

In fact, Danny was the only one who ever rose above the air of factionalism, fast-tracked from Reception and now another of *NME*'s star turns. He belonged to every camp and none of them. Working-class, like Parsons and Burchill, he didn't give a toss about the paper's brow-mopping existential woe. He liked any kind of music. As far as Baker was concerned, Rick Wakeman, The Ramones and Earth, Wind & Fire *all* added to the gaiety of nations, and he quoted aloud from the novels of P. G. Wodehouse, where the drowsy stillness of afternoons among the landed gentry could be 'shattered by what sounded like G. K. Chesterton falling on a sheet of tin'. He lampooned the old guard too but with the softest of touches – one of Pink Floyd's hour-long stage projections looked like 'an apple decomposing'.

The collision between the mid- and late-seventies played out on stages all over town. I went to the Marquee one night where four types in matching boiler-suits called Roogalator were plying their complex pub-rock and I could feel their audience melting away. The wind had changed. The harder they worked, the more pointless it sounded. Six months earlier I would have loved them, now they had the doomed aspect of that great Turner painting *The Fighting Temeraire* in which a ghostly, outmoded sailing-ship is towed to the breaker's yard by a new-fangled steamboat. Their faces didn't fit. No one wanted musical proficiency, especially from anyone over twenty-five with a Steely Dan album. I went back a few days later and the place was packed. Cartoon punk act Slaughter and The Dogs were onstage rubbishing every aspect of the outside world with three chords and some cheap theatre. A knot of spike-topped supporters sprang about trying to nut the light fittings, but the club was mostly full of blokes in denim jackets wanting to see what all the fuss was about. A hail of phlegm showered the stage as they delivered their B-side 'You're A Bore'.

Behind me was Chris Welch from *Melody Maker*, the legend who'd championed Cream, Yes and Deep Purple. He must have been thirty years old. He was being nudged gently into the fray by the band's publicists, his hoofs dug in like a panicked pit-pony entering the seventh stomach of Hell.

11

'Move Too Fast And You're In The Past'

Outside the office, life was good. No intimidating section editors, no constant tyranny of cool for the freelance at the bottom of the food-chain. I went in occasionally to drop off my copy, frantically re-scribbled on the bus, and hurled myself into the all-consuming world of the trainee rock writer.

Motorbikes from record companies would rumble to my door with foot-square packages full of test-pressings of albums coming out months later, 'white labels' that appeared with badges, stickers, publicity pictures and little handwritten notes from PRs I'd never met with names like Toni which they signed with a string of hearts and a smiley face in the *o*. Pre-release records had a particular cachet.

'The new Ruts' album's just arrived!' I'd tell a friend.

'Never heard of them.'

'Angry and challenging punk four-piece, signed to Virgin.'

'Sounds dire.'

'It's not out till March.'

'*Stick it on!*'

Live reviews were my main source of income. One week I saw twenty-seven bands, nine on one day at the Reading Festival when they were experimenting with a new twin-stage which allowed one act to play while the next was setting up. Sham 69 supporters were packed on the left and their bitter rivals, the Jam fans, below the one on the right, a cordoned-off pizza-slice of grass between the two serving as a press enclosure. Each side rained missiles and insults on the other until dusk when the barriers broke and the Sham Army came windmilling over the railings. Panicked reviewers dashed down a passage below the boards to the backstage area, one with a leaking head wound. Violence was a regular fixture at gigs, as it was on the football terraces; some writers talked with the hardened air of war reporters, as if mentally wearing a flak-jacket – 'You should have been at the Pistols in The Nashville Rooms, mate. It all kicked off *big*-time!'

My parents' idea of a rock concert was based solely on *Top of the Pops* and they struggled to picture my working environment.

'Do you just jig around with the other dancers while the music's playing?' Mum wondered, on one of the rare occasions I rang home.

'I don't "jig around", Mother. I'm a professional writer! I'm a rock critic, read by millions! I'll have you know I'm being sent to Birmingham next week on an *assignment*,' though I stopped short of telling her it was a group called Bram Tchaikovsky's Battleaxe.

'Your father says *The Times* are looking for new writers. And *Punch*.'

'Mum! Dad!'

Occasionally I'd be asked to write a news story, which required 'doing a phoner', a problem as the house in Applecrumble Street had no phone. I got the inside of a loo-roll, cut it in half and made a hole in the side, pushed a microphone into it, wedged it between my ear and the receiver and managed to tape the odd quote above the noise of angry queue members banging on the window of my foul-smelling phone-booth, wondering how much longer I was going to be. I'd ram a coin in while the PR put me through and try to wrap it all up before the money ran out.

'So, Chrissie Hynde, if you were to sum up your career in just one sentence . . .'

Pip-pip-pip-pip-pip . . .

Pause.

Hynde (*aggrieved*): 'Are you in a *call box*?'

I tried to be professional but I didn't know what professional was. I poked my cassette-recorder gingerly at rock bands and was thrilled I'd simply got them talking, then transcribed screeds of nervy, self-promotional waffle steered by me saying, 'Amazing' every two minutes, like a frightened parrot. When I interviewed The B-52s and singer Cindy Wilson didn't turn up, I was inconsolable. I'd seen them twice and gazed up in gormless, weak-kneed devotion at this vision of a young Julie Christie with a beehive, but only four-fifths of her pop group were shepherded into their label's press office in a blaze of lime-green nylon and boot-sale tat. Conversation got off to a wobbly start.

'So anyway,' singer Fred Schneider chirruped, 'our first hit, "Rock Lobster", was like bubble-gum pop meets Dick Dale surf guitar and . . .'

'Is Cindy coming?' I asked anxiously.

'Be along in a minute!' her guitarist brother Ricky said brightly. '. . . with some electronics thrown in and a brittle top-mix to point up the danceability with . . .'

'Do you think she'll be long?'

'You know Cindy! Buys shoes *on* the hour *every* hour,' drummer Keith Strickland chipped in. '. . . using this compressed rhythm sound for club market appeal so . . .'

'She's *shopping*?'

'Only till she drops!' said the keyboard-player Kate Pierson, ignoring my pain. '. . . and then we added some synth melodies and a slice of dime-store style and . . .'

I could have made rich comedy from the no-show of the band's star attraction but stuck firmly to their record-selling spiel. Fellow *NME* junior Deanne Pearson was left gaffer-taped to a tree in a Portuguese desert by The Stranglers during the filming of their 'Nuclear Device' video but at least she had the brains to put it in her opening sentence. I couldn't see a news angle if it was staring me in the face. I was called up one night by the King's Road bar I'd just left and asked if I'd be a waiter at the Berkeley Square ball, and couldn't help noticing one of my tables featured a stubbly, sweat-stained geezer stretching the buttons of his grimy white suit, barely identifiable as the drummer of The Who. I brought him two bottles of champagne, most of which he drank himself. A few days later he keeled over and died. 'Keith Moon: My Fizz-Filled Night With Tragic Sticksman' might have made a good headline but it never crossed my mind to suggest it.

A delicate balance existed between the journalists and the rock stars we interviewed: we entered their world on the understanding that we could write about any amount of booze or hotel-wrecking but sex or drugs were to be cloaked in the vaguest terms available. When another junior, the great Paul Du Noyer, was sent on the road with Thin Lizzy, he dutifully ignored the fact that Phil Lynott kept nipping into the next hotel room to help a series of girls with their 'school projects', but his piece about The Damned revealed that, maddened by the tedium of motorway travel, their drummer had poured lighter-fuel down the back of his jacket and set the long-suffering reporter on fire.

My encounter with Rat Scabies took place in a palatial, split-level suite at the Montcalm Hotel in Marble Arch. His band made good money and he'd laid on quite a show, all of his own devising. I was directed up a spiral stairway to a loft by his PR man to find a king-size bed strewn with flowers. Above it was a bastardised version of the Woodstock Festival logo, its famous guitar neck broken and its white dove replaced by a dead bat on a piece of string beside the legend 'Three Years of Chaos, Anarchy and Destruction'. On the table, a Scotch bottle with about an inch left. Scabies and a female acquaintance were stark naked between the sheets, both wearing wigs – his a John Lennon one, hers Yoko Ono. I cleared some petals and sat on the counterpane, fumbling with my tape-recorder.

'Peace!' Scabies declared, with a two-finger salute. He had a flint-eyed look about him and was spilling ash on the pillowcase. 'Lennon had a bed-in once and I thought I'd see what it was all about.'

What *was* it all about?

'Wreckin' things,' he cackled. 'When Keith Moon died I was grief-stricken. I was just lying there in this lonely room one night and this white dove comes fluttering in and throws the telly out the window. That's the message, mate – big drum kits, smashin' hotels, great fun. I love breaking things. *Everyone* does when they have a chance. Cheap publicity. What's the meaning of life? The answer's in the soil.'

He picked up the Johnnie Walker and drained it.

'Move too fast and you're in the past,' he said, looking around him. 'I've been here two days, poncing about trying to decide how lovely I am.'

Bored by the proceedings, 'Yoko' got up, removed her wig and tottered *au naturel* down the staircase to the floor below. When Rat and I followed twenty minutes later she was having it off with his press representative in a circle of empty wine glasses and trays of untouched food. We tiptoed softly past them, sniggering, and went to the pub. Did this paragraph go into the piece? I'm ashamed to say it didn't.

An even greater dereliction of duty occurred at the '78 Knebworth Festival, scene of riotous past excursions on the other side of the barrier. I could see some old friends near the front, in fact, waving at me, having a whale of a time.

Suddenly I wanted to be with them. I didn't want to be standing there with the other hacks, jotting down clever adjectives for Tom Petty and The Heartbreakers' drum sound while trying to find out the name of the new song they were playing. I missed my old relationship with music where it was purely entertainment. I clambered across the metal barrier, tripping over beer-coolers and folding chairs, and picked my way to their sodden compound, which was well stocked with strong drink. Refreshed and relaxed, I slept soundly through the entire set by Jefferson Starship and woke to find ninety thousand people watching Genesis. Back home, with the mother of all hangovers, I knocked out my review, including brief but fulsome praise for Starship's lead singer Grace Slick – bewitching stage presence, shimmering top notes, faultless deployment of the tambourine – and was about to board the 19 bus to Piccadilly Circus and hand it in when a mate from *Record Mirror* dropped by.

'I thought it was good,' he said. 'Devo were great, Petty played a blinder, but I've given the Atlanta Rhythm Section a right old shoeing. Managed to get a few quotes about Grace too. She'd had a bust-up with the band apparently and just went AWOL. Never got on the flight from Frankfurt. Weird watching them muddle through without her.'

Even on the lowliest rung of the *NME* ladder I felt an astonishing sense of power. I might have been naïve and overawed but I now crackled with the peculiar static of minor celebrity. Press officers twice my age beamed expansively whenever I spoke. Blokes at gigs bought me drinks and talked about Stiff Little Fingers. Girls in leather jackets pretended they fancied me. It was like being in a rock band. And I was an office junior in 1978: what was life like for the star writers of the early seventies? Some of them had egos the size of America and I was starting to understand why. If they acted as though their weekly pronouncements might shift the parameters of popular taste, it was only because they could and did.

But the paper's relationship with the bands was often tense and thorny – we were known, in that tortuous pun, as 'the enemy'. Acts on the way up might seem snide and confident but were mostly cautious and desperately keen to please. Even the bolshiest bunch of political herberts became fawningly co-operative as they were fearful I'd 'do a hatchet job'. Bands at the top of their curve were warily tolerant, *NME* a necessary evil to keep the ball rolling, and those on the way back down were fractious and sore about being yesterday's heroes, assuming it was 'barbecue time', and I was there to tip more petrol on their funeral pyre. Quivering with excitement, I was led backstage at Oxford Polytechnic to meet my great heroes The Kinks – and then introduced as 'the guy from *NME*', at which point silence fell and four pairs of eyes swivelled accusingly as if every syllable of bad press ever dumped on their doorstep could be neatly blamed on me.

For so much of my teenage life I'd fantasised about being in a band, but the more time I spent on the road, the less attractive it seemed. The tensions were complicated and the pressures huge. I spent four days in Scotland with pop darlings Squeeze and started to feel sorry for them. Racing onstage, hitting a chord and watching fifteen hundred people leap into the air as if they'd stood on a power cable, that part looked fun, but the rest seemed like paranoid drudgery. Was the venue full? Was the album selling? Was the contract safe? Whose nose was out of joint if only Glenn Tilbrook and Chris Difford talked to the reporters? How dispiriting were the damp, barebrick dressing rooms that reeked of Dettol? They all rang their other halves from the hotel each night but if they told them they were miserable they wouldn't believe it, and if they told them they were having a ball, it smacked of girls and booze. Beneath the surface of even the most presentable groups a kind of madness was waiting to break out, a result of that routine switch from adrenalised showtime followed by nerve-soothing drink to endless hung-over hours of slightly anxious tedium in which you were constantly being told to hurry up and wait. Squeeze had different ways of defusing it. Their keyboard player, the twenty-year-old Jools Holland, bashed out Ray Charles songs on pub pianos while smoking cigars; their drummer, Gilson Lavis, tied himself to the roof-rack of a mate's car on the Australian tour to see what it felt like at ninety miles an hour.

The most extraordinary band I travelled with were Steel Pulse, who were exactly the same off-stage as on. Life was tough enough on the road in Germany but their dreadlocked code of living made it tougher. I adored those people but they couldn't switch off. They played their magnificent pumping reggae in an old Berlin cinema, supporting a new trio with dyed blond hair and striped T-shirts called The Police. I fondly imagined we'd be heading off for beer and *bratwurst*, but the teetotal Hansworth revolutionaries piled back on the tour bus to read passages from the Bible aloud and discuss His Imperial Majesty Haile Selassie, the Rastafarian godhead and late Emperor of Ethiopia. Eating out was a nightmare: they couldn't just go to vegetarian restaurants, they would only eat where *no contaminating meat product had ever been served in the entire history of the building.*

Even those enviable moments in the spotlight could be tricky. Joe Jackson's taut pop hits had catapulted him into the charts straight from the club circuit so he blinked with astonishment as he stepped out at the Crystal Palace Bowl. An enormous crowd was on the sloping lawn, sinking cans of Red Stripe, waiting for Bob Marley and The Wailers. The heat was so intense that a gaggle of pissed and sunburnt revellers had waded into the shallow lake below the stage and started splashing about, the water up to their waists, one of them dredging a large, gloopy-looking object from the mire below. Only when he began swinging it by its neck, like an Olympic hammer-thrower, mud flying in all directions, did it become obvious what it was: the rotting remains of a dead swan. A chill fell upon the crowd as they sensed where this was going, like some uncontrollable movie in slow-motion.

Last to notice was Jackson himself. Hitting a piercing high note, a triumphant climax to his first number, he looked up in horror as this festering carcass sailed through the air and piled into his microphone stand.

12

See You In Court!

An imposing new figure came bowling into the *NME* office, the gangling two-metre frame of Anton Corbijn, a rock photographer lured from Holland by the sad, stately sound of his heroes Joy Division. His destiny, his Holy Grail, was to meet them and take their portraits. He was twenty-three, just younger than me, another son of a preacher, thin and optimistic, always telling Tommy Cooper jokes. He wore buttoned-up polo shirts and flat, pointed shoes and spoke English in the delightfully dislocated way of the Dutch.

'Captain Beefheart comes soon to London and I am thinking to make pictures of him.'

'Dream on,' I told him. 'The *NME*'s a meritocracy. You have to start at the bottom and work your way up.' I could have added that I, personally, seemed to have started at the bottom and *remained* there, and was still only given assignments the star writers wouldn't touch with a bargepole.

Anton and I were thrown together as a words and pictures unit, and booted onto the road with some godawful Californians called The Dickies, blocking up the charts with a novelty punk version of 'Banana Splits (The Tra La La Song)'. Even its title brought me out in hives. I shuffled off to my dismal hotel room, with its nylon sheets and stale-cigarettes smell, to scrawl my thousand words on hotel notepaper, and pray that next week we'd get something glamorous like The Selecter or Joan Jett and The Blackhearts. When I came down, Anton's photo session was in full swing.

Junior photographers mostly went for the rock press clichés – the band on a fire escape, or five heads above a graffitied wall, or the lead singer glimpsed through a window-blind, or blokes with beer cans making internationally recognised hand-gestures. With great care and imagination, and some antique face masks he'd found upstairs, he transformed these idiot frat-boys into enigmatic godheads of art-rock. His textured black and white prints would do for The Dickies what they were about to do for countless other musicians in need of mystification: they made them look deep and meaningful.

Anton moved into my new pile, a four-storey legal squat at 144 Richmond Road, Dalston. The council let us have it for eight pounds a month to keep the burglars out before it went on the market, ideal for moneyless *NME* stringers. My old college friends moved in too, Nick and Mary, and the four of us had a floor each for fifty pence a week. We named it the Roach Motel after some traps we'd had to buy, little cardboard boxes with cheery cartoon insects on the side clutching luggage beneath a sign that read 'Roach Motel: they check in but they don't check out!' Someone had nicked the letterbox so I nailed a slice of carpet over the hole but chill winds still tore through the place like the Kazakhstan steppes. Next door was a brothel run by a woman with trowelled-on turquoise eye-liner who looked like *Coronation Street*'s Bet Lynch. Lone figures in raincoats would ring the bell and her accommodating other half would slip out the back and mooch about in the garden till her popular work was complete.

The Roach Motel had no hot water so we pottered down to the public baths on the corner where, for twelve pence, they gave you a towel and a cake of soap and cranked a handle in the passage outside filling your tub from a brass tap. Anton and I played out the scene in *Quadrophenia* where the guy in the next cubicle drives Jimmy mad with his wobbling versions of Gene Vincent's 'Be Bop A Lula' and 'You Really Got Me' by The Kinks sung over the partition. We were fired up with excitement about life, the two of us on this quixotic quest, reporters from the rock and roll frontline, him with his little darkroom in the attic where he developed his pictures in trays of strange-smelling chemical, and me with my typewriter and wall of albums on planks. When the summer arrived, I built a sound-system. I put the huge wooden speakers on the window-sill and we roasted out the back, listening to records. Memories of that blistering heat – the dandelions, the bees, the peeling paintwork, the smell of long grass and warm tar on the fence – seem wedded to the music we played. There were the mournful minor-chord excursions of The Feelies, New Jersey nerds in plaid shirts and big glasses. There were the thundering bass-heavy hymns of the Cool Ruler, Gregory Isaacs. There were the sprocketing guitars and inscrutable words of *Ashes To Ashes* by David Bowie, who Anton reminded me was a genius. And there was the household favourite, the sweltering jungle soundtrack of a song called 'The Monochrome Set (I Presume)' by Hornsey art-rockers The Monochrome Set whose immortal chorus ran,

THE Monochrome Set, Monochrome Set, Monochrome
Se-e-e-et
THE Monochrome Set, Monochrome Set, Monochrome
Se-e-e-et . . .

with the emphasis not on the key words 'Monochrome' or 'Set' but the single word 'The'. We all joined in, playing it over and over again, lying in the tall, flower-filled meadow that passed for our garden and crying with helpless laughter.

At painful expense, Anton and I bought tickets to see Frank Sinatra at the Albert Hall, though we didn't dare admit it in the office. Confessing to a fondness for the tight-skinned old crooner was only marginally better than saying you liked Genesis or The Eagles. We dressed up as best we could, his tousled mop above a cream coloured jacket and me in a sheer polyester white suit bought for the occasion for nineteen pounds from Mister Byrite in Oxford Street; it had stretched out of shape by the interval. We were twenty years younger than anyone else and gazed down at the strange and exotic crowd, mostly comprising embarrassed, put-upon business-men with shrieking, jewel-studded wives who seemed to have blown their entire life savings on a frock and a hairdo, the middle-aged equivalent of my Golden Earring nightmare six years earlier. Some of these women had even brought presents with them – champagne, cigars in cedarwood boxes, top-end malts tied with ribbons. Sinatra took his place at the music-stand, a shiny fellow in a tux and bow-tie with a bright orange face.

'Hey, Mister Tangerine Man!' Anton sang, a little too loudly.

It was a preposterous cash-pumping pantomime, wonderfully funny. Rock music would never sink to this kind of soulless, high-priced cabaret, we laughed! Sparkling matrons began tottering up the aisle to present their gifts to the over-tanned idol, who'd respond with a lingering handshake. But it was quite a hike to the front and one got her timing badly wrong, setting out just as he was ending a song.

'Chicago is one town that won't let you down,' went Frank, with a flourish, 'it's *myyyy* kind of *tooown*!'

Cymbals crashing around him, he strolled back to pal around with the orchestra and stir a gin and tonic. Slowly, unsteadily, she heaved her vast crystal vase with its bouquet of red roses onto the lip of the stage. It must have cost a fortune. But Frank was now firing up a Camel by the horn section, radiating a monstrous, seedy, casual decadence that would have given Byron Ferrari a run for his money. Ten thousand eyes were on her as she started the long, tearful return journey, her lavish offering lost and unnoticed. Frank shimmied back to the microphone and stared down at it quizzically.

'Hmm,' he sniffed as a minion whisked it to the wings. 'I don't know whether to drink it or smoke it.'

There was, however, a downside to living with Anton: his career was in overdrive, possibly something to do with his enormous talent and immense personal charm. The section editors severed our budding partnership and 'The Flying Dutchman' was fast-tracked to higher things. We met every few days in the Roach Motel local to compare notes.

'How goes zer work?' Anton asked, sipping warm English beer.

'Terrific,' I said. 'Just been to the Isle of Man to do Manny Charlton of Nazareth! Another thousand-worder. Little prop plane, six seats. The whole place is a tax haven. Look up the street and there's three members of Status Quo stepping out to get their milk bottles! How about you?'

Anton had been in Chelsea photographing Mick Jagger and Keith Richards. This was *extraordinary*. Nothing had been heard from the stratospheric world of the Stones for ages. He pulled out his gravelly prints of the two of them looking impossibly old and weather-beaten, both thirty-eight, an enormous damp patch on Keith's trousers where he'd spilt his beaker of bourbon. The entire pub gathered round and just stared.

'How is your journey viz the girl who seems like she stays in zer sixties?' he wondered a week later.

'Not bad,' I said bravely. 'We went to Colston Hall in Bristol!' The Tourists had moaned the whole way down about 'those cynical bastards at the *NME* who hate pop music' but their singer seemed a nice enough sort. 'Annie Lennox – vocals, keyboards, flute, blonde hair, huge eyes, huger grin, multi-coloured jewellery, red mini skirt,' my breathless copy read.

Anton had been to Chicago. The pub crowd sidled over again as he slid another set of shots from an envelope and there was David Bowie. He looked bleak and wounded, dressed in a loincloth like some persecuted saint about to be strapped to a cross and filled with arrows. He'd taken the role of John Merrick in a stage production of *The Elephant Man* and this astonishing image was the first anyone had seen of it. And there was more. Anton had been to Joshua Tree, a national park in the Mojave Desert. Back at the house in his darkroom, I watched him pull a print from a dish of developer and out of the red-lit gloom appeared the gaunt, haunted figure of Captain Beefheart, the gnarled trunks of giant cacti bunched in the sky behind him. I'd never seen a better portrait in my life. He'd been in the country just eighteen months and he'd already photographed most of his heroes. Twenty minutes with Joy Division and he might as well stick a flag on the summit and retire.

I, on the other hand, was going nowhere. Occasionally I got days on the 'T-Zers' desk which I loved, compiling the news and gossip, ringing the Boomtown Rats' singer Bob Geldof for reliably caustic quotes or finding out the track titles on an upcoming Ian Dury album, which earned a 'splash' on the cover. I was in the horn section of a little soul band and was asked by a mate at Arista if I'd mime the sax parts for a Nona Hendryx video. I spent a happy afternoon leaning on a plastic lamppost in a powder-blue zoot suit while the former Labelle star sang 'You're The Only One That I Ever Needed' umpteen times – a flop, tragically – but the hundred pounds they paid me was more than I'd earned writing in a month. To compound my agony, the head of press at Island Records, Rob Partridge, called and offered me a job as a PR. The wages sounded like science fiction and I think there was a car involved. I'd be flying round the globe, staying in expensive hotels and representing four of my favourite acts – Steel Pulse, The B-52's, Marianne Faithfull and Bob Marley and The Wailers. On days off I could maybe take Cindy Wilson for a spin in the company convertible and inspect my vast, teetering piles of not-very-hard-earned cash. I returned to the Roach Motel, sat heavily on my mattress on the floor and stared long and hard at the mound of *NME*s in the corner that featured less and less work by Mark Ellen.

'You can't join the other side,' Anton agreed. 'I'm taking pictures. You're writing. This is what we do.'

'Good luck,' said the cordial Partridge when I dropped in to see him. 'You'll do pretty well.' He gave an inscrutable smile. Was that 'pretty well' as in you might make a features editor? Or the 'pretty well' that says, 'Don't come crying to me in four years' time, pal, when no one's even offering you a phoner with the bass player of Secret Affair, and you wake from your sweat-stained slumber, thinking, *I'm the clown who turned down a job with Bob Marley?*'

I had no idea which and it worried me. I'd chipped away at the coalface for two years, covering worthy, well-intentioned acts lugging amps through the get-in of the Pegasus in Stoke Newington, the pinnacle of whose career was a review from a stringer like me (The Carpettes, The Dandies, The Tea Set, The Bollock Brothers, Writz, Agony Column – where were they now?). *NME*'s engine was oiled with a wit and cynicism I was never going to master. The invite to their Christmas party at Dingwalls captured it perfectly: 'Dress Modern!' it advised. 'Cool and convenient, comfortable and exciting! The *NME* Xmas Offensive CLEANS you, THRILLS you, FUNS YOU! Falling over gets you accepted. No invite, no party,' warned the photocopied card. Glued to the bottom was a newspaper cutting: 'HOW TO GET GIRLFRIENDS – what to say, how to overcome shyness, how to date any girl you fancy!' The star turn was Chas and Dave (*oh*, the irony).

Weekly rock-press writers were gun-slinging mavericks riding roughshod over everyone, and the readers loved it. They were radicals, malcontents, firebrands, activists. They emptied both barrels from the hip. They were always right. They never apologised. They weren't fresh-faced goons who'd volunteer for anything. Even when I *tried* to be aggressive, and with the softest of targets, I just couldn't pull it off. A tear-streaked letter arrived from an Osmonds fan appalled at the weeklies' treatment of her toothsome heroes' recent tour, my 'nonsensical blabberings' in *NME* singled out in particular – I'd described the God-fearing sextet as 'ceaseless torment' and their dance routines 'like the death throes of a Lurex locomotive' so I don't know what she was so touchy about. A second one turned up a week later which exposed my shamefully diplomatic approach to reader-relations.

'Thanks for the nice letter, Mark,' it read. 'I didn't really expect any replies when I wrote to the music papers and I certainly didn't expect the one I got from Dave McCullough of *Sounds*. I enclose a copy.'

Indeed she did, from Spotlight Publications in Covent Garden. McCullough had informed Ms Bowerman that he *did* like The Osmonds and didn't give '2 fucks' whether she disagreed with what he'd written or whether he should be 'hung upon the cross of Donny', signing off with 'only God knows and God is DEAD!'

And then came the court case, just to bang home my final coffin-nail. Write something illegal, as I was about to discover, and two parties are held responsible: the paper that chose to publish it without changing a word, and the pillock who wrote it in the first place. My review of the so-called Great British Music Festival contained the assurance that one of its stars,

Frankie Miller, had been the worse for drink when he wandered onstage at Wembley Arena, and M'Learned Friends were soon in touch. I figured this was fair comment: the Glaswegian brawler was a well-known soak, as celebrated for his 'pints o' heavy' as his paint-stripping rhythm and blues. In fact, he'd written a song called 'Drunken Nights In The City'. I thought he'd sue if I said he was *sober*.

But things had changed since his hit single 'Darlin'' – 'I'm feeling pretty lonesome, I'd call you on the phone some', it quavered, lest we forget. It was bought by a whole new market of doting suburban mums who fancied the craggy roustabout and wanted to cook him a nourishing stew. Any suggestions of his wayward past had been airbrushed out. Miller, we were darkly informed, was on the wagon. It was raining writs. But legal letters were never a staff priority. They'd arrive, be passed around and get buried under a Crispy Ambulance album and sometimes nobody got round to replying. The next thing I knew I was summoned to appear in court. Miller arrived in a large black hat; I turned up in a shiny purple drape jacket, black plastic trousers and red shoes with yellow laces. Whatever contemptuous look the judge had in store, he now had to dig even deeper.

'The case between Francis John Miller, popular entertainer, and . . .' he seemed to shiver '. . . the weekly *rock* publication *New Musical Express* is constructed upon a phrase appearing in that periodical on the sixth of December, its author one Mark Henry Ellen.'

I'm bang-to-rights here. Put the bracelets on.

'Mr Ellen, you said in an article in the aforementioned newspaper – and I quote – that "a decidedly boozed Frankie Miller swayed onto the stage" at the Arena in Wembley upon the night of the thirtieth of November. Would that be correct?'

Of course it's correct! If NME *had bothered to respond to your perfectly reasonable allegations, we'd have settled out of court for a few quid and I wouldn't be standing here in this ludicrous pair of trousers.*

'Yes, m'lud, those were the words in question.'

'Mr Ellen, what was your vantage point for this observation? The backstage area? The *wings* of said theatre?'

'Out in the audience, sir! We like to keep a critical distance from our subjects in order to maintain an unbiased—'

'So if you had no proximity to Mr Miller prior to his performance, how could you have seen him imbibe the beverage that apparently resulted in his *swaying onto the stage*?'

'I – I didn't, m'lud.' Beads of perspiration were popping from my brow.

'And yet . . . "decidedly boozed"?'

'Naturally assumed so. Seemed that way to me, sir!'

There was a rustling of papers and a piercing look from a pair of flashing spectacles.

'And upon what do we base this natural assumption?'

Use the word 'research'. Sounds impressive.

'My extensive *research*, m'lud. While *researching* Mr Miller I discovered a very public enthusiasm for alcohol was a routine part of his performance so . . .'

'*Was*, Mr Ellen, *was*.'

It was like something out of *Bleak House*.

'And yet someone whose first sight of the plaintiff was when he stepped from the wings to perform – and was thus unable to observe the consumption of *the very stimulant Mr Miller has now so assuredly foresworn* – sees fit to cast a gross calumny upon his re-burgeoning career via the suggestion that he still appears in a manner that might taint his professional reputation, reduce the value of his concert tickets and . . .'

We lost. *NME* paid damages and handsome court costs and I shuffled back to the office feeling horribly responsible, only to find that one of the newsdesk hadn't turned up. When I asked where he was I got a shrugging response.

'He's shuffled off his mortal coil, mate.'

I'd never heard this expression and it didn't sound good. 'Unlucky! I *hate* it when that happens. Still . . . calls to make, stuff to write, press day and all that,' I said, rolling a sheet into the typewriter. 'When's he back in?'

Blank looks all round. 'He isn't. He's brown bread. Overdosed on Tuesday.' A phone rang offering tickets for Teardrop Explodes at the Music Machine and we quietly got on with our work.

The next day I arrived to deliver copy to the features editor and found the place deserted. A staff meeting was under way. He was about to go on holiday and a book lay open on his desk full of detailed notes about all the contributors for his replacement. There was no one around so I took a quick look. Paul Morley was the first entry, oceans of praise for his capabilities and freewheeling gonzo prose. Then Kent, of course – 'Can't type and busts deadlines but, hey, he's Nick Kent!' Eulogies for Anton, Danny Baker, Charlie Murray, Burchill, Parsons, *yada yada* . . .

No mention of hard-working, dependable me.

. . . Goldman, Salewicz, Du Noyer, Penman . . .

I turned the page anxiously.

. . . Pennie Smith, Penny Reel, Robert Elms . . .

Robert Elms? Who'd turned up in a big girls' blouse and a pair of jodhpurs? Only one thing published and that was about Spandau Ballet? Been here a week? Younger than me? *Elms?*

. . . Andy Gill, Paul Rambali, Deanne Pearson ('hates being tied to trees') . . .

I turned *another* page, panicked, to find three final names, one of them mine. Followed by five words I could see chiselled on my gravestone.

'MARK ELLEN – Sarcastic, OK on general stuff.'

It was time to move on.

13

Our Father, Which Art Garfunkel . . .

'Mark, it's Mark Williams. We've started a new rock weekly and your stuff in *NME* looks halfway decent. Want to jump ship? We're in a basement off Tottenham Court Road. Hundred and fifty quid a week in cash.'

This seemed worth a shot. Mark was a devilish, handsome character whose drainpipe jeans, sideburns and crêpe-soled shoes gave him the louche air of a rockabilly on a three-day bender. Nick Logan had left *NME* to launch *Smash Hits* and he'd been lined up to replace him, but a run-in with the law now labelled him 'too rock and roll'. It was the sweltering summer of 1980 and *NME* and *Melody Maker* were on strike in a pay dispute, so Mark had launched *New Music News* to fill the gap.

I nipped down to *NMN*'s steaming, subterranean lair to take a look. Smoke-clogged, watery light filtered from the pavement above and a gaggle of red-eyed souls were cobbling together the final pages in a circle of clanking electric fans. They clearly hadn't slept for days but the mood seemed impregnable. Paper-thin girls wearing big T-shirts as dresses with belts round the middle bashed at typewriters. Stubbly blokes sliced cardboard layouts with scalpels, some working on the carpet surrounded by ashtrays. Publicity shots of Paul Weller and Ozzy Osbourne were pinned to the wall, doctored with speech-bubbles. It seemed noble and heroic, a scene of wild, frazzled madness. It was a shambles, complete and utter chaos. It made *NME* look like *Wedding Day & First Home*.

'When can I start?' I asked.

'Start now if you like,' Mark said. 'Going to press as it happens. Why don't you give Tom Hibbert a hand in the Department of Finishing Touches?' He pointed to a murky little cubicle where a hunched figure, about five foot ten and weighing eight stone, was prodding a Remington. A row of vertical butts stood beside him on the desk, two of them alight. I watched him for a while, tapping away with a mischievous smile, then stopping to read what he'd written and rubbing his hands with glee.

'What's happening here?' I wondered, banging my head on the ceiling.

'I'm writing the readers' letters,' Tom said, without looking up.

'Why?'

'Because we don't have any.'

'Readers or letters?'

'Either,' he said, unconcerned, and soldiered on. I leafed through his sheets of paper and offered to supply the 'black type', the flip editorial replies music papers usually added to any post they printed. If there were no real readers there didn't seem to be much point in real writers either, so why didn't I do it as a fictional character?

Tom looked up, delighted. 'Dear fellow,' he announced, 'follow me,' and he rummaged in his pockets for some loose change. His speech was peppered with quaint expressions – 'old chap' or 'what the juggins'. Food was 'tuck'. Cigarettes were 'snouts'. Booze was 'sauce'. Too much sauce and you were 'in your cups'. If he was tired he was 'plumb tuckered out' and, soon after, 'fast a-kip'. We headed to a photo-booth in Oxford Street where he decided I should edit the letters in the imagined personality of the first person we could persuade to have their picture taken. We'd invent a name for them and put their shot at the top of the column. An amused student eventually sat in the chair and we raced back to the office where I assumed the crushingly dull personality of 'Guest Editor Richard Carlisle', a theology scholar from Reading University.

Sleepless subs passed us proofs with little notes attached saying, 'Captions here!'

'What sort of thing do they want?' I asked.

'Whatever you like, old fruit.' Hibbert shrugged, lighting up a snout. 'Any old tippety tappety typing.' He rolled another sheet in and began clicking away. A newspaper with no readers, clearly a bad thing. A ship with no rudder, that wasn't great either. But a risk-taking rag where you could do anything you wanted and they published it? That seemed wonderful. Drunk on each other's company, we put helium-filled rhyming nonsense under all the pictures, one writing the first half, the other the second – 'Bashi bazooks! The Thompson Twins: some you lose and some you wins' – then cooked up a rock and roll Lord's Prayer appearing a line at a time at the bottom of each page and starting 'Our Father, which Art Garfunkel . . .' Nobody was chasing the big commercial cover stories but a lot of effort went into writing fried psychedelic messages and packing them off to the printers. This seemed like time well spent.

Tom moved into the Roach Motel alongside the now stratospheric Anton. I don't remember inviting him: he just followed me to the 38 bus one night with a couple of carrier-bags, got off at Dalston and asked where his bedroom was. He called everyone 'man', regardless of gender, but with the withering 'we mean it, *maaan*' sarcasm of Johnny Rotten in the Pistols' 'God Save The Queen'. His domestic skills were off the scale and soon the stuff of legend. Tom's signature dish was 'burgers' – instant sage and onion stuffing moistened with tap water and pan-fried in marge. Lucky diners often got 'something from the trolley' to follow, a dessert he called 'electric pancakes' – standard pancake mix but with Martini Bianco instead of milk. He kept the winter fires stoked with a hopeless invention called 'logs' – tightly rolled copies of *Time Out* magazine tied with string. But his knowledge of music was peerless and his quality control vicious in the extreme. He homed in on my record collection and gave it the once-over.

'Dear boy,' he said, 'this is abysmal.'

Hundreds of albums, fondly arranged on a framework of bricks and old floorboards. And much loved, by me at least.

'Abysmal?'

'There are records by Squeeze.' He shuddered, as if the word was contaminated. '*And* Paul McCartney. I rest my case.'

Even at the *NME*, I'd never met anyone so opinionated or convinced they were right. All my life, the same cycle had happened: I'd develop a fondness for certain records then either grow out of them or be forced to reconsider them by someone who appeared to know better. But this was my greatest challenge. Tom channelled all of his love of music into a dozen acts and mercilessly ridiculed the rest. About five per cent of the rock landscape was raw and uncompromised and, thus, acceptable – the Stooges, the Pistols, The Kinks, Neil Young, MC5 and, at a pinch, Vanilla Fudge; the remaining 95 per cent was polished and proficient and, hence, laughably awful – Bowie, Steely Dan, Kate Bush, anyone you'd care to name. And he loathed all pop music after 1966 with the sole exception of Abba as he fancied the girls. He was appalled to discover I had records of every stripe and therefore lacked discernment and perspective. I loved the great boards of noise that came off Iggy Pop singles but I couldn't see anything wrong with Blondie either. I once played him 'I'm Wishing On A Star' by the disco floor-fillers

Rose Royce and he got quite aggressive. What kind of juggins, he asked, finds some kind of merit in everything? We'd sit up all night spinning scratchy long-players and arguing the toss. I tried Sam Cooke on him but he thought all soul was rubbish. I tried country music – the Flying Burrito Brothers, Commander Cody – but he went weird at the sight of a cowboy hat. The computerised pulse of Kraftwerk was kicked straight into touch – 'Frightful non-rock bores pretending to be robots, dear chap. Fingers crossed, they might touch a bit of faulty wiring.'

By dawn he'd be taking tiny, tottering dance steps round the turntable on his spindly legs, swinging his arms about and dropping the needle on huge psychedelic walls of sound by Crazy Horse or The Replacements. '*Real* music, my dear fellow!' he'd shout above the din, thrashing an imaginary guitar. It was one-way traffic: I liked his stuff, he hated mine. The pinnacle of all greatness, he announced, was the now-defunct Big Star, thin, lackadaisical men from Tennessee who played chiming melodies with a mournful cadence and a doomed, romantic sheen. I loved them, too, but not as much as Hibbs. When 'in his cups' – which was often – he would shake a fist at the sky and declare them 'too beautiful for this world', as if some sinister cartel of sugary hit-makers were keeping these pale underachievers from the mass market they deserved. Big Star, he added sourly, 'was what The Beatles *could* have been if they'd improved a bit and hadn't split up'.

Endless heated debate inspired a new leisure pursuit, 'clay pigeon shooting', a ruthless expression of musical taste. One Roach Motel resident was a biker and, for some reason, had a rifle. Every time Tom or I did the singles reviews, we'd remove anything we both liked from the pile – The Cramps, The Fall, The Slits, The Comsat Angels – and one of us would cart any miserable offenders that hadn't made the cut to the bottom of our garden, which backed onto a four-storey wall. The other would stand by the kitchen window with a pocket of shells.

'Pull!'

A shiny new 12-inch of 'In The Air Tonight' by Phil Collins was hurled aloft and peppered with gunfire.

'Pull!'

'You Drive Me Crazy' by Shakin' Stevens was blown into shards of splintered plastic.

'Pull!'

Up went the fearful 'Xanadu' by Olivia Newton-John and the Electric Light Orchestra, shattered fragments lodging in the fruit trees. That seemed fair enough, a justifiable one-in-the-eye for the wretched chart-cloggers. There was something intensely satisfying about filling a record by The Korgis full of holes, or watching 'Sexy Eyes' by Dr Hook explode in mid-air and scatter across a cabbage patch.

Instantly, exhaustively, *New Music News* consumed my life. It was published by a bearded tycoon called Felix Dennis whose maverick empire was built on poster-magazines about the martial arts pin-up Bruce Lee. Felix had been one of the figureheads of *Oz*. I'd taped a news picture of him and his fellow editors to my wall in 1971 when their 'Schoolkids Issue' stuck them in the dock on a high-profile obscenity charge. Much of the romance of the underground press came from this harsh hippie scandal-sheet, its wit, bite and satire. Now Felix was trying it again with *New Music News*.

The 'press schedule' was ridiculous. We stayed up three nights in a row bashing the whole thing together in a frantic fireball of smoke and booze, then collapsed in a heap for three days to recover. And did the same the next week. And the week after. The less I slept, the more I felt I was suffering for my art and the more rock and roll the end-product. If I wrote my pieces alone and in the cold light of day, it seemed like a profession; if I hammered them out at three in the morning in a room full of skinny girls crashed out on cushions, I felt I was changing the world. The old order would end, we all reckoned, the dour music-press obsession with Devo and Bauhaus, and a brave new golden age would be trumpeted in by our ragged little fanzine led by groups like Doll By Doll and Young Marble Giants! I felt charged up and invincible!

There was another reason for this manic energy: the frayed routine was kept afloat with piles of amphetamine sulphate. I was never much good around drugs – dope seemed to kill conversation and speed produced far too much of it and, being fairly accelerated anyway, made me start burbling and bouncing off walls. The office tipple was not the top-drawer 'Berwick' deployed by well-heeled connoisseurs for a gentle lift of a morning but a damp, yellow, head-splitting pharmaceutical knocked up in a bathtub in Leytonstone. Too much of this and you couldn't sleep for a fortnight. Your eyes bulged like peeled boiled eggs, blood poured from both nostrils and your central nervous system collapsed. Otherwise, tremendous. It was like being plugged into the mains.

'I'm off to Liverpool to do The Teardrop Explodes,' I told Tom, expecting a warm response. The psychedelic voyagers were one of the few new acts with the Hibbert seal of approval.

'Well-known lovers of the old Billy Whizz,' he confided, '*famed* for it, in fact. It's always beak o'clock at Château Teardrop – which I think you'll find on *Chisel* Beach. I wouldn't try to keep up if I were you,' he added darkly.

'Fancy a line of chop?' Julian Cope asked before I'd even taken my coat off. The damp yellow speed had made its way to Eric's Club in Mathew Street, too, and the band were having a pre-interview 'nose-up'. Cope, their charismatic leader, had wide eyes, big boots, a flying jacket and a grin like a suspension bridge; he was tipping huge, conical mounds of chisel onto a plastic table-top.

'Why not?' Seemed rude not to, but this made our home fare look like talcum powder. I turned pale and began perspiring.

'Anyone for a top-up?' Cope suggested.

They hoofed down another so I followed suit. Waves of adrenaline surged through my body and my hair stood on end.

'One more for luck?' The Teardrops were seasoned consumers of eye-watering stimulants and seemed barely affected by it, but three dibs of this and my heart started rattling my ribcage. Sweat stains the size of Shropshire appeared on my shirt and I'd lost the use of one leg. We filled both sides of a cassette with fizzing gibberish and I sprang back to my hotel room and lay vibrating on the bed, staring at the ceiling till nine in the morning, teeth gnashing like a steam-hammer, brain mushed to guacamole. I creaked my way painfully to the station feeling as though my internal organs had been taken out, pummelled with a milk bottle and then put back in the wrong places. It was an omen. Drugs and I didn't seem to get along and I never took any ever again.

Back in London there was another omen. The strike was over so *NME* and *Melody Maker* had returned to the streets. We couldn't last five minutes and we knew it. *NME*'s comeback cover had an eerie portrait by Anton of Joy Division in a tube station, Ian Curtis looking back at the camera. He'd taken his own life a month beforehand.

Within days there was a message from Felix. He wasn't running a charity, he was running a business. We couldn't take on the weeklies and win.

'Bless you,' he said, 'and please don't nick all the typewriters.'

14

The Party On Paper™

So *New Music News* folded, the autumn closed in and chill winds blew again through the Roach Motel letterbox. And the big new hits tinkled from the radio – 'Don't Stand So Close To Me' by The Police, 'Talk Of The Town' by the Pretenders, and Blondie's 'The Tide Is High', along with the strident sound of '9 To 5' by the brassy Scots singer Sheena Easton which, according to Tom Hibbert, signalled the end of civilisation as we knew it. If still employed as reviewers, he pointed out, we could have got the clay pigeon shoot back up again and taken at least one copy of this miserable disc out of circulation.

Work was thin on the ground but one afternoon our newly installed telephone suddenly sprang to life. It was David Hepworth, the editor of *Smash Hits*.

'Do you fancy tea and cakes with Sheena Easton?'

Hibbs eyed me with contempt as I set off to Manchester Square with my tape-recorder, though I could tell he didn't know which was worse: that a principled taste-maker flying the flag for rock's outer limits should lower himself to that kind of drivel, or that I was earning money and he wasn't.

'Dear fellow,' he sneered, 'when Easton calls, can Bonnie Tyler be far behind?'

I wandered into EMI Records, gazing fondly at the stairwell where The Beatles had posed for *Please Please Me*, and was ferried to a room full of gold discs and glass-topped desks where girls with big, fizzy hair were dialling up the music press and talking brightly about Pink Floyd, Kate Bush and the Gang Of Four. How thrilling to meet any of *them*, but I tried to focus on the job in hand. Sheena Easton was whisked in, her boyish locks teased into spikes and wrapped in a leopardskin headband. She had a taut, school-marmish tilt about her and gave me a cautious glance: her three hits had been the subject of some barbed, hand-wringing editorial in *NMN*, much of it written by me. I kicked off, still in rock-press mode, with a tough, take-no-prisoners agenda.

'Isn't there a confusing, mixed-message kind of *discrepancy*,' I said, 'between the free-range independent woman of "Modern Girl" who, and I quote, "don't build her world 'round no single man", and the outmoded, almost *servile* standpoint of "9 To 5" and "One Man Woman"?'

Easton was the daughter of a steel-mill labourer from north Lanarkshire and probably ate bolts for breakfast. She shot me a withering look that said, 'Since when did *Smash Hits* do dull sexual politics instead of asking people if they'd got any hobbies?' I'd set off her bollocks-alarm.

'Singers sing about any situation!' she hissed, in her rasping brogue. 'If I sing about my dog dying it doesn't have to mean *I kill my dog every night before I go onstage!*'

The red mist was coming down and the tea and cakes were untouched. I thought she was going to thump me.

'Don't think every time I sing something I'm trying prove something, because I'm not!'

There was a deafening silence. 'Favourite food?' I gulped.

'Sweeties, tuna fish and brown-bread sandwiches, apricot jam and toast,' she trotted out tartly. 'Want my pet hates too?'

I supposed I did.

'Lumpy custard and spiders in the bath.'

This was a whole new ball game. The rock press was aimed squarely at people my age but *Smash Hits* was a fortnightly colour pop magazine for kids who bought singles. Some were around eleven, the oldest maybe sixteen. Nick Logan had launched it in '78 and it ran news, interviews, songwords and posters. He'd recommended me to Hepworth, who'd published my less than classic Sheena Easton piece and asked me to keep contributing. The more I saw of the place, the more I liked it. It looked directly across Carnaby Street and through *NME*'s windows.

A great sea-change was occurring and my old employers had been painfully slow to acknowledge it. Sensing the warm trade winds of the new video boom, a lot of the late seventies rock acts were now aiming for the singles chart. I'd seen Adam and The Ants in tiny, sweat-filled cellars, sex-obsessed punks with a Hitler fetish playing tracks like 'Whip In My Valise' for art students; they now dressed as American Indians, wrote for teenage girls and had a limousine at 'on-stage temperature' to ferry them from hotel to venue. *NME* presented Madness as noble Cockney ska-revivers on the lash; to *Smash Hits* they were a riotous dance-machine in likeable hats. The Human League were an audio-visual art-collective; to us they were the synth-prodding sideline to a bold home-haircutting experiment. They saw Gary Numan as a fragile Bowie-descendant ploughing brave new furrows in electronica, but when I met him in his pile on the Surrey 'rock-broker belt', he was sporting a Bogart-style Panama and belted mackintosh, and his personal empire included a helicopter, his 'Numan Air' fleet of three planes ('for tax reasons'), and investments in restaurants, record labels and a Formula One racing team.

Pop music was taking over in late '81 and the old landscape was looking deserted. Led Zeppelin had disbanded, the Stones were mostly abroad, The Kinks had run out of steam, Dylan was in his Christian phase, Bob Marley and John Lennon were dead and The Beatles' song catalogue would soon be sold to Michael Jackson. And the British reggae boom had bust and the punk heroes were disintegrating – the Jam, The Pistols, The Clash and The Stranglers. None of this suited *NME*, who were happiest promoting acts at the fringes who quacked on about Kierkegaard – if, these days, they were happy at all.

Smash Hits, however, was on a fond, full-colour mission to squeeze the maximum amount of fun out of everything and it seemed like a blessed relief. It called itself 'The Party On Paper™' with a little trademark symbol. Being there was like crawling into the sunshine, blinking, from underneath a boulder. I tumbled off to Covent Garden for a Debbie Harry album launch and the message was crystal clear: there was big money in hit singles. Debbie tottered in – her head, strangely, way too big for her body – and gazed at the lavish spread laid on by her record company. The rooms were hung with flowers and there were tables of champagne and uniformed chefs carving saddles of meat beneath a wall of lobsters. Hundreds of large, ruinously expensive lobsters – in a wall. I tried to take one but it was quite a stretch to reach the top.

I'd brought along another Roach Motel resident – not Hibbs or Anton but an ex-art student called Clare Belfield who liked Debbie Harry a lot. We'd met at college where, for some reason, she'd had me down as an irritating, loud-mouthed twerp and non-stop party animal, but now I'd reached the ripe old age of twenty-seven she thought I wasn't quite so bad. She wore a bandana wrapped round her head and a carved bone necklace and looked like the two girls from Abba merged into one. She was adorable. Clare worked as a sign-writer, hand-painting shop windows. I'd come along to help and pretend she'd spelt 'mayonnaise' wrong fifteen times but, despite this, the two of us were going out. Levels of hygiene in Hackney being what they were, she suggested I cart my records over to her place in

Shepherd's Bush and stick them alongside hers – two Blondie 12-inches, some Television, Talking Heads, Patti Smith, the Velvet Underground, a Stones' cover by an Italian band called the Lunatics that she'd bought on holiday, and seventeen studio albums and thirty-nine bootlegs by Bob Dylan, the latter purchased with a nod and a wink from a bloke in Portobello Road market who kept them under his table in a milk crate. She'd designed her own covers for a lot of them, hand-drawn and lettered. I thought *I* liked Dylan but this was impressive. Her favourite bits included Bob and Robbie Robertson writing songs in a hotel room and some funny things he'd said when tuning his guitar at a soundcheck in Melbourne, Australia.

Clare was highly amused by *Smash Hits*, though she thought Toyah looked 'a state' and Simon Le Bon of Duran Duran could maybe lose a few pounds.

'Lou Reed centrespread?' she'd suggest, with a wry smile. 'Dylan personal file? Tom Verlaine songwords? "Stars and Their Cars" with Leonard Cohen? What about a fashion special – "Patti Smith, Looking The Way She Likes and Liking The Way She Looks"? It's what the kids *want!*'

Whatever I was doing I must have been doing it right as Dave offered me a full-time job. Motorcycle messengers clattered into Reception dropping off packages, and there was a warm hum of activity at 52–5 Carnaby Street. Tinny little radios played above the symphony of phones, the walls were papered with posters and every desk had a wobbling pile of cassettes, miniature tapes in a plastic cartridge – when they snapped you put a biro in the cog-wheels and twizzled till the broken ends appeared, then stuck them back together with Sellotape. A smell of glue drifted from the art department as they designed pages full of glitter or sweet wrappers or headlines pressed out of Dymo labels, then rolled the layouts with melted beeswax and stuck them on cards. Just past the design desks in a little office of his own, Nick Logan, the noble champion of my boot-stained copy at *NME*, was launching his new magazine *The Face*.

Dave Hepworth had been at the weekly rock press too, *NME* before me and then at *Sounds*. Fast-driven Yorkshiremen and breezy southern types tended to eye each other with mutual curiosity and we'd hit it off from the start. Dave was funny and immensely bright, a great engine of ideas. He knew instinctively what appealed to the teenage viewers of *Top of the Pops*. A picture of Toyah turned up, her face painted with seagulls and her hair a bright-orange, vertical explosion as if she'd been connected to the national grid. The black and white music papers called her a histrionic harpie of no audible talent but *Smash Hits* readers thought she was the liberated sister they'd never had. Dave slapped it on the cover and it sold 150,000 copies. He decided the next issue should have *two* covers, Kim Wilde on the front, the Stray Cats on the back: the two half-magazines met in the middle, one printed upside down. His next stroke of genius was his coverage of the tooth-rotting pop medleys of the Dutch novelty act Stars On 45. They'd taken fragments of hits – Beatles, Abba, soul, disco – and joined them at the same relentless beat and these dispiriting discs were never off the radio. Dave felt the tortured public should have the right to reply so I took some copies and a photographer round Soho asking music-lovers to destroy them in imaginative ways. Some were snapped, scratched, trodden on or simply hurled, frisbee-like, into heavy traffic. One was pulverised with a road-drill, another sawn in half by a fabulously camp window-dresser from a shop called The Foundry, wearing a ballgown and a black felt hat. He looked like a Dickensian pickpocket crossed with a Hollywood starlet and told me he was forming a pop group. I put his name in the picture caption and the letters poured in – 'More photos of "clothes-seller Boy George O'Dowd" please.'

Alongside Dave there were two other key members of the *Smash Hits* central lobby. One was *Melody Maker*'s Ian Birch, who had an amused, slightly shrugging Irish sensibility. He was as fascinated as I was by the demands of our new readers: in his first week he dashed off dutifully to interview Japan when a reader announced she would leap from the Forth Road Bridge if rumours of the pale quintet's split weren't officially denied. The second big wheel was Neil Tennant, a wildly entertaining former editor at D. C. Thomson, home of *The Dandy* and *The Beano*. He had big glasses and a mop of hair, and was from Newcastle, now living in a cheap flat in Chelsea. His baptism by fire was being sent on the road with Kajagoogoo, a new pop sensation mobbed wherever they appeared by girls in distressed clothing. 'The *noise!*' he sighed comically. 'The *people!*'

Neil and I cooked up a fantasy about the savage, unforgiving world of stardom. Every issue of the magazine needed the big chart fixtures of the moment, ten key figures riding what we called 'The Giddy Carousel Of Pop'. If one of them had two flop singles in a row – the hapless Howard Jones, the doomed Shakin' Stevens – they were transferred to another imagined location known as 'The Dumper'. Here they eked out their fading celebrity in a run-down boarding-house that smelt of gas and cabbage. 'Down The Dumper' was where the former hit-maker languished until their name fell off the radar completely and their room was made available for another starlet on the slide. Occasionally an act would reverse their fortunes and come kicking back with 'a new sound' and a highly expensive makeover, like Bucks Fizz or Shalamar, in which case they'd be 'Up The Dumper' – or, indeed, 'back, *back*, BACK!' – and reinstalled in a vacant saddle on The Giddy Carousel of Pop. There were no more chilling words in the showbiz lexicon, Neil believed, than the phrase that ended a damning *Smash Hits* singles review: 'The Dumper beckons . . .'

'Would you say, Neil,' I'd ask him, 'that Gary Numan was still Up The Dumper, for the ashen-faced android hasn't troubled our charts since April?'

'Up The Dumper? *Au contraire!*' he'd trill. 'The pallid pop trooper couldn't be more Down The Dumper if he tried. That last single, oh pur-lease. *Poor* old Gazzer,' he'd shiver. 'See me – could do better.'

Warming to his theme, he'd begin pacing the office and flinging his arms about.

'IF one was to visit LA DUMPEURE *ce matin* and tap gently upon its hallowed portal – which would be opened, incidentally, by Buster Bloodvessel of Bad Manners, possibly still in his pyjamas – THEN one would find that not only has *dear* old Gaz Numan JUST checked into Room Number Six but the neighbourly Midge Ure has been helping him choose some wallpaper. And Phil Collins has popped by with a cup of sugar. And Renée *and* Renato.'

One pop act that couldn't be further Up The Dumper was Meat Loaf. His hit-spinning *Bat Out Of Hell* album had sold fractionally less than Fleetwood Mac's *Rumours* and long negotiation eventually secured us a 'world exclusive' at his east coast American home. On the road to Connecticut I tried to picture what the place might look like. Where would you live if the heavens opened and it started raining royalty cheques? And with such success, what levels of pride, contentment and peace of mind?

The New England terrain was studded with huge cedarwood cabins with names like 'Deepwood Eagle Drive' – it was rock-star country: we passed Ian Hunter's place – but we eventually sank into the gravel of a modest slice of real estate known locally as 'Loaf Ranch'. It was tiny, with a little garden and pick-up truck outside. If you were just the singer, and not the song-writer, in a gazillion-selling franchise then clearly someone else was buying the yachts. *Bat Out Of Hell* had been written and arranged by Jim Steinman; 'Meat', as everyone called him, including his wife, was merely the frontman. Nobody sang a Steinman song like Meat and no one wrote for Meat like Steinman, but relations over its mountainous profit had soured into a very public soap opera of feuding, suing, counter-suing, catcalling and farce. On no account must this subject be raised, my chauffeur insisted, the doleful man from Epic Records in New York. Not a word about his finances. Not one. None. Meat Loaf would 'go mental', I was warned.

The door was opened by the big-boned showman in a baseball cap, apparently in good spirits. A huge, silent TV flickered in his shag-piled living room; a quad bike sat on the grass. Meat's long-suffering wife Leslie – Leslie Loaf? – was piling fruit into a blender, a baby slept in a cot and a flaxen-haired child named Pearl was prodding a computer game called Slalom Skiing. There was a wholesome scent of fresh coffee and apple juice, and the portly troubadour seemed to be enjoying many aspects of his wall-to-wall ubiquity.

'I stand on the street with Peter Frampton, they don't recognise him,' he told me. 'I stand on the street with Bruce Springsteen, they recognise me first. Stand on the street with John Belushi – me first, Belushi second.'

Why was this?

'Hey!' Palms upturned. 'I weigh two hundred and eighty pounds!'

The profile was high, the celebrity pals in place, but where were the trappings of rock success – the staff, the fleet of jeeps, the polo ponies, the studio in a converted barn? Even

Gary Numan had a helicopter. Land one here and you'd knock off a chimney-pot.

I couldn't help myself. I asked about the money. Big, *huge* mistake. The man from Epic began to wobble visibly.

'Money?' bellowed Meat. 'I don't *have* any money! Are you kidding? My money,' he pointed at the house, 'you're sitting in it! In 1978 *Bat Out Of Hell* grossed sixty-four million dollars. Let's break that down, OK? Let's say the record label get seventy-five per cent so that leaves me twenty-five per cent.'

He'd changed colour and was overheating.

'But out of my twenty-five per cent along comes . . . hey, the manager! He gets ten per cent.' He was counting on his fingers. 'Then along comes . . . hey, the agent! *He* gets ten per cent. And the business manager. He gets five per cent. And then you got your legal fees and they want a quarter of a million dollars. And then the government comes along and says, "Give us our fifty per cent," and out of that sixty-four million dollars you got a buck and a fuckin' half!'

He stormed upstairs for a shower, slamming the door. The man from Epic gave me a sour look, as did Mrs Meat. Pearl was prised from her console and bundled into another room. There was silence, apart from the weeping of Infant Loaf and the distant din of her father going about his ablutions. Then another noise, a station-wagon crunching up the drive. A nervous envoy in a padded jacket hopped out to deliver a letter and waited while Leslie opened it and read the first line in a quavering voice.

'Meat!' she yelled. '*Meeeaaat!*' It was a writ claiming owner-ship of Loaf Ranch and she told him so. The soap-smeared singer banged open a window to see the messenger leaping into his car and starting the engine. There was an almighty roar from upstairs, a great soulful human wail, followed by the sound of a well-built man in his underpants taking the stairs five at a time. He tore open a hall cupboard full of tumbling sports equipment, grabbed a blunt instrument, charged down the drive, bellowing like a wounded bull, and jumped into his pick-up. 'I'm gonna get that sucker,' he howled. 'I'm gonna nail his ass to the floor!'

Leslie dialled Meat's personal minder. All rock stars of a certain level had an all-purpose gofer and The Loaves had 'Uncle Freddie'.

'Freddie!' she screamed, as the PR tried to stop me taking notes. 'Freddie, get over here right away, ya hear me? Meat is . . . a little upset. Meat has a baseball bat. Meat is . . . Meat's getting in his car. Meat is driving *awaaay*. UNCLE FREDDIE, I THINK HE'S GONNA GO OUT AND *KILL SOMEBODYYY*!'

The press guy and I beat a retreat to a chorus of twin-generational tears, but at least Uncle Freddie was on his way. We powered through the gates and out to the open road. The man from Epic was livid and I was quietly thrilled with my preposterous scoop – AT HOME WITH MEAT LOAF, WHERE IT ALL GOES HORRIBLY WRONG! – but I felt a lot of sympathy for the poor soul in the bear-pit of this miserable drama who'd naïvely imagined, as *I* had, that he'd get a larger slice of the pie.

The return trip to New York passed in almost total silence.

Back in London another surprise was in store. I went to interview a new rock act doggedly plying their trade in the face of the pop explosion. They were promoting their second album and playing a half-filled sports centre in Bracknell, Berkshire. I'd seen them at the Lyceum the year before, above Delta 5, below Echo & the Bunnymen, the night their singer clambered up the PA system to create some spontaneity and split his leather trousers. *Sounds* called him 'the new Rod Stewart', and not in a good way.

Bono sat hunched in his tiny hotel room before the gig.

He had pointy boots, a zipped leather jacket and a soft Dublin accent, pronouncing his name 'Bah-no'. He had an open copy of Gideon's Bible on the bedside table by the kettle and teabags. Every now and then he'd read a passage from the Old Testament to illustrate a point he was making. I was amazed. This wasn't what I'd signed up for at all. I'd spent a lot of my youth hearing extracts from the Good Book and I'd thought rock and roll was an obvious way to escape it. But in the new age of cork-launching decadence and Pan Stik frivolity, here was an earnest twenty-one-year-old peering at the world with sober, God-fearing scrutiny. Pop music, to U2, was an overdressed sham, a vulgar video-based charade with no strategy or substance performed by people mostly required to mime. He referred to his voice as 'an instrument' and took great pride in playing it live. Fakery had poisoned the wells of his happiness. I couldn't work out if he was enjoying life or simply on a religious crusade for passion and authenticity.

'The ceremony is about to begin,' their PR whispered at showtime. Bono disappeared alone into a little store-room full of gym equipment and paced up and down, running through his scales. In the punk-rock days, singers used to charge onstage and start shouting; *this* guy spent fifteen minutes 'warming up my instrument'. He stepped into the lights in the same clothes he'd worn all day.

'We're here to rekindle people's hopes in progressive music,' he told me. 'They're seeing someone on stage in shabby jeans. *That*'s reality. That's where music *ought* to be.'

I might have bought all this ten years earlier but where was the fun in it now? Honesty, sincerity, artistic purity – in 1981?

I couldn't see it catching on.

15

Shelter From The Storm

Clare and I set up home in Greenside Road, W12, our little bedroom crammed full of albums. They were slowly taking over so their sheer number was a pressing concern.

'Do you think you've got *enough* records now?' she asked sweetly.

'*Enough?* Enough *records*?' This was unthinkable. 'You can *never* have enough records!'

'Well, maybe every time you get a new one you could find an old one that you maybe don't play as much cos you've maybe gone off it a bit and maybe pass it on to somebody else who, you never know, might maybe *enjoy* it, maybe.'

This was a tough one as she'd often take one of my albums out to have a listen, then put it back in the wrong place, and I'd point out that that way madness lay as they were all racked alphabetically. And she'd run a finger randomly across the spines and note that although, yes, the Glitter Band did come conveniently between the Glaxo Babies and the Global Village Trucking Company, hell would have to freeze over, thaw out and possibly *refreeze* before even *I* let any of them near the turntable.

For me, music was mostly part of a particular activity – cooking, talking to people, getting ready to go out, or even simply sitting in a chair listening intently to what it sounded like. Clare played music to suit a frame of mind or a time of day, and she danced adorably round the kitchen while she heard it. The mood she was in when she played Bob Dylan's recent *Saved* could be described as merciful. I felt anyone with all his other albums – among them the peerless *Blonde On Blonde*, *John Wesley Harding* and *Blood On The Tracks* – could be pardoned for thinking this turgid and featureless work was, by some margin, the lowest point in the great man's catalogue. But I was wrong: a year later *Shot Of Love* had appeared which was even worse. But Clare took a long, forgiving and fascinating view of them. Men like me, she said, impatient types, tended to fit albums into a neat mental sequence we felt we controlled. We expected them to follow a certain logic we'd imposed on them and were miserable when they turned out differently. She, on the other hand, saw Bob's music from *his* point of view. Whatever he was going through, he had to go through it to come out the other side and be able to write another masterpiece. It was part of the process. These two records might be a challenge she said, but if you dug deep and put in the hard yards, there were pearls to be found – all the more magical as so few others had found them.

'If you expect life to be wonderful,' she smiled, 'then you're always going to be mortified when it isn't. If you think it'll be disappointing then you wake every morning with a nice surprise. It all works out in the end,' she said, '*trust* me,' and she put her arms round me. 'Just you wait and see!'

This was wise and precious advice, and I adopted it imme-diately. I couldn't have loved her any more if I'd tried.

16

Disco Lungsmiths And Pantomime Dames

Mottled with gum, rich with the scent of warm asphalt, the sunny side of Carnaby Street was a good place to be in the summer of 1982. Its boutiques bristled with striped T-shirts, black hats and espadrilles and were run by dark-eyed girls with fake tans and big hair. Everything was cheap and cheerful.

Across the way, just below the windows of *NME*, was a shop called Cascade selling tourist tat – cardboard bowlers, Union Jack mugs and postcards of Charles and Di. Above its awning was a line of plastic upside-down legs in petticoats and high heels in a metal tank which became the clock that measured our working day. At ten every morning, whirring machinery would crank into action, jets of water shot into the air and the legs began their creaking choreography, waving from left to right like windscreen wipers, and we'd roll sheets of paper into typewriters, stick on a tape and start making phone-calls. When they wobbled to a halt at half past six, we took this as the signal to knock off and wandered into Soho to drink Budweiser and munch peanuts at record companies with an act to promote. The new decade was brash and had an amateurish charm about it, records produced by bass guitarists, videos shot by the boss of the label, bands managed by the mate from school, photos taken by someone who happened to have a camera.

A single screening of a video could now reach the same number of people as a lifetime of live performance so the studio was now the instrument, the promotional clip the main stage and the rusty old concept of a 'band', with cumbersome luggage like amps and a rhythm section, was falling apart at the seams. The new pop unit was the two-piece: one sang and the other prodded a synthesiser or played a guitar that wasn't plugged in. 'Young Guns (Go For It)' by Wham! was all over the radio, along with 'Mad World' by Tears For Fears, 'Only You' by Yazoo and Soft Cell's 'Tainted Love'. We'd have office conversations about how if The Beatles had started in the eighties they'd be a duo called Johnny and The Moondog, and the Stones would be the Glimmer Twins. The Hollies would be a pair called Bus Stop and there'd be only two Kinks, The Davies Brothers. Jethro Tull would be Flutes 'N' Boots. Dr Feelgood would be Brilleaux-Johnson.

Some records we covered were magnificent, like 'Dare' by the Human League or ABC's 'The Lexicon Of Love', and some seemed thin and self-satisfied – by Spandau Ballet or Duran Duran – but those weren't aimed at people our age and the bands who made them didn't expect us to like them. I'd wander out towards EMI and run into John Taylor in full Duran livery – cream linen suit with sleeves shunted up to the elbows, flapping shirt cuffs, jangling pendants and huge, artfully streaked hair stuffed under a trilby. I'd stroll up to Chrysalis and bump into Gary Kemp in official Spandau uniform – capacious suit with silk hankie, hand-made shoes, no shirt but a waistcoat with a large gold watch-chain. They told sparkling tales of photo shoots on yachts and pool parties in California, high as kites on their fame and success, and I couldn't have been happier for them. They needed us and we needed them, and we were making hay together. The rock press moaned loudly that the new groups were 'manufactured' and their clothes and musical direction governed by devious gold-diggers. Nonsense: they'd manufactured themselves.

One act alone sent the pop revolution through the roof.

Its singer bowled up at a music awards but I didn't see him at first: I was too busy watching Princess Margaret on the top table. The Queen's sister was a wild card by any standards. The press were obsessed by rumours of her tangles with Mick Jagger, Peter Sellers and the actor David Niven, and the Incredible String Band had told me they'd been living in their commune on the Scottish estate of Lord Glenconner, gone to his Christmas party and found the fun-loving Countess of Snowdon with a large drink to hand, bashing a piano and singing 'The Ferret Song' by Monty Python. The starters arrived at my media-packed lunch, she tapped a glass and suddenly stood up, thanked Britain briefly for its musical exports, proposed a toast, sat down and lit up a Chesterfield. There was a house rule, I discovered: no smoking till after the speeches.

Boy George then swept into view. The Carnaby Street clothes-seller had formed a group and was trying to publicise their new single, 'Do You Really Want To Hurt Me'. A chunky six-footer in a scarlet hat, a long white dress and eye-shadow, he had the room's attention anyway, but the place roared with delight when he came to a halt below two neon signs for the toilets and then trundled theatrically between them in a show of mock-confusion – Ladies? Gents? *Decisions!* The press loved a pantomime dame, sparky but harmless, and from that moment he was never out of the papers, the wit, crackle and colour of Culture Club making the last gasps of punk rock seem boorish and stale.

And if Boy George sold newspapers, why wouldn't Wham! or Duran Duran? The *Daily Mirror* discovered the father of Wham!'s unshaven leader was Greek – 'a bubble and squeak' – so George Michael became 'The Bubble with the Stubble'. With echoes of Beatlemania and T.Rexstasy, a new sensation was apparently sweeping the nation – 'Duran-demonium!'

None of this harmed *Smash Hits*, of course. The more eccentric and imaginative the magazine was, the more it sold. The more it cooked up its own parallel universe, the more The readers posted their fond and whimsical letters to The Party On Paper™ written in coloured biro, the boys often asking if we had Kim Wilde's home phone number as they seemed to have lost it, the girls attaching elaborate collages of John Taylor with their own head glued to the body of whoever he was pictured with. Gasping postmen hauled huge sacks of mail up the office stairs every morning.

We created a whole new coded language. Sexual relations between pop stars were known as 'a snogathon'. When they broke up it was 'a blubathon'. If they fell out of a taxi they'd been drinking 'harmless fizzy pop'. Trails for the next issue promised fictional acts like the Flying Saveloy Brothers and Janet, or wonders of the world like the Human Saucepans Of The Orinoco, or just random collections of objects – 'a duck, some tractors and a pound of lard!' For years I answered the readers' letters in the guise of the 'Black Type', a complex, waspish individual who claimed his mother was a bottle of Tipp-Ex and his father a visual display unit (Tom Hibbert took over when I left). Dave commissioned a cartoon version of the Human League story in which Phil Oakey had his famous lop-sided haircut at the age of four, as did everyone else in his household including his parents, the cat, the canary and the flying ducks on their sitting-room wall. *Smash Hits* came with free stickers, saying, 'Put the kettle on, Mother, I'm parched!' A middle-of-the-road ballad-belter like Bonnie Tyler was 'a disco lungsmith'. Ridiculous hair was 'a fright-wig'. The exotic lead singer of Queen was 'Sir Lord Lucan Of Mercury'. His androgynous rival was 'Dame David Bowie'.

The readers listened to them all on their radios or new portable tape-players called Sony Walkmans but still had to endure, as I had, the weekly agony of *Top of the Pops* round the family's sole TV set. The more their fathers mocked the preposterous garb of Marilyn or the Thompson Twins, or the rubber dress and eyeliner of Depeche Mode's Martin Gore, the more they loved and defended them and thought them brave and misunderstood, and wrote in their thousands to tell us so.

Occasionally, if the strain of organising a 'phoner' with the dumper-bound Shakatak proved too much, Neil, Ian and I would reminisce about the groups *we'd* loved as teenagers, trotting out old stories about Bowie, Marc Bolan and Roxy Music gigs like grizzled old war veterans. All three of us had adored the String Band and felt it our educational responsibility to mention these sitar-plucking pals of Princess Margaret's in every issue. Alongside the entry forms for the annual readers' poll, we ran reminders of acts who'd had a good year to jog the memory of the voting public.

'Don't forget Nik Kershaw,' we'd write, 'and Kool & The Gang and Scritti Politti.' There'd be little pictures too. 'And, of course, Hazel O'Connor, Blancmange and the Incredible String Band . . .'

Neil had loved these Celtic hippies so much he'd formed a school group in Newcastle called Dust. If asked why, he'd trot out the same priceless response, emphasising the odd word with 'quote mark' fingers.

'Because, *as any fule kno*, the Increds had a ten-minute track called "Maya" on their SEMINAL 'sixty-eight double-album *Wee Tam and The Big Huge*, and the opening line – lest we forget, people – is "The dust of the rivers does murmur and weep" . . .'

He also had a band in 1982 though he kept very quiet about it. His friend Chris Lowe would wander into Reception in a baseball cap at precisely the moment the Cascade legs shuddered to a standstill and they'd slip off to a studio in Marshall Street. Neil thought *everyone* in the office should be in a band and designed imaginary names for them. There was the Saturday Girls, a trio of bag-swinging ragamuffins in the mode of Bananarama featuring the junior writers Bev, Lisa and Kimbers. Our receptionist, he reckoned, should be a Lulu for the eighties and present a bow-and-arrow-based TV quiz called *On Target With Samantha Archer!* Ian Birch should be launched as the new Bryan Ferry, moody and windswept in stylish winter-wear, pulling reflectively on a Gauloises and renamed A Man Alone – he even drew a cryptic one-word logo: AMANALONE.

The sales raced upwards and piles of the magazine appeared in teenage bedrooms. For anyone too young for gigs, it was perfect – they had the music, we provided the people, the pictures and the lyrics and brought the whole thing to life, the missing link in the circuit of their imaginations that switched on the fairy-lights. Art students even started buying it, delighted by its psychedelic gags and cartoon sense of absurdity. There was still, however, the odd note of concern.

'How's it all going on . . . what's it called again? *Smash Hits?*'

My dear old Dad. He'd just seen the new issue and was baffled to discover that his son's version of journalism was taking Bananarama to a Burger King and asking other pop notables hard-hitting questions like 'What colour is Tuesday?' and 'Have you ever felt like a roundabout?', this for a publication whose idea of a news story was not the sinking of *The Belgrano* but the release of 'a 12-inch remix' by something called the Lotus Eaters. He was glad I was in gainful employment but still dropping hints about *Punch* and the paper he called *The Thunderer*.

'*Punch*, Dad,' I pointed out, 'is still running the same old jokes about pipe-smoking men on lawnmowers and even *you* only read it at the dentist's, and *The Times* hasn't the faintest interest in music beyond Brahms, Verdi or the Ronnie Scott

Quartet. I'll have you know *Smash Hits* now sells a quarter of a million issues a fortnight,' I trilled, desperate to impress him. 'Four readers per copy!'

'Well, your mother seems to like it anyway,' he said fondly. 'She's taken to wandering the byways of Hampshire wearing a free badge that was taped on the front of it, saying, "SIMPLE MINDS". No idea what it means but she says it rather suits her.'

The only frustration with *Smash Hits* was that I couldn't write about the bands I loved that were too far from the mainstream, like a thunderous new Irish folk-rabble called The Pogues or the curdled power-pop of The dB's from North Carolina. Dave Hepworth felt the same and was contributing to a Radio 1 show on Saturday afternoons with the lumbering title of *Rock On*, which let him enthuse about the full range of his record collection. He invited me to tag along and watch him interview Greg Kihn, a low-level rock and roller from Baltimore.

'I'll introduce you to the producer,' he said kindly. 'They like people like you at the BBC: you're from the south and you've got one of those *deep, resonant voices.*'

I sat in the control-booth watching the tape-spools spinning while Dave talked to Greg and took instructions through his headphones. In the gap when they played a track I managed to give the producer's paw a vigorous shaking and babbled manically *in my deepest southern tones* about what a crying shame it was that The Pogues and dB's weren't on the programme's thrusting playlist, and how it could do worse than find a keen young reporter to hack through the undergrowth and discover some exciting new acts – 'tomorrow's sounds today', that sort of thing.

A week later, amazingly, he gave me a call.

17

Wearing Facepaint On The Radio

Everyone has their radio memories, indelible moments they can summon in a second. Here's one of mine.

On a cloudless afternoon in August '82, Clare and I climbed into a blue Ford Escort and headed for the docks at Southampton. Strangers honked their horns and gave us a thumbs-up and we waved back excitedly. We stopped at a petrol station near Winchester so I could hose down the car, which was plastered with rice and shaving-foam. Our hair was full of confetti. As we motored south, I kept checking my watch.

At exactly three minutes to six I switched on Radio 1 where 'Mark Ellen, sitting in for Tommy Vance' was lining up a track you wouldn't normally hear on the *Rock On* programme. It was Billie Holiday back in 1933 with the Benny Goodman Orchestra playing a rowdy old slab of showboat jazz, a favourite song of ours. As the clarinet whistles around her, the singer sounds resigned but upbeat: she has a boyfriend who'll never make much money in life – creative type, probably, limited earnings – but it's a situation she's accepted and she'll take him the way he is.

You don't have to have a hanker to be a broker or a banker
No siree, just simply be . . . my mother's son-in-law!

'Thanks for listening,' Mark Ellen said. 'That was a song for anyone getting married today – and might be a surprise for one of them, Clare Ellen!'

She shrieked and we hooted with laughter as the trombones parped their way into the pips. An hour earlier the *Smash Hits* staff had posed behind the married couple in the shape of the Madness Nutty Train, a giant dancing locomotive, arms flying, legs pumping, the girls with their flat shoes and hairbands, Dave with a hand out, Neil in the middle raising a tea cup from a saucer in the droll manner of an eighties Noël Coward.

But there hadn't been much joy from my producer the week before.

'You're getting married? Next *Saturday*?' He had a meat pie on a cardboard plate and was chewing distractedly. 'Fuck's sake, we'll have to pre-record.'

He was no great romantic, Pete Ritzema, and hard to please so I was flattered he'd taken me on. When he called he'd said I had the 'the right voice for radio' – right face too, probably – and asked if I fancied interviewing someone for a 'try-out'. I mentioned Pete Wylie who seemed the dream ticket. I'd met him before and knew you had merely to light his fuse and the motor-mouthed singer of Wah! Heat would fire off a deathless stream of deliberation until physically hauled from the room. I told Ritz he was 'shy and retiring but I might be able to coax something out of him' and that his band had what Radio 1 called 'a chart-bound sound', part of which was true.

The red light came on and I started my introduction.

'We're joined today,' I quivered, 'by a Liverpool living legend, leader of the mighty Wah! Heat, Pete Wylie . . .'

'And, as if by magic, here I am!' Wylie chipped in, and talked non-stop, apparently without breathing, for the best part of twenty minutes, at which point Ritz made wind-up signs from behind the glass, sending a shower of pastry to the carpet. He always had a sausage roll on the go.

'The mighty Pete Wylie there of Liverpool legends Wah! Heat,' I signed off, 'whose new single "The Story Of The Blues" is in the shops on Monday!'

Ritz was delighted – 'You really got him going!' – the piece was aired and I was hired as *Rock On*'s roving reporter, working at *Smash Hits* in the daytime and for Radio 1 at nights and weekends. I was charmed by his weather-beaten view of the world, the polar opposite of mine. He felt the Golden Age had been and gone and all we had left were crumbs from the great table. Tapes of sessions he'd engineered in the sixties gathered dust in the cupboard behind him. He'd tell wistful tales about Led Zeppelin and Tim Buckley while I suggested a few up-and-coming acts for his programme, like Aztec Camera, The Higsons or Everything But The Girl. I could see him twiddling knobs in the room behind them, smiling in his crumpled way and munching baked confections from the staff canteen. Whatever he'd felt wrestling with the controls as the Jimi Hendrix Experience played 'Spanish Castle Magic' ten feet away from him, it wasn't going to be revived by white-rasta pop-vendors Haysi Fantayzee.

Broadcasting House was a whole new world, the base for Radios 1, 2, 3 and 4. Occasionally you'd see a Member of Parliament stroll into Reception, past the little stand with free postcards of Simon Bates and Noel Edmonds. There was a brisk, wider-world efficiency about the place, and a real thrill in telling someone you were interviewing them for the BBC. Dad was overjoyed when I said I'd bumped into Brian Redhead from the *Today* programme in the lift. If I fancied going 'out in the field', Ritz gave me a portable Uher reel-to-reel recorder; it had a little metal plate on the front with a diagonal groove so you could slice the tape with a razor blade and re-splice it if you had to edit in a hurry. I lugged one down to the Bath and West Showground near Shepton Mallet where Peter Gabriel was launching his new WOMAD festival and watched its little needles dance to the sound of CND clowns, sitar players in tepees and gurgling hippie children trying a sizzling new invention called 'the veggieburger'.

The *Rock On* studio was a revelation. Conversations for magazines with anyone of note often went in one direction – frantic enquiry from the interviewer met by lofty indifference, sarcastic evasion or long, enigmatic silence. Try any of that on the radio and you got acres of agonising 'dead air'. This wasn't a battle so much as a joint venture. You were in it together. You had ten minutes of national airtime to forge some entertainment and it was in both your best interests to succeed. And this was fine with seasoned old troupers who lit up when the red light came on. Grumpy though she was, and darkly fringed, the Pretenders' Chrissie Hynde was chippy and characterful when the nation was listening in. Lemmy of Motörhead was alarming in the warm-up, a bristling physical presence in clanking chains and boots, but warm and magnetic on air, like some whiskery old actor in the presence of his public. Nick Lowe was charm itself, the first musician I'd seen onstage. His carrier-bag gave an ominous clink as he settled it on the floor beside him and retrieved his first bottle of warm white wine. I asked long and complicated questions to give him time to top up and drain his paper cup out of range of the microphones. A grinning Ritz gave me a thumbs-up behind him: *this* was the stuff, proper rock and roll, like his booze-filled memories of Hendrix and Jimmy Page.

But there was always going to be someone who'd test the mettle and upset the gentle rhythm of Ritz's pastry consumption. In fact, there were two of them, wild, erratic and with exotic pseudonyms, both heroes of mine. I tracked down the first at a soundcheck at The Venue in Victoria, a sixty-eight-year-old jazz musician from Alabama called Herman Poole Blount. Back in the forties he'd played piano in the Fletcher Henderson Band, then erased his whole back story and relaunched himself as the mystic, robe-toting leader of an avant-garde collective called The Arkestra. He now claimed to come from Saturn and answered to the name of Sun Ra, the kind of behaviour I felt should be encouraged. But he'd been a hard sell at Radio 1, 'cult act' written all over him. Run a piece in a magazine and people could turn the page if they didn't like it, but stick a lunatic like this on daytime radio and they might switch off or retune to another station. Ritz noticed his just-released seventy-third album had a hand-painted sleeve.

'How many copies of this record exist?' he asked.

'It's a limited edition,' I told him.

'*How* limited? Five? Ten? Are they available in a shop somewhere or do you have to ring Saturn and get so-called Sun Ra to press one up personally?'

To his credit, Ritz gave eccentrics a national audience. He sat there, grimly munching a meat pie, playing the section of my badly recorded tape where Sun Ra claimed to have changed his address. He'd left Saturn, apparently, and now simply occupied a space-time continuum.

'I wasn't born,' he twinkled. 'Spirits, like drops across the water, can't be born, And I am from The Omniverse. I am ten thousand years old.'

It was a long old day in the edit suite.

Next week's problems were even worse. Just before the show we'd had disturbing news: full of refreshment and the joys of spring, our guest had ran amok at Chrysalis Records. One of those old-school hippies who found clothes restricting, he'd rampaged round the press office stark naked, startling the girls with the stupendous size of his manhood. 'It was like a penis,' one of them shivered, 'only *bigger*.'

His American manager arrived to tell us 'Jim' was very excited about appearing on *Rock On*. He was a liability at the best of times so Jim being 'excited' didn't sound good. Drink must be involved, and maybe some powerful chop. Things might get broken. Pictures of James Osterberg as a high-school senior in the mid-sixties had looked preppy and presentable but a Doors concert at the University of Michigan had sent him hurtling off-track. The spectacle of a topless Jim Morrison had made him form his own band, taking the stage name Iggy Pop. He sang, abused the audience and writhed around semi-clothed in broken beer bottles. He'd invented the stage-dive. When I saw him at the Music Machine in '79, he'd performed 'I Wanna Be Your Dog' while crawling on all fours in a dress, his bare, hairy legs ending in crimson stilettos. He looked like a prostitute playing charades.

And now he was on his way and 'very excited'. In what way? I asked the manager.

'Jim feels *colourful* today,' he said, eyes lowered. 'Kinda theatrical.'

'Acting or acting up?'

'He's put a lot of thought into how he looks today,' he said slowly.

'He does know it's a radio show?'

'*I* know it's a radio show, *you* know it's a radio show, my friend, but *Jim* . . .' He trailed off. 'Work with me here. Jim thinks he's appearing on television.'

'Television?'

'He's wearing face-paint.' He looked up, pain behind his eyeballs. 'Jim has painted his face with woad.'

'*Woad?*' I said.

'Woad.'

An explosion in the corridor announced the arrival of an

extraordinary-looking man, part Iggy Pop, part primitive tribesman. Had he carried a blowpipe or a dead lizard, you'd have thought he'd come straight from the Amazonian rainforest. His face was a mask of green, red and white lines, crudely applied. His eyes were huge, his body vibrating. He'd taken what's technically known as a 'fuck-load' of drugs. The manager was keen to start immediately. I sensed this powerful cocktail could be about to wear off and then things might get worse.

'Iggy Pop is here!' I squeaked, over the bruised and sunless poetry of his new single 'Run Like A Villain', a raw, mordant work about how the shockwaves of a nuclear accident would bury you in a melting coffin. 'Iggy Pop's in the studio and he's very excited!' I wanted musicians to be the way they appeared on record but this was only an inch off method-acting. He was like someone who'd taken a crash-course in Iggy Pop and was hamming it up for an Oscar.

'The shining moon, the dead oak tree,' the record barked, 'nights like this APPEAL to me!'

The author of this magnificent verse was now swinging from side to side in his swivel chair, one knee pressed against his chin, his facepaint loosening in the heat. The interview lasted seven minutes. Ritz's steak and ale pie was abandoned. Like some fevered, gripping nightmare, like some battery-powered robot running out of juice, Iggy Pop began to slow down, his speech getting more and more slurred, his voice deeper and deeper, his movements grinding to a halt. My headphones rattled, Pete telling me to abandon ship. I signed off hastily – 'And that's where we'll have to leave it!' – as the woad-plastered 'Jim', sensing he'd been cut off, clambered onto the table spilling glasses with his knees, grabbed my microphone and delivered one last stream of unintelligible speech, the final words – but of course – being '*Raaahk and rooowlll!*'

★   ★   ★

Radio 1 was flying high. Its reach was massive and its support of a new single crucial to the industry. It had a crackle about it and a sense of its own importance. Long black cars delivered rock stars to its entrance hall. Record-pluggers in T-shirts gossiped in the lobby. Paunchy men in anoraks clutched autograph books outside and girls with Lady Di fringes mooched about, hoping for a glimpse of its ever-tanned DJs – Peter Powell, maybe, or 'Woo' Gary Davies.

The studios and offices were all in Egton House, a monstrous glass and steel box lashed to the carved stone portals of Broadcasting House, and the station was divided into two quaintly labelled sections on different levels. You could still feel the echoes of the old BBC, the days when its output was split between Gramophone Programmes (or 'Grams') and Variety Shows. The fourth floor was 'pop', the daytime slots, mostly fronted by blokes in their mid- to late-thirties wearing baseball caps and expensive trainers – Steve Wright, Mike Read, Paul Burnett and Simon Bates. Beside them was *The Radio 1 Roadshow*, the whole place like a cross between a college campus and a Butlins holiday camp. The floor below them was 'rock' – the weekend, evening and night-time shows – where I'd run into Kid Jensen, Janice Long, Richard Skinner, Noel Edmonds and *Rock On*'s presenter Tommy 'TV On The Radio' Vance, who referred to himself as 'The Larynx on Legs' and had a voice like *crème de menthe* on a bed of warm gravel. On my second visit, the doors opened and there was Alan 'Fluff' Freeman in a fabulously unfashionable satin tour-jacket promoting prog-rockers Camel. The sound of his voice sent me spinning back to the school boot-room and the magical transistorised twang of The Kinks.

Pluggers were allowed up in waves to deliver their packages to the producers, their pitches carefully tailored for each programme. The same Iron Maiden single that was a 'balls-out floor-filler' for *Rock On* was a 'muscular ballad' when offered to *The Breakfast Show*. Huge amounts of money were lavished by labels on promotion: the first Radio 1 heard of the new ZZ Top single 'TV Dinners' was when the band's plugger hired a hydraulic lift to raise him to each programme's window in turn where he tapped on the glass and offered them a tray of fried chicken from the outside of the building.

The producers sat in their little cubicles sorting through Jiffy-bags and compiling playlists. I'd assumed that even the daytime DJs were firmly involved in this process but this was wide of the mark. There were times when Dave Lee Travis strolled into his studio ten minutes before the red light and was already pulling his coat on as he bade the nation a fond farewell. He simply played the records in the box prepared for him and read notes his producer put between them about where the Bucks Fizz tour was headed next or how great the Fun Boy Three were 'if you're lucky enough to catch them live'. A lot of these DJs were national celebrities and had lucrative sidelines on the club circuit, so the main priority for the self-styled 'Hairy Cornflake' seemed to be maintaining his profile with the aid of his grating 'quack-quack oops!' sound-effect and gormless snooker-on-the-radio feature, and endlessly reminding his lucky listeners he'd been voted 'Pipe Smoker Of The Year, 1982'. I wondered if these people still lived in the real world. They seemed drunk on their own ubiquity. When not treating a multi-million audience to his own terrible songs sung to an acoustic guitar, *Breakfast Show* host Mike Read wittered on about weekend tennis tournaments with his neighbour Cliff Richard.

'It's pouring with rain in Manchester,' a caller once told Dave Lee Travis, as it was all over the country.

'Lovely and sunny in London!' trilled the Cornflake, without looking up.

* * *

The 'rock output' on the floor below had more credibility. Night-time radio was where new acts were first played before reaching the mainstream via the pop slots above, the most cavalier supporter being *The John Peel Show* on Mondays to Thursdays from ten till midnight. I hadn't seen Peel in the flesh since those early seventies festivals and peered out excitedly from the *Rock On* office, hoping he'd wander past.

'Just follow the sound of the trumpet,' Ritz told me, between mouthfuls, and pointed down the corridor.

I poked my head round the door of Room 318 to find Peel's producer John Walters tootling an old showtune – he'd been a member of the Alan Price Set – and the crumpled figure of John Peel in a faded T-shirt sifting through a gigantic mound of Jiffy-bags, postcards, cassette tapes, albums and singles, assisted by their secretary Sue Foster who, for some reason, they both called 'Brian'. Their programme's mantra, they told me, was 'We're not here to give the public what it wants but what it didn't *know* it wanted.'

Peel was a *huge* hero. I'd followed him since his late-sixties show, *The Perfumed Garden*, and knew the droll, melancholic delivery that now introduced challenging records by the Dead Kennedys and Shriekback had been through a few transitional stages. Residents of Dallas in 1959 tuning into WRR for John Ravenscroft's R&B show *Kats Karavan* heard someone who, by his own admission, sounded 'like a minor member of the Royal Family', with an accent that could chip bone china: 'We hev some *mahvellous* blues platters here from the purely excellent Big Bill Broonzeh!' By '64 he was co-presenting *The John and Paul Show* with his mate Paul Miller for KOMA in Oklahoma City and had changed his name to the less posh and fashionably English John Peel. He'd got the job by claiming to be a friend of The Beatles, though he wasn't from Liverpool but the nearby village of

Burton. Five years later his tones had morphed into what he called his 'princeling of hippiedom voice': on one memorable show, his effete, practically lisping delivery enjoined you to 'throw wide the windows and whisper, "I love you," at the stars'. And when the first Ramones single arrived in '76, he'd developed his classless, mid-tempo mumble. Radio 1 colleagues said the main force in his courageous adoption of punk had initially been his producer – indeed, Walters described their complex relationship as 'a bit like a master and his dog, each believing the other to be the dog' – but slowly Peel's mailbag had begun to change: people no longer wanted 'more Purps, Zep, Heep and Dr Strangely Strange'; they wanted 'more Clash, Jam, Damned and Christians In Search Of Filth'.

Everyone listened to Peel – the bands, the press, the nation. His show reached two and a quarter million people and, with an irony not lost on the man himself, was the only Radio 1 programme broadcast in FM stereo. This new-fangled signal was designed for acts with the pin-sharp separation of Boston or Dire Straits. Peel, of course, championed the uncommercial, discs so obscure he could barely get hold of them and often cycled to Rough Trade in Notting Hill to buy a copy for that night's show. So what you heard on your high-end home entertainment system was not just *not stereo*, it was deliberately, mutinously mono – raw, rampaging monologues from Attila The Stockbroker or cacophonous fusillades from Einstürzende Neubauten who sounded like four sets of cutlery tossed down a mineshaft. You couldn't find more low-fi and unsuitable records if you tried.

Peel was proud of this, and rightly so. It was the very tent-pole of what he stood for, the polar opposite of Air Supply, Toto, Rick Springfield and whatever else was being spun by the perma-tanned, tennis-playing, mullet-sporting, daytime staples on the floor above. The man was irreplaceable. His show was unique. If he ever took days off he pre-recorded it as even *he* thought he was irreplaceable.

So it was a shock all round when they decided to replace him. With me.

18

Play 'Misty In Roots' For Me

In its own strange way, the fact that John Peel never took a holiday was linked to the Radio 1 calendar. If you'd imagined, as I had, that his talent and his status as one of the few surviving cornerstones of the station's first broadcasts might have allowed him a sense of his own worth, you'd have been sorely mistaken.

Peel operated on an undercurrent of paranoia, a quiet, low-level suspicion that he might be replaced at any moment. A new director general could arrive, a new broom sweeping Egton House, and some upstart could end up in his chair. And there was no clearer demonstration of a DJ's value than the network's yearly calendar, sold to listeners across the country. The more I worked for *Rock On*, the more I hung around the office and the more I understood the chilling significance of this annual ritual.

To the outside world it was a random collection of portraits of the station's most famous faces; on the inside it was the writing on the wall, an indication of your professional life expectancy. Twelve months, twelve DJs – but which ones and in what order? If you appeared in the winter months then clearly your contract was safe for at least another year, indeed the cheery disc-spinner picked for the Santa suit seemed virtually unsackable. If they asked you to pose in sturdy knitwear kicking a pile of leaves then best give the controller a big smile if you passed him in a passage. If they told you to bring a surfboard to the photo shoot, then your agent was on red-alert – that year Peel was 'June', astride a racing bike and wearing shorts and a look of fake sincerity. But if you were a 'spring pin-up' – so long, Pat Sharp; farewell, 'Me' Mark Page – you might as well start packing now.

Peel's insecurity was so great it was hard to get him to take any time off, but astonishing news arrived that he was heading to the seaside for a fortnight with a pile of battered paperbacks and I was signed up to sit in for him. The trumpet-toting Walters was now presenting his own programme, *Walters' Weekly* – 'An oik's eye view of the arts,' he called it – and Chris Lycett was brought in as the new producer, a kindly soul Peel called 'the Adonis-like Lycett' on account of his elegant mop of Grecian locks (it was all surnames at Radio 1 – Peel, Walters, Lycett, Bates, Ready, Wrighty). And so began a delightful cycle of pint-filled lunches as I was coached to scale this monumental crag.

The first thing I noticed was that everyone in Peel's orbit seemed to talk like him. His speech was full of extraneous phrases that gave a dash of colour but were actually a clever device to buy him a few split seconds to think when he was on-air. He'd ended up talking like this all the time: why use one word when you can use sixteen? Peel took the scenic route through dense verbal shrubbery, a masterclass in procrastination and space-filling where he emphasised the odd RANDOM word and each sentence trailed off in a mournful cadence that made it hysterically funny. Instead of 'This is the new single from the Polish punk band Tilt', he'd say, 'In *my* book, in *my* understanding, if *I*'m any judge – which coincidentally has yet to be proved with any degree of CONVICTION – then the show's next "hot platter" will set toes a-tapping in right-thinking households the length and breadth of Radio 1's PROFOUNDLY enviable FM-stereo reach, a waxing if I'm not entirely mistaken on Warsaw's block-rocking TONPRESS label, and the robust and bracing work as you might have surmised of person or persons of POLISH extraction. I give you . . . the mighty TILT!' At the beginning of this link he'd have had no idea what he was about to play but, while speaking, would have sifted through his box of records, slipped one out of its cover, slapped it on the 'grams', cued up the needle and hit the play button when he finished speaking.

Lycett spoke just like him. So did Walters, who accompanied us on every trip. I started doing it too. The murmuring rhythms of Peel's speech were infectious. The three of us would loaf about in the Yorkshire Grey on Langham Street, sinking pints of furry ale and having the same circular conversations.

Walters: 'On a purely PERSONAL level, I'm pondering an investment in some of this hostelry's *highly* rated haute CUISINE . . .'

Me: '. . . quite possibly a *meat*-filled product of PASTRY-based persuasion . . .'

Lycett: '. . . and surely floating said comestible on a fresh draught of their endlessly potable falling-DOWN water!'

Peel himself never appeared, a merciful relief as the thought of seeing the man I was about to substitute was paralysingly frightening. The pair of them knew I idolised him as I regaled them with star-struck memories of him hosting festivals and of his late-night shows in the sixties. I even quoted things he'd said on the previous night's programme: he'd played Neon's 'Don't Eat Bricks'– 'Sound advice in *my* view' – and followed it with 'the new one from David Bowie called "Cat People (Putting Out Fire)" – Fire, one *imagines*, being the name of the cat in QUESTION'.

The big day approached and we started choosing the music. I couldn't play precisely the same records as he would but I couldn't be that different either as, judging by his fan mail, devoted listeners might march upon Egton House and hurl me from a top-floor window. And there were a lot of them, from the tip of Scotland and the west of Ireland right across northern France, Holland and Belgium. Lycett suggested I replay an old Peel session in each of my shows and gave me the key to a cupboard packed with magical white boxes full of quarter-inch tape, among them the Hendrix and Tim Buckley recordings by Pete Ritzema. To Lycett's horror, I picked ones I'd remembered from when I was a teenager, like Led Zeppelin and The Faces, now jarringly off-message for *The John Peel Show* of the eighties – in fact there was a sense of embarrassment that he'd ever commissioned them in the first place. Though he'd never know, Lycett pointed out, as he wouldn't be in Peel Acres, Stowmarket, with the radio on but on his relaxing and much-publicised holiday. I pictured him shrimping gloomily, probably on the Suffolk coast, a knotted hankie on his head.

All four of the network's studios were off the same corridor in the control room at Broadcasting House, which you entered via a dingy tunnel from the Egton House basement. I arrived with my records on my first night, Monday, 14 June, and peered through the windows one by one. Humphrey Lyttelton was in Radio 2 rounding off *The Best Of Jazz* in a pale pink jumper. He gave a friendly wave. Reels of symphonic music revolved in Radio 3 while a 'tape-op' read the paper. *Kaleidoscope* was in Radio 4, highbrow arts reviewers hunched in a circle. I opened up the fader at ten o'clock and had barely got to the second record when there was a commotion behind the glass. Lycett appeared looking tight-lipped and holding a piece of paper.

'We have to go over the newsroom at exactly ten twenty on the dot.'

'Ten *twenty*? We'll miss most of "Hesitate" by Boots For Dancing!'

'Special announcement,' he said. 'No idea what but we're all going to the news in five minutes.'

Loud whooping down the passage suggested Radios 2 and 4 were ahead of the game. We looked out to see cheering network personnel with their arms linked singing 'Anchors Aweigh'.

'Read exactly what it says on the paper,' Chris cautioned, 'and don't refer to it, just stick on the next track.'

'That's all we can have from Boots For Dancing as we're going over now to the newsroom for a special announcement . . .'

'BBC News Extra at twenty past ten. After seventy-four days, the war in the Falkland Islands has officially ended. Troops surrounded the Argentine garrison at Port Stanley at noon where white flags were seen flying, then advanced on the capital. Nine thousand eight hundred soldiers led by General Mario Menéndez have surrendered to the British forces.'

'Play something sensitive when you come back!' Lycett shouted. This wasn't the moment to be going, 'So, yes, the old Falklands War's finally slung its hook. Onwards and upwards, here's the new one from Xmal Deutschland!' I glanced at the running order:

- 'Wasn't Tomorrow Wonderful?', The Waitresses
- 'Cokane In My Brain', Dillinger
- 'I'm An Old Cowhand', Dan Hicks & His Hot Licks (With The Lickettes)
- SESSION: 'The Pictures On My Wall', Echo & The Bunnymen (REPEAT FEES PAYABLE!)
- 'The Drastic Haircut (Of Mr Doomed-Alright)' by Clive Product

I rummaged through the box and picked the safest option, 'The View From Her Room' by ambient Welsh jazzers

Weekend, a song so inoffensive you could barely tell it was playing.

There were two more curveballs on the Wednesday. News arrived that James Honeyman-Scott of the Pretenders had died; Lycett charged off to the library to find 'Brass In Pocket' while I wrote and delivered an obituary of the hard-living guitarist I'd once met in Paris. Ten minutes later, another ripple. We had a visitor. I looked up to see movement in the control room. There in the shadows – with no bucket, spade or evidence of shrimping equipment – was the unmistakable silhouette of John Peel watching morosely from behind the glass, a shrugging Lycett beside him. To compound his misery, I was playing one of his favourite acts, Southall reggae band Misty In Roots. I slapped on a 12-inch single and went through to meet him for the second time in my life, completely thrown and overawed.

'It's like letting someone borrow your toothbrush,' he said, nodding at the microphone. 'It's like letting someone sleep with your wife.'

It was bad enough trying to amuse the listening millions when they were expecting someone else; now I was doing it in the baleful gaze of the man himself. Peel was clearly *not* on holiday. The BBC had ordered him to take two weeks off, a break would do him good, but he was mooching about at home consumed by the hunch that the stooge sitting in for him was being groomed to take his position. That was how much he cared about his job. But I could see why he was attached to it. My romantic image of late-night radio was built on Peel, along with Clint Eastwood in *Play Misty For Me* and advance copies of a Donald Fagen album called *The Nightfly*, all lone figures in the lamplight sending messages across the ether to other lone figures in cars or on nightshifts or simply drifting off to sleep, launching music like paper darts to float through countless opened windows. Peel himself had heard the midnight howl of Wolfman Jack who'd set up a huge transmitter over the Mexican border and whose dark-sky broadcasts had swamped much of the south-east United States in '63 – 'You got The Wolfman whether you wanted him or not,' he once told me. 'You could probably get him on your fridge.' The moonlight slot had a luminous sheen to it. The whole building felt empty apart from its night-watchman and his box of records, his soft voice murmuring in some distant room.

And you could see why the listeners were attached to Peel: he was so *good* at it. They wrote to him in their thousands, God knows how many letters a week. Even *I* got hundreds, and most of those from people saying they missed him. I got cards, paintings, drawings, tapes, discs, poems, fanzines, rubber-stamped dispatches from HM Prisons, great heaps of the stuff in bulging envelopes, some carefully typed, some scrawled in coloured felt-tip. And with them came passionate requests for Joy Division, The Mekons, Au Pairs, The Fall, Mood Six and Killing Joke. My dredging up of the Zeppelin session sparked demands for my painful death. As did my suggestion that 'No member of The Clash can actually sing.'

'Here's your post,' Brian said brightly, and she sat and listened while I read bits out.

'Paul from Pewsey wants me to ask Jane Fox of the Marine Girls to get in touch. He's included his address and phone number.

'Nikki Sudden from Harbury says he "was making some toast and things" so missed what I said about his new single. "You're probably getting ten million letters a day now you're a fabby swinging DJ," he adds sarcastically.

'Liz from South Glamorgan says she's sorry about the "slagging off" I've been getting, adding that *she* "quite likes Wreckless Eric – and Peel hasn't played him for years!"

'"Mark Allen, from within this network of infinite black

boxes you may catch the fleeting whimper of convulsing muscle as it pulses with the relentless anticipation of hearing Peter Hammill sometime after eleven p.m. this Thursday – yours, S. Ferenczi."

'Nikki from Carshalton – "your fan FOR TWO WEEKS" – wants me to play "Charm" by Positive Noise for Gary, Mole, Spy, Mr Anon and the Frog Children.

'Pete from Romford says I have "a monotonous voice and the ability to play chronic records at the wrong speed so you may go far – hopefully SIBERIA!"

'Dave says, "Please improve or it will be the rat torture."'

But it wasn't all bad news. Pamela from Carmarthen sent me a snap of herself in a photo-booth 'because you probably won't get any fan mail'. And Jackie Howitt from Matlock, Derbyshire, said I was 'better than Andy Peebles'.

Slings and arrows aside, the whole thing was slightly addictive, another reason why Peel couldn't bear the thought of losing it. I loved evangelising about records I liked. I loved the comforting, half-lit fug of the studio and the sunset pace of the programme. I loved the winking lights and dials, the soft whirring of tapes and clicking of switches, the crackle of static, the whistling in my ears as the record ended and I slid up a fader to speak. I even liked the 'carts', big box-like cartridges with trails and jingles for the next day's shows in a little wooden case by the console: you clattered them into a slot, hit a button and they trilled about the 'Radio One-derful sound' of Simon Bates. Peel and Walters had a withering collective name for any dull BBC jobsworth in a cardigan but I loved it when 'Blair Lawnmower' came bustling in from the Motoring and Travel Unit and gave me a 'flash' to read about a pile-up on the A30 near Hartley Wintney. The audience were mostly alone in a bedroom somewhere – in Dorking or Glasgow or Bruges – with just a radio and the dark outside, and there was a peculiar intimacy. I could sense their presence. I could feel them listening. They hung on every note and every word. They wrote to me, quoting me back, wanting the conversation to carry on. It gave me a ridiculous sense of my own importance. I had power. I was high as a kite. I'd hear the booming, three-dimensional sound of my own voice in my headphones and think everything I said had some actual significance. When the red light came on I was talking to *two million people* – and this was a late-night cult show, not the daytime when half the country seemed to be listening.

No wonder radio bred such egomaniacs. No wonder it produced bores like Dave Lee Travis, magnetised by attention and so convinced they were fascinating that they still seemed to be broadcasting even when off the air, advancing their daft opinions in voices *ever so slightly too loud*. The fearful 'Cornflake' would enter a room and visibly sag if it was half empty. Why waste time speaking to so few people?

The Adonis-like Lycett got hold of the Radio 1 'reaction profiles'. A staggering 15 per cent said I had a 'likeable personality' – probably the ones I'd written to – and only three per cent ticked the 'poor DJ' box. I don't want to brag or anything but I got higher marks than Emperor Rosko. I was now officially on the subs bench. Whenever the overanxious Peel was shepherded to another 'holiday', or Annie Nightingale had an evening off, or Kid Jensen was sunning himself in the Algarve, I was ferried in to occupy their chairs and keep the big red beach-ball of entertainment off the sand.

There was one minor hitch but I think we got away with it. The big record in the autumn of '82 was a ground-breaking hip-hop single called 'The Message' by Grandmaster Flash and The Furious Five, about a rotting tenement full of pimps, whores and dealers. After countless calls to the Sugar Hill Label, *The Kid Jensen Show* secured a phone interview. I was so excited I trailed it as a 'world exclusive' before we'd even got it recorded. After hours of hanging around I was eventually put through to the pioneering hit-maker but seemed to know more about his career than he did.

'Is it true,' I asked, 'you had the legendary Melle Mel in the original line-up?'

'I *did*?' The Grandmaster seemed unsure. There was a pause and voices off. 'Fo' sure, guy, I *did*!'

'Last year you sampled Queen, Chic and Blondie on one seven-minute single. Explain how that works, this new mixing-on-turntables thing.'

'Who knows, man? Hey, that's a tough one!'

There was barely any information at all. After a savage edit we were left with two minutes of spectacular waffle but we'd trailed it so we had to put it out. A week later I ran into some rock hacks in a club. One had just been to New Jersey to write a piece about Sugar Hill for *The Face* and was full of some story about they'd 'stitched up Radio 1'.

'Flash couldn't be arsed to do this phoner, right, so he got his mate to impersonate him. Wasn't even a member of the band. Wasn't even in the *music* business. Nice one, yeah?'

'Classic,' I said nervously. 'Wasn't *The Kid Jensen Show*, was it?'

'Correctamundo, squire!'

'Ha!' I nudged in quick. 'Do these wankers know *nothing*? *Chuh!* . . . Another pint, anyone?'

The next night the *Jensen Show* got another spanner in the works. Reception rang to say a visitor had 'dropped by' and was heading our way with a chinking carrier-bag. The heavy door heaved open to admit the boyish figure of Mike Appleton, head of the BBC's rock television, who gave a warm hello and said he was passing. He fired up a TV in the corner as he had to watch a documentary he'd made about the Stones, and settled in, levering the top off a beer bottle.

'Don't mind me.' He beamed. 'Keep calm and carry on!'

He pointed to the telly telling me what was about to happen and chatted about cricket and his collection of old gramophones as if we were in a pub rather than a studio entertaining the nation. I kept my links as brief as I could – 'Two more from Dolly Mixture later in the programme' – and returned politely to Mike's latest *bon mot* from Charlie Watts or the score from the Ashes in Perth. I was so breathtakingly stupid I hadn't realised it was an audition. He was lobbing obstacles in my path to see how I coped under pressure.

Two weeks later he rang and asked if I wanted to present *The Old Grey Whistle Test*.

19

Music To Send Children To Sleep By

Only one musician wouldn't talk to *Smash Hits*, David Bowie, though we asked questions with no wrong answer. And only one act played hard to get, the authors of one of the most life-changing records I'd ever heard.

When it first came on the radio I was thirteen all over again. It was like hearing 'Sunny Afternoon' by The Kinks, or 'Eight Miles High' when it finally made sense. It was a haunting, inscrutable tale on a springboard of chiming guitars, its opening line painting a soft, dramatic picture – 'punctured bicycle on a hillside, desolate'. The more I played it, the more cryptic it became, a beguiling journey in an old-fashioned motor-car involving a 'jumped-up pantry-boy' and the return of his mystic ring.

No one understood pop music better than Morrissey. He'd bombarded the music papers with emotional letters when *he* was thirteen, one describing a 1972 Marc Bolan concert in Manchester as 'messianic and complete chaos' – T.Rexstasy indeed. But now The Smiths had some hits of their own and he was an object of affection himself. He wanted to be adored but only by students, not by kids who might have a picture of Boy George on their satchel, and his rare interviews with the magazine were fraught and painfully self-conscious. He came across like an eighteenth-century romantic poet stretched upon a day-bed, a damp paw clamped to his brow, gauging the depths of his existential sorrow before perishing from melancholy or consumption. He thought he was different and he was. He wore a hearing-aid onstage and waved gladioli but they were an arch intellectual statement, not a bunch of attention-grabbing props. Morrissey would only board The Giddy Carousel Of Pop if he could have a little roundabout of his own in a less gauche part of the fairground, nowhere near Galaxy or The JoBoxers.

I listened to 'This Charming Man' over and over again and, for the first and only time, I missed my old employers over the road. *Smash Hits* was beneath him but he saw the *NME* as an equal. He wasn't fractious or bored when they interviewed him. I wished I was back there and he and I were shaking this magical record by its ankles to see what fell out of its pockets.

The single now had another use too: it was part of the complex, cassette-based process of getting a small boy off to sleep.

Clare and I had moved into a little house in Chiswick with a new arrival at the end of the bed, who gurgled peacefully in the daytime but wept and trembled at night. When we got Tom home from the hospital, his mum stuck a postcard of Bob Dylan by his pillow, the first thing he'd see when he woke, and I gazed into his cot for hours in a great cloud of happiness. I thought about the long dawn as the quivering needle sketched his heartbeat, the teary call to his grandparents and the inexplicable urge to smoke a cigar. And I thought how every record until now had appeared in a world without him, and about the music that might carry him through his life as it carried me through mine, music that already existed, music that was still to be made. And how the hits of the day seemed to telegraph moments in time. 'Every Breath You Take' by The Police poured from taxi windows the week he was born, along with 'Sweet Dreams (Are Made Of This)' by Eurythmics. I wondered if they'd ever sound as quaint and archaic as the bestsellers when I'd arrived twenty-nine years before – 'Flirtation Waltz' by Winifred Atwell and 'Dragnet' by Ted Heath and His Music.

I padded up and down the living room at two in the morning trying to get him to drift off to a tape I'd compiled, a carefully paced arrangement that gradually slowed in tempo and started with 'This Charming Man'. Next was XTC's 'Making Plans For Nigel', then the fragile 'Computer Love' by Kraftwerk, then the creaking tones of Willie Dixon, the murmuring hymns of Pentangle, the soft echoes of 'Davey' by Roy Harper, the heart-slowing 'Hush Darling' by Gregory Isaacs and, finally, the lagging, soporific tug of 'Cry Me A River' by Julie London, a sequence of tracks so pacifying it was impossible to keep your eyes open.

And it worked every time. Blinking in her nightie, Clare would patter downstairs, nudge me awake and snatch the howling child from my arms.

20

The Terrible Curse Of Paula Yates

The Old Grey Whistle Test had kicked off in 1971. Its first presenter was Richard Williams, a dashing cove from *Melody Maker* with a moustache who looked like Dickey Betts of the Allman Brothers and conjured up the late-night vibe of a jazz club while working through a packet of Marlboro.

His successor smoked even more, the man we'd watched at college. The dry-ice would clear to reveal Bob Harris mumbling sincere and admirable things about a brand-new 'waxing' with an ashtray close at hand. 'Whispering Bob' was never happier than when a band sported the blue-collar work-wear of the southern-rock foot-soldier – denim, checked shirt and the occasional cowboy hat. There were close-ups of finger-plaiting guitar solos, hairy men chatting on flight cases and stoner-friendly *Betty Boop* cartoons synched to tracks by Little Feat. Next in the chair was Annie Nightingale, in her hippie weeds and psychedelic shades, but the show still clung to its rule that no musician could appear unless they'd issued that great artistic statement, the album. Any new band with just singles – The Clash, The Sex Pistols – was considered flighty and superficial and didn't qualify. In fact, punk rock was only grudgingly acknowledged in '78 when The Damned and The Adverts trundled on for some chin-stroking perusal of their 'debut LPs'.

Even in the eighties, *The Old Grey Whistle Test* seemed stuck in the past, saddled with mental images of Bob enduring the New York Dolls or flickering black and white footage of forties' showgirls cut to Led Zeppelin's 'Trampled Underfoot'. The name didn't help either, a dog-eared throwback to the days when Tin Pan Alley agents sold songs as sheet music: publishers had pianos so the salesmen could audition the tune; if the silver-haired doorman was whistling it when they left it felt like a hit – it had passed the 'old grey whistle test'. Had you paid market-research experts to cook up a title for a thrusting new rock show, it's unlikely any of these four words would have been chalked upon their blackboard. The next stage in its overhaul was the arrival of my old pal Dave Hepworth. At a New York press event he'd buttonholed Mike Appleton who'd thought him the perfect foil: Annie would provide the froth, Dave the wisdom and perspective – and when she'd slung her hook, Mike had rolled up at Radio 1 with his expansive banter and relaxing drinks.

The first show Dave and I did together was 'August Bank Holiday Rock!', a live broadcast from the Regal Theatre, Hitchin, featuring Squeeze. We were hustled into a caravan for Hair and Makeup where kindly girls worked long and hard to make us presentable and warned us our striped shirts might 'hum' on camera and give viewers a seizure. My first link was in the car park outside, the band playing in the background. No one gave me any advice: I was just told to look at the camera and speak. Two teenage girls elbowed in front of me.

'Fuck off, mate, we're trying to watch the telly.'

They could have stood inside and watched the group onstage but they seem magnetised by the monitors. Seconds later *I* appeared on their little screen, too, and this brought a sharp change in attitude. Over they came, blushing, simpering, flicking their hair, hopping from foot to foot.

''Ere, you, can we have your autograph?'

They stared at it intently, wondering who I was. I got back late to London and a school friend rang me, filled with a strange mixture of awe, spite and envy.

'I was with some other mates from the old place last week who didn't know we were still in touch,' he told me, 'and one of them said, "Did you hear Mark Ellen's the new presenter of *The Old Grey Whistle Test*?" And the other guy winked and said, "Well, you know how he got *that* job."'

They didn't. Neither did I.

'*He dropped his trousers for Elton John!*'

It took me a while to get to sleep that night. The idea that the BBC wasn't a talent-based organisation but a knocking-shop run by a randy pianist, that was hilarious, of *course* it was. But everyone at my school – maybe all over the country – thinking I'd only been hired as I'd been bummed by a big man in comedy glasses, for some reason that was disconcerting. Telly had a peculiar effect on people. The next day a thoughtful package arrived from my sister Al: a disguise kit with a false nose, beard and moustache.

Billed in the *Radio Times* as 'a sideways look at the rock scene and beyond', Dave and I began our first joint series of *The Old Grey Whistle Test*. The idea of a 'rock scene' was immaculately awful. A 'sideways look' was even worse. We tried to send this up in a promotional photo-shoot on the Television Centre roof, posing in profile, pointing and squinting at the horizon. The first shows had an audience, many of whom had queued for hours to see Wogan or Noel Edmonds's *Late Late Breakfast Show* and been bundled into our studio instead as the others were full. In they trooped, grumbling audibly, with bags of West End shopping. When bee-hived soul-belter Mari Wilson came on, some looked bored and homesick. When Scots proggers Marillion appeared, they seemed frightened and confused. This wasn't how I'd pictured it. I'd imagined everyone would be as excited to see the Buzzcocks as I was but we were surrounded by the Noel Edmonds fan club, and pipe-smoking, middle-aged cameramen in armless padded jackets. The floor crew could suck the fun out of things too. The BBC was so firmly in the grip of the unions that only Props was allowed to move the set, several of its members loafing in the shadows, lit only by the glow of their cigarette butts, yet leaping into frenzied action if you tried shifting your own sofa as it 'threatened their livelihood'.

The show dropped its audience and recorded late-night in a studio about the size of a kitchen. It went out after live snooker from Sheffield so, if Cliff Thorburn and Dennis Taylor were locked in a nail-biter, we weren't on till after midnight. Packed with that new staple of low-cost television, the promotional video, a typical night went something like this: single from Yazoo, a cheery exchange with Mark Knopfler, a Level 42 clip, archive footage of Rory Gallagher playing 'Bullfrog Blues' followed by Dave and I enthusing about his lumberjack shirt, a brief chinwag with Thomas Dolby dressed in a belted mac and trilby, an item about the ruinous cost of 12-inch singles and then – see you next week! – the new video from Fun Boy Three. We built quite a head of steam but I felt sorry for the bands. Simple Minds were used to playing their last ringing chord to a club full of drunk and deafening supporters, not to complete silence or a cameraman asking for tea and a bun.

Then a giant boulder crashed into the BBC's trouble-free rock pool. For ten long years, *The Old Grey Whistle Test* had had the road to itself, the only programme showing bands outside the mainstream. But not any more. A throbbing neon-lit cocktail of music and fashion called *The Tube* was coming live from Tyne Tees in Newcastle with an audience who dressed up and danced and hadn't been bounced from a recording of *Coronation Street*. Their first show featured the last TV appearance of The Jam. Its ratings were going through the roof.

One of the anchors was former Squeeze pianist Jools Holland, though some bloke making flip asides didn't bother our production team as they felt they'd got two of their own. But Paula Yates was a different story. Everything about their other presenter was extraordinary. Her mother was a showgirl who wrote erotic fiction. The man she thought was her father, Jess 'The Bishop' Yates, had hosted *Stars On Sunday*, which he'd open playing a church organ. When his affair with an actress was exposed, 'The Bishop' was sacked amid such press furore that he had to be smuggled from the studio in the boot of a car. Born of this showbiz chaos, Paula had turned up at *Record Mirror* at the same time as I had, filing a sauce-filled weekly gossip column called 'Natural Blonde'. We ran into each other in clubs. Her progressive approach to news-gathering was a revelation: eighteen, razor-sharp and a colossal flirt, she'd start conversations with male musicians by squeezing their biceps and telling them they were gorgeous. She'd posed naked for *Penthouse* and published a book called *Rock Stars In Their Underpants*. To cement her standing as a thermonuclear sex-kitten, she released her version of 'These Boots Are Made For Walkin'' just before signing with *The Tube*.

The difference between the two shows was fairly marked. *The Tube* was fast and fizzing and featured Paula in short, meringue-like frocks; *The OGWT* was unhurried and stubbly and presented by blokes wearing Boz Scaggs and Orange Juice T-shirts. They were from the fashionable north, prime-time and live; we were pre-recorded in a cupboard in London and aired when Hurricane Higgins put his cue to bed. We asked about gigs and new albums. She talked about haircuts and suntans, and once interviewed someone in bed. If *The Tube* was a clubbing teenager who bought clothes and singles, we were its older brother in his bedroom with his long-playing records.

They were fantastic telly. We were in big trouble.

21

The Empire Strikes Back

But the BBC decided to fight. Cash rained down upon *The Old Grey Whistle Test*. It was ripped from the night-time schedules, slapped into Tuesday evenings at half past seven and broadcast live. The words 'Old' and 'Grey' were quietly dropped and the shiny new *Whistle Test* was hauled, kicking and screaming, into 1984. Even its title sequence was updated: the sign-of-the-zodiac humanoid cavorting in space that had made us leap, hooting, from our chairs at college to kick invisible stars was replaced by a synthesised version starring a robot.

And new presenters were recruited, so many we couldn't all be on at the same time and took weekly turns on the subs' bench. There was the charmingly shy Ro Newton with her big hair, white pixie boots and belted tops, who had even less TV experience than we did. There was Radio 1's softly crackling Richard Skinner, who'd had a love affair with Sheena Easton and was soon to marry 'Delightful Deborah' from *The Steve Wright Show*. For bank-holiday specials there was the flinty Janice Long, who'd shot to fame when Frankie Goes To Hollywood tore their clothes off on her Liverpool radio show demanding to be interviewed naked. 'It's been said by many,' she told our audience, 'that Bryan Ferry is a national treasure and should be mounted in the Tate. I'm sure many of us would go along with that . . .' And in a knee-jerk reaction to *The Tube*'s street philosopher Mark Miwurdz, we occasionally got *NME*'s ranting poet Seething

Wells, though he was 'let go' after a sketch with a plastic skeleton he claimed was the late John Lennon.

But the key new arrival was a powerful presence from Rochdale, the gruff and charismatic Andy Kershaw. The entertainments secretary at Leeds University, he'd famously walked out of one of his finals to make sure Elvis Costello's gear had turned up. He'd worked at Radio Aire and as Billy Bragg's roadie and, when Bragg appeared on the formerly *Old Grey Whistle Test*, he'd impressed new producer Trevor Dann with his bristling opinions, been auditioned and signed a week later. Dave and I were magazine editors and used to the idea of presenting music we didn't personally adore. If we liked stuff, we enthused; if we didn't, we might drop the odd hint – 'Sting there with his new single "Russians",' Dave announced. 'They should never have given that man a library ticket.' But Andy was mortified if he had to introduce anyone that wasn't dead-centre of his universe, in fact refused point-blank even to be *on* a show that featured the 'glutinous bed-wetters Tears For Fears'. Viewers were in no doubt as to his personal taste – boyish joy for his favourites, amusing sarcasm for everything else.

'More from middle-of-the-road maestros Hall & Oates later,' he winced. 'Now it's Sade, about to perform something new and suitably sophisticated.

'After having a hit in Britain, Pat Benatar disappeared for a bit. Now, I'm told, she's back!

'The new one from Midge Ure. I'm not sure why men grow moustaches. You might as well write "I'M A DICKHEAD" on your upper lip and have done with it.'

He referred to Dave on-screen as 'Cuddly David Hepworth' or 'TV's Mr Music' and myself as 'Yummy Mark Ellen'. There was something infectious about his brazen self-confidence. The more we were told to refer to the show as *Whistle Test* on-air, the more he and I called it 'the *Old*

Grey'. The two of us built Richard Skinner into a comic-strip hero, our twin-handed links into his chart rundown getting more idiotic by the week.

'As ever on the *Old Grey*,' Kershaw kicked off, 'we have the man with the hits, the headlines, the picks to click, the uppers, the downers and the just-hangin'-arounders, your one-stop switchboard to the stars . . .'

'. . . he's the Housewife's Choice,' I'd chip in, 'the Forces' Favourite, the very big deal on the wheels of steel, the man who – for literally scores of people – has come to personify the chart that counts and where the hits are made and played. We have a name for that man. We call him . . . Richard Skinner!'

Dave devised a character known as 'the lovely Veronica', an unseen presence conducting on-air raffles. Kershaw was so enthralled by this *Dad's Army* conceit that he found a blouse and some bracelets in Wardrobe and thrust an arm into shot to select the winning ticket. On one New Year's special, he and I delivered a link while juggling. I once found owlish weatherman Ian McCaskill wandering the Television Centre corridors and made him introduce a Robert Palmer video. We had no autocue and used what was laughingly called 'the card system'. We'd bash out rough scripts the night before, scrawl giant 'prompts' onto three-foot boards with magic-markers and busk the rest. These wobbling contraptions were then held beside the camera by helpful office staff:

PET SHOPS BOYS – mention their hats!!
NEXT WEEK . . . KERSHAW IN TEXAS WITH ZZ TOP
– beards, beer & barbecue
HEPWORTH MEETS SPRINGSTEEN – again!
ME IN NEW YORK WITH SUZANNE VEGA
THE RETURN OF DON HENLEY – new solo album,
The Eagle has landed, etc.

ONE MORE FROM MICRODISNEY – THIS IS 'BIRTHDAY GIRL'!

Kershaw broke all records by once delivering a 'four-carder' with a posse of board-wranglers. We'd managed to bring all the cartoon nonsense of magazine life to the screen and we seemed to be holding our own in the fierce ratings war with *The Tube*. Some of the bands never quite took off – the Roaring Boys, the Mystery Girls, the Frank Chickens – but a lot of it was epic telly the whole country seemed to be watching. REM began 'Pretty Persuasion' with a chunk of 'Moon River'. The Jesus and Mary Chain used squalls of pre-recorded feedback, Bobby Gillespie standing up to play the drums. Bauhaus had the novel idea of drifting round the dressing rooms with a Super 8 film camera compiling a self-shot documentary. Pogues' bassist Cait O'Riordan brought her boyfriend Elvis Costello to the show and sat on his knee when they weren't performing. When Elvis himself appeared he wore the crown on the cover of his *King Of America* album. He crept up behind Kershaw as he addressed the nation and lowered it onto his head.

The new and improved *Whistle Test* seemed to be flying but the press still didn't approve. *The Tube* was sexy and hip. We were clunky and dull.

'I wouldn't look at this if I were you,' Trevor Dann advised.

Trevor was a Radio 1 producer who'd transferred to telly, super-bright and with a huge record collection. He looked like Graeme Garden of *The Goodies* in a baseball cap. A double-page spread in *Melody Maker* lay open in the Wood Lane office, bits of it underlined, squiggles in the margin. It was a review of a *Whistle Test* special called *Rock Around the Clock*, an all-night broadcast with a live phone-in, the Video Vote. A recent invention and still not for sale, videos could only be hurriedly home-taped if they happened to be showing, so there was real value in ringing in at three in the morning for a screening of 'Master And Servant' by Depeche Mode, or 'When Doves Cry' by Prince, or Propaganda's magical 'Dr Mabuse' by my old pal Anton Corbijn.

'Grossly unfair, monstrous,' Trevor huffed, 'we're complaining, of course,' though I sensed a sing-song note of joy in his voice, the sense of relief that, when the critical guns get blazing, it's the 'on-screen talent' that takes a bullet for the team. 'Never, *ever* read this,' he said, pushing it across the desk towards me. Unusually their review of the 'multiple agonies' we'd inflicted opened with a blistering attack on senior producer Mike Appleton, later named and forcefully shamed.

'Whichever paunchy executive in a satin tour jacket and turquoise jewellery punched out the idea for this programme on a digital watch,' it scoffed, 'he thought he was onto a racing certainty for promotion. Said executive is now probably working for Radio Botswanaland, condemned to the aboriginal outback by the resounding failure of this massive flop.' This 'grossly misconceived 15-hour marathon' was 'a tedious stodge of old pop videos, uninspired documentaries and variable live footage, and the show was a turkey whose wingspan defies any conventional measurement. In a studio that looked like a cross between a Filipino brothel and *The Eurovision Song Contest* and with the artificially hyped atmosphere of an Election Special' were 'the fidgety David Hepworth and the ingratiatingly cherubic and insufferably glib Mark Ellen, perfecting his Katie Boyle impression beside an electronic scoreboard'.

That was the good bit. As its 'increasingly tousled' presenters soldiered through the night, the writer sharpened his pencil. Trevor savoured my expression, a kaleidoscope of agony beginning with shock and horror and blending, eventually, into resignation and crumpled defeat.

'Allan Jones, eh?' he scoffed supportively. 'Ha! What does *he* know about anything?'

Allan Jones! Couldn't it be somebody else? What he knew about anything was quite a lot. The funniest, most respected writer in the music press, whose career I'd envied, whose life I'd wanted, whose on-the-road-with-Mott-The-Hoople anecdotes I'd virtually memorised, had seen fit to tell the rock nation I was a challenge to both watch *and* hear. And if that wasn't the general consensus already, it soon would be, as the highly influential and much-loved 'Jones Boy' had said so. In cold, hard print. Sensing my pain, the office PA approached nervously with some post.

'Got some mail for you, Marcus,' Karen said brightly. 'These'll make you laugh. They're a funny old lot, the viewers!'

The first item was a picture postcard of a young couple in colourful leisurewear grinning on a ski-lift. The back of it read:

Tschau Mark! I wish you are well. I was by England for 2 weeks and I sawed you on a music show. I hope to see you one day by me apartment because you are nice looking. I am 22, single and name is Heidi Fuhrmann – PO BOX 206 8025 ZURICH. I love you xxxx
PS I think this picture is us too!

The second was from Basingstoke, on purple notepaper with a floral motif.

Dear Sir or Madam, Do you think that it would be possible to have a photograph of Mark Ellen? Many thanks, Sue Darley (Miss)
PS Is Mark Ellen free at the moment? If so, could you ask him to give me a call on . . .

There you had it, the absurd impact of television. Even on its lowliest rung, it ramped up reactions out of all proportion. If you warmed to someone on telly it could slide into uncritical devotion, the way it did when I'd gawped, besotted, at Julie Driscoll or Cindy Wilson of The B-52's, but it could escalate the other way just as rapidly. There didn't seem to be much middle ground. Appear on TV and you were either a grotesque buffoon with a personality disorder or someone complete strangers in Switzerland wanted to sexually molest.

It was far worse for Kershaw. Dave and I were just frontmen who knew a lot of stuff, chatted to rock deities and told you what was coming up later. Kershaw actually *stood* for something, which magnified his relationship with the audience to an alarming degree: he was either unimpeachably brilliant or intensely offensive, a corrosive little cocktail if ever there was one. Whenever I went to gigs with him, blokes in denim jackets would either hug him and give him a demo cassette or try to floor him with a single punch for saying something unkind about Ultravox. Girls in flat shoes and Clash T-shirts would slip him their home numbers or harangue him loudly for being a 'sexist git'.

Whistle Test battled on, overtaken in the ratings by the ever-ascending *Tube* but still managing to land its quota of legends. Most of these appeared in the interview slot, gently shepherded into a corner of the set the crew called 'the Comfy Area', a cushion-stuffed compound apparently fashioned from the props department of an old seventies sitcom, possibly *Robin's Nest*. Kate Bush explained how didgeridoos were made from wood hollowed out by termites. Ray Davies told me America liked him because of his hair and that he only wrote songs for his uncle. Lemmy said it was the God-given right of heavy-metal videos to feature 'dodgy girls astride powerful motorbikes'. But some were simply too stellar to come to the studio and would only be interviewed on home turf so, at crippling expense, a film crew was dispatched to meet them.

'We've landed what I'm calling a *Whistle Test* world exclusive,' Trevor said excitedly, 'and you've got the job!'

'Why me?'

'Two of your old heroes,' he said. 'A marriage made in Heaven.'

22

The Lake District And Ancient Ruins

The journey up to Ambleside was tense. Trevor and I footled along in a BBC hire-car full of film reels trying to figure out a plan of action.

Whistle Test had originally been offered Roy Harper on his own but Trevor had turned him down. I'd spent nights on end in my chicken-filled college commune wallowing in the pastoral charm of his *Stormcock* album and the psychedelic *Flat Baroque and Berserk*. I'd seen him playing to eighty thousand people at Knebworth; he'd arrived backstage on a white horse wearing a cowboy hat and joined Pink Floyd later to sing 'Have A Cigar'. But that was in '75 and even *I* had to admit his golden years were behind him. Then his press people had rung to say Roy's old pal Jimmy Page might now be joining him on his rambling jaunt in the Lake District, and they were both bringing guitars. Trevor couldn't have rung back faster.

Page was piping hot. Little had been heard of him for four years. Led Zeppelin had disbanded and he'd slunk back to his two country piles. One was an old mill in Windsor where John Bonham had died after a night on the quadruple vodkas and half a ham roll which the drummer declared was 'breakfast'. The other was Boleskine House, the former home of Aleister Crowley on the shores of Loch Ness. I imagined him up there in a satin suit festooned with dragons, hauling symphonies from the clouds with a Les Paul and a theremin, or conjuring black magick with potions, thunderclaps and dark rituals involving the blood of virgins. I couldn't believe the old hell-raiser was still alive. That he was above ground, vertical and on his way to meet us made me wobble with nerves. Trevor talked hard about how we could divert Roy from his usual weed-stained, hectoring theories about the government to the higher-rating topic of Led Zeppelin, while I prepared to meet two rock godheads of my youth who'd apparently taken up fell-walking. My mind raced with more unsettling images, the folk-sage who'd written 'Me And My Woman' with knee-high socks and a rucksack, the author of 'Whole Lotta Love' nibbling Kendal Mint Cake.

Trevor parked the car at the pub in Ambleside and I strolled into Reception. A girl in rock-chick jeans asked me if I was with the BBC and then announced she was 'going out' with Harper. Gentle enquiry revealed she was nineteen; she'd hooked up with the forty-three-year-old troubadour when he'd played her local venue, Leeds Bierkeller, and he'd asked her along for a weekend in the Lakes. He'd got a mate coming, Jimmy who played the guitar, so why didn't she bring a friend too? So she had. Who was even younger than she was. Neither appeared to know the first thing about Page and his illustrious catalogue and assumed my knowledge was much the same.

'You know "Stairway To Heaven"?' she asked.

I did, as it happened.

'Jimmy *wrote* that,' she told me.

I wandered slowly back to the drive to report. There was good news and bad news. The good news was that our rock legends were in residence and had asked us to drop by their private dining suite around nine o'clock, the back room of the inn. The bad news was that the forty-year-old guitarist of Led Zeppelin was on a blind date with a girl of eighteen.

The scene that greeted us was like the cover of *Beggars*

Banquet. The two minstrels sat before a roaring fire strumming guitars, the bearded Harper in faded denim, Page in riding boots and a battered leather jacket with a long white knotted scarf. Before them in the candlelight were the remains of a medieval feast – half-eaten meat pies, hunks of bread, abandoned vegetables and a forest of empty wine bottles. Around them were the two girls and a bleary-eyed entourage of stubbly mates, roadies and fawning acolytes, who laughed excitably at anything they did or said and eyed the BBC gang with an airy, sneering contempt.

Page and Harper presided over this bacchanalia like lords in the ramparts of a castle. All that was missing were some suits of armour, a spit-roasted deer and a pikestaff with somebody's head on it. When either of them craved refreshment, a cry went up and a lowly factotum busied themselves delivering the tipple of choice. There were two gears to their recreational palate: if they shouted, 'Red tackle', generous goblets of claret were ferried their way; if 'White tackle', one of the serfs produced a small pouch of a potent powder, upended it on the table top and fashioned some lines for consumption. The rest of us sat there nursing our pints of Coniston Bluebird, spectators on the sidelines allowed to bathe gratefully in the warm glow of some card-carrying rock deity. It was as if they cruised at a certain altitude but had deigned to alight briefly on our lily pad and give us a glimpse of their glamorous world. Except it didn't look very glamorous. It looked a bit seedy and baggy at the knees. I gazed at Harper and the scales fell from my eyes. I felt the tragic, heartrending jolt of pain of a small child discovering there's no Father Christmas or that everyone mimes on *Top of the Pops*. I felt deceived and used and disillusioned. The man I'd listened to night after night, whose canon I'd defended, whose soft hippie maxims I'd bought and adopted, whose songs I'd painstakingly learnt on guitar, whose voice had ferried my son to sleep, seemed – in real life – an absolute arse, a griz-zled, rancorous, crashing old bore with an ego you couldn't fit outdoors. And Page wasn't a vast improvement either. On close inspection, the dazzling guitar god of 'Since I've Been Loving You' came across like a prize twerp frozen in a changeless adolescence.

So the evening rolled on. 'Red tackle!' Fresh supplies would be rushed from the cellar. 'White tackle!' Another massive mound of chop. Trevor and I munched our crisps and had another Bluebird. By one in the morning, the roof beams rattled to the sound of merriment and Trevor gingerly broached the subject of the filming. The crew were arriving at eight, he said. Was everyone happy with that? Strangely, they all seemed delighted.

'So that's sorted,' he beamed. 'I'm turning in. See you all at breakfast!'

'*Breakfast?*' Page looked horrified. Whatever 'breakfast' was, he didn't like the sound of it. He'd assumed Trevor had meant eight in the *evening*. So had Harper. Used liberally, red tackle is a well-known sedative, but the same couldn't be said of their other favoured pick-me-up. White tackle brings with it many things but the gift of sleep is not among them. They looked tight-lipped and ashen-faced.

'Eight,' Trevor said. 'Eight in the *morning*.'

There was an awkward, head-scratching silence while two men who'd never risen before the crack of noon pondered their fate.

'Tell you what,' Page decided, and then delivered words to chill the spines of even the hardiest film unit. 'We'll just have to stay up all night.'

Soon after dawn I headed out to meet the camera crew, a local father-and-son team with a jeep and a driver. Fresh-faced individuals with side-partings and quilted jackets, they rubbed their hands expectantly. They'd just done another job for the BBC, they told me: a ten-year-old girl had asked the *Jim'll Fix It* programme if she could shear a sheep like a French poodle and the kindly Jim had waved his magic wand. They talked fondly of their wool-clipping adventure.

'What's on the cards for today, mate?' they wondered. I glanced up at Page's window to see the top half of his coltish paramour wandering about in a bra. She caught my eye and gave a sarcastic wave.

'This,' I said, 'this . . . might be a bit different. You know what rock stars are like – mavericks, wild cards, punctuality not really their bag and all that. Strong chance of some overtime, though!'

Two hours later Harper materialised, announcing he'd only do the interview in the ancient ruins of a nearby castle.

'The Roman fort of Galava,' he declared theatrically, pointing at some distant horizon, 'which guarded the road from Ravenglass to Brougham in ancient times.'

Page stumbled out and joined the fray, cutting the most dissolute figure imaginable, his teenage pal padding along beside him. Whatever quantity of sex had been available in the Ambleside area, they'd had all of it, then rung down for some more. The very sight of them seemed to scream debauchery. The film crew swapped anxious looks.

'Why a Roman fort?' I asked.

'The vibes, man,' said Page, tucking in his shirt.

'It's got a magnetic force-field,' Harper said mysteriously, tapping his nose, 'which assists the performance of *beautiful music.*'

With a deafening clink, a bag of red tackle was packed into the boot of their car by their minder-cum-driver, then Harper, Page and the girls clambered aboard, claiming to know the location of the vibe-dispensing relic. The crew's jeep followed in hot pursuit, behind them Trevor and I in the Volvo. Orientation wasn't Harper's strong suit, especially after a night on the Bordeaux and bugle. For what seemed like an eternity, this shambling caravanserai bumped along the tiny lanes, reversing into gateways, executing six-point turns and occasionally lurching to a standstill in a cloud of exhaust. At which point Harper would step out, sniff the air, decide no Roman had ever set foot in the place – hence he wasn't 'feeling it' – and off we'd bump again, up hill and down dale, scanning the skyline for music-boosting ruins. Another hour and still no filming, *Whistle Test* was feeling the heat. The crew were bored and confused and Trevor, who'd removed his baseball cap and was fanning himself, now faced the looming possibility that we'd come to the Lake District with a four-man team, racked up a sheaf of expenses, and would return to London with not a single square inch of footage.

A showdown ensued. The Harpermobile was flagged down and told to follow the jeep: the crew knew a picturesque hillside pasture that might make an attractive backdrop for their duet. The car-train rumbled to a halt, doors flew open and out came cameras, tripods, metal film canisters, sound baffles, clipboards, gumboots and, from the motor at the back, empty bottles of red tackle and the unsteady figures of Harper and Page. After an epic amount of arsing about, they settled down in a brisk crosswind and declared themselves ready to roll. Trevor asked for some live performance but, for some reason, he'd only packed thirty minutes of film, so it wasn't ideal when Harper kicked off with his rambling twelve-minute '71 album track 'Same Old Rock', Page tinkering in the background. After ten minutes they gave up, saying it 'wasn't working'. Fresh tackle was uncorked, Harper relieved himself in the bracken, and we had a crack at the interview, my patience now replaced by an adolescent sense of fury and disappointment. Cheery enquiry about their interest in rambling fell on stony ground, particularly with the chain-smoking Page: they'd chosen Ambleside for its scenic double-rooms, ley-lines and abundance of claret. The more lofty and self-deluded they sounded, the more chippy I got. And the more bitter and defensive this made them and the more the wheels came off and the whole thing fell apart. Mentally totalling the number of hours of my life I'd clearly wasted listening to the music of the preposterous Harper, I began to understand why the big bucks had eluded him. I must have said this out loud as he stiffened slightly and shot me the evil eye.

'My own idiosyncratic behaviour precludes me from international stardom because all of a sudden I'd take a bend in the road and go a different way,' he announced. 'I'm a sparrow in the gutter, really. It's not imperative that I become a multi-millionaire.'

I turned to Page, who was slurring slightly and fiddling with his fretboard, and suggested the last phase of Led Zeppelin had been pompous and overblown. This had a disastrous effect on both of them – Page started mumbling sourly about the subtleties of their music, and Harper began answering on Page's behalf as if he'd been a member of the band, annoyed that an item about his new album had lumbered off-road in a cheap bid to prise some quotes from his lead guitarist. He then switched to a broadside on the soulless nature of eighties music, with a tortuous gag involving the new pop darlings and the key battle of the Wars of Scottish Independence.

'What I'd like to do in this day and age right now,' Harper revealed, hair flapping in the wind, 'is create something more live and human and down to earth than has been seen for the last six or seven years. You don't need Bannock Goes To Frankieburn!'

'It's still verses and chorus like it was in 1960,' Page

complained, 'and with all the technology they've got and all the outspoken statements they make, I think they ought to come up with something special. They all sound the same to me.'

All of them?

'Yeah, they've just got different singers.'

I wanted examples.

'Bannock Goes To Frankieburn!' Harper grumbled.

'They all sound the bloody same,' Page shrugged, spoiling for a fight. 'They've all got computers! Why don't they come on out,' he said, like a pissed old lag at closing-time, 'with their batteries?'

This was terrible. It was awful stuff. They weren't just tedious egomaniacs, they were reactionary old curmudgeons whose livelihood was under threat. A raft of electronic nerds with brains made of printed circuits had pulled the rug from under their feet. Their own *fathers* had probably said, 'They all sound the bloody same,' about the rock guitarists who'd kicked out the jazzers.

'What are they doing?' Page whined. 'Just verses and choruses! Well, that's the same as Herman's Hermits as far as I'm concerned. And the pop charts at the moment sound like that to me.'

It was gridlock. We were stuck and we were all to blame. We'd fallen out so badly we couldn't fall back in again. They'd labelled me as a goofy flag-waver, cheering anyone who'd helped sever the old guard's power cables, and I'd labelled them as bitter and twisted old scrotes stuck in a time-warp. A ghostly silence fell on Ambleside, broken eventually by Roy Harper.

'Mmmaaaaaarrrk!' he bleated.

A flock of sheep had wandered into shot. He'd decided they were calling my name.

'Mmmaaaaaarrrk!' he echoed. 'Mmmaaaaaaaaaaaaaarrrrrrk!'

I took the frantic throat-cutting signals from Trevor to have three meanings – rightly, as it happened. First, this was the worst interview in the entire history of interviews and must end immediately. Second, I couldn't be heard anyway above a chorus of real and impersonated livestock. And third, there was four minutes of film left and no decent music in the can.

'Mmmaaaaaarrrk!' said Harper.

'Well, for the benefit of Bannock Goes To Frankieburn . . .' I said, retreating.

'Mmmaaaaaarrrk!' said Page.

'. . . we'll have a few more verses and choruses from you and I shall leave you to it.'

'Thank you, Mmmaaaaaarrrk!'

'Don't get exhausted on the walk back!' Page scoffed, and stumbled off for a piss in the hedgerow, his aim directed by the delicate hand of his girlfriend. The father-and-son film crew were frozen with horror. The old sheep-shearing caper now seemed like a distant dream.

Trevor rang a week later. 'Think we've managed to salvage something,' he sighed manfully. 'And you know that bit at the end where they start bleating?'

I'd had nightmares in which a man playing a guitar with a violin bow had turned into a series of giant farm animals so yes, as it happened, I did remember it.

'Well, this'll make you laugh. The sheep weren't actually very loud on the soundtrack so, guess what, we had to dub some on! Otherwise you wouldn't know why they were going "Mmmaaaaaarrrrrk!"'

'And they *are*, are they – going "Mmmaaarrrrk", I mean?' Maybe I'd imagined it.

'Oh, yes,' he said, 'quite a lot.'

If I'd kept a log of career lowlights, an office junior being sent to the BBC Library for an Agricultural Sound Effects record to allow two rock stars to take the piss out of me on national television would be fairly high among them.

23

Frankie Goes To Italy

'Bob Geldof,' I announced, back at *Smash Hits*, 'is making a charity record.'

Dave had left to launch *Just Seventeen* magazine, taking Ian Birch with him, and I was now the editor. We'd been invited to cover its recording and it seemed like a good idea.

'Bob Geldof?' Neil Tennant asked, just checking.

'Bob Geldof.'

'Is our beloved Boomtown Rat still aboard The Giddy Carousel Of Pop,' he asked mischievously, 'or is he, ahem . . . down *La Dumpeure*?'

The floodgates opened and there was a barrage of complaint from the rest of the office, the gist of it being that *if* one was to crack open the door to The Dumper – at number 71, Chart Failure Avenue – then just past Hazel O'Connor's room, past Toyah, past dear old Steve Strange, past even Leee John of Imagination, right at the end of the passage and lit only by a bare light-bulb, there I would find the lead singer of a group who hadn't had a hit since 'Banana Republic' some four years earlier. His name, Bob Geldof. It was a fair point and I knew it. The man couldn't get arrested. If he'd capered round Leicester Square stark naked waving a banner saying, 'Kill the Pope,' no one would have taken a blind bit of notice.

'Spandau Ballet are coming,' I pointed out. '*And* Heaven 17 and, supposedly, Dame David Bowie.' All I knew was that the backing track was already recorded, a democratic slice of the new pop aristocracy – Phil Collins on drums with samples from Tears For Fears, John Taylor playing bass, Gary Kemp on guitar as The Edge couldn't make it, and the song's co-author and producer Midge Ure of Ultravox adding some keyboards. Paul McCartney had sent a contribution by post. It just needed the vocals.

The main architect was, indeed, the Dumper-dwelling Geldof. Horrified by a TV documentary about the Ethiopian famine, he'd pulled together an old-fashioned supergroup and, on the bright winter morning of 25 November 1984, they filtered into Sarm West in Notting Hill Gate, a church converted to a studio by Island Records – Nick Drake had made an album there, as had Free and John Martyn. Only two publications were present, the mass-circulation giants Geldof thought would sell his record, *Smash Hits* and the *Daily Mirror*.

This was highly entertaining to watch, partly because the singers he'd asked weren't used to collaborating. His main inspiration had been George Harrison's Concert for Bangladesh in 1971 where you'd imagined warm, self-supporting hippies locked in a bear-hug, but the place was filling up with people normally at great pains to avoid each other now nudged into a stiff political truce. The pop boom was so massive, so confident and all-conquering, that its frontliners were rammed full of piss and vinegar. Profits were huge and there was room for everyone. They rarely met outside an awards event or a TV studio and all fired shots across each other's bows in the press. The old guard thought the young guard were overdressed and workshy. The young guard thought the old guard were knackered, pensionable gits in denim jackets, and used the rest of their column inches to rubbish their contemporaries. A special edition of the BBC's *Pop Quiz* had just brought together bitter rivals Duran Duran and Spandau Ballet. The papers made it seem like a world peace summit.

And now thirty-eight pop stars had to be in the same room for a day. I watched them troop in, all glancing round nervously. Paul Weller arrived in a blazer with his hair slicked back, the look of his new duo the Style Council. He'd spent the last seven years lambasting anyone whose world-view differed even slightly from his and cowered sheepishly in the corridor.

'I'm hardly everybody's favourite person,' he told me, whispering. 'They just seem to ignore me, to be honest, and I don't blame them.'

Kool & The Gang rolled up in a ball of noise and came face to face with Bono. A shrieking Bananarama queued at the coffee machine with Francis Rossi from Status Quo. The briefly chart-troubling Marilyn appeared – uninvited but he came anyway – and had to swish his blond mane past Rick Parfitt. In a noble bid to break some ice, Culture Club drummer Jon Moss shouted 'My hero!' and threw his arms round Phil Collins. Sting, his new wife, a baby and some dogs bowled up in a black Range Rover. Duran Duran flew in from Germany, two of them wearing ski goggles. Spandau Ballet arrived in a pair of chauffeur-driven limos with four minders between them.

'I get it,' Gary Kemp observed, scanning the country's *crème de la crème*. 'It's all a ploy by Island Records. Get every pop star except Frankie Goes To Hollywood into one room and blow the place up.'

A quiet, fizzing tension filled the air, everyone trying to work out the pecking order or finding some distraction that made them look cool and detached. Nick Rhodes stuck some money in the Asteroids machine. John Taylor ordered chilli con carne. Weller and Bananarama watched a TV set with the sound off. Status Quo, the Duran rhythm section and some Boomtown Rats found cans of lager and went out for a smoke. Midge Ure tried to soften the mood by flinging open the door to the studio, a sumptuous suite full of classical pillars, and saying, 'It's just like my bedroom!' A TV crew swept past, led by Nigel Planer in the waist-length wig of his character Neil from *The Young Ones*, pointing a microphone and asking people if they had any herbal tea.

One by one, the lead singers were summoned for their parts, Paul Young now offered the opening line as David Bowie hadn't managed to make it. But Tony Hadley stepped up first and I felt for him – could any audience be more terrifying than his peers and chart rivals squinting from the control room? The whole thing had the undercurrent of a penalty shoot-out: they had to put one away for the team but also, ideally, ram as much of their own personality into their few seconds as possible.

'Female vocals!' Midge Ure barked through a talk-back, twiddling knobs, and Bananarama trooped up. 'Coming, Marilyn?' they shouted down the stairs.

Boy George burst in direct from the New York Concorde, effortlessly upstaging everyone with his scarlet hair. He charged straight to the console, pausing to pick up a glass of brandy.

'My God, it's so trippy seeing all these faces in one tiny room!' he shrieked and, spotting Marilyn, 'Hello, Doris.'

Finally the massed ranks of musicians – Band Aid as they'd become – were called to record the chorus. 'Feed the world,' the guide-vocal told them, 'let them know it's Christmas time.'

Francis Rossi turned to me in mock-horror. 'Feed the *Welsh*?' he said, and drained his beer can.

I wandered out into Tavistock Gardens and back home feeling peculiarly moved. For all its self-interest and squandering of cash, for all its cheap public squabbles and hairdressing bills, the pop fraternity had done something extraordinary. The patricians of the old rock vanguard had been forced together with the brazen upstarts and briefly formed a mobilising superpower. And it had taken someone with a foot in both camps – Geldof, whose fading career had posed no threat – to make it happen.

But there was one strange dimension to the Band Aid story: the act of the year hadn't been invited. They'd had two world-conquering hits, 'Relax' and 'Two Tribes', and released a third, 'The Power Of Love', the week before Bob called his troops together – in the very studio where they'd recorded their entire catalogue.

No act expressed the new age better than Frankie Goes To Hollywood – brash, political, newsworthy. They shocked on every level. Their album artwork contained wriggling sperm and Radio 1's Mike Read had snapped a copy of their first single on-air to keep the nation's youth from its corrupting agenda. And no act had gained – or suffered – more from the rise of the new technology. Trevor Horn's production was crisp and captivating, full of sweltering sound effects and pumping textures to pack any dance-floor, but in some ways this had sidelined the group themselves. Holly Johnson provided the vocals but the music was mostly machine-driven or supplied by Horn and various session-playing stalwarts from Yes and the Blockheads, seasoned back-room boys about as far from the group's thrusting eighties image as you could picture. Symbolically, the Frankie album *Welcome To The Pleasuredome* included a tiny sound-sample of the other four band members jumping into a swimming-pool. I wanted to write a piece about what the pop circus now asked of its leading lights so Island Records invited me to go on the road with them.

On the morning of 6 February 1985, a plane took off for the north Italian border. I was sitting at the back with a perfect view of the cabin. Beside me was Holly Johnson, who'd emptied some crayons out of the plastic Superman bag he'd nicked from Milan airport and was sketching in a notebook. He was wearing a baggy pinstriped suit and red bow-tie. Under 'Distinguishing Marks' in his passport he'd written 'great beauty and freckles'. It slowly dawned on us late-arrivers that the flight's only freight appeared to be other chart-topping pop stars bound for San Remo, a key promotional opportunity. Appear at its Festival della Canzone Italiana and you'd reach a national audience of around 16 million, with an additional 24 million when the show was networked across Europe. These were the mechanics of the new industry. The live-circuit days before video were now a dim and distant past.

Through the thick smoke I could make out all five members of Duran Duran, no ski goggles but a lot of pixie boots and big scarves. Two rows in front were the lugubrious Talk Talk, next to them the giant frizz of Chaka Khan and, just behind, the generous application of hair product that betokened Spandau Ballet. A cautious Bronski Beat were up the front, loudly mocked by Frankie Goes To Hollywood in their latest round of press. Phil Collins should have been aboard – decrepit old granddad, he was thirty-four – but he was travelling out later in a private jet. Alongside Holly and I were the other members of Frankie, smoking, drinking and dishing out some Liverpudlian lip. We were in the back row, appropriately, as they seemed like the Bash Street Kids: if paper pellets needed flicking or plaits dunking in inkwells, these were the boys you'd want on your team. In front of us were various personnel from their ZTT record label, including manager Jill Sinclair, for some reason their sworn enemy.

Imagine the insurance. If this barge spiralled into the Alps it would be game-over for British pop music. On the bright side, I told Holly, it might clear the decks a bit and allow Pigbag to have a hit. And maybe the Cocteau Twins.

'Well, at least Jill Sinclair's on board,' he drawled, without looking up. 'If *I* go, *she* goes.' And he stirred his gin and tonic.

A member of the cabin crew wandered down the aisle in an ankle-length skirt, her soft Nigerian features offset with eye-shadow, hair wrenched back in a ponytail. Strangely, she was only carrying one drink. I nudged Holly again. How funny that all air stewardesses looked like Sade.

'It *is* Sade,' he hissed, and carried on sketching. She called to him as she drifted past and raised her glass.

Tense and explosive, the superstructure of Frankie was like the pop industry itself, a collision between the old world and the new. The back line were rock musicians, Mark O'Toole and Brian 'Nasher' Nash, hard-living Scouse heterosexuals on the razz. Presumably drummer 'Pedro' Gill was the same but he hadn't shown up; he'd 'injured his ankle falling downstairs', though Nasher told me this was self-inflicted, like the fight-shy infantry of the Crimean War, as he'd wanted to stay at home and watch football on telly. Nasher and Mark were both twenty-one. They were sharp but felt obliged to be idiotic. When we landed they set themselves to work spraying reporters with Coca-Cola. Billy Idol had come over to their flat once; when he started smashing the place up, they'd lent him a hand. Nasher had red eyes and a face the colour of grout. How was he feeling?

'Rough as a scrapyard Alsatian.'

Reason being?

'Not enough blood in my alcohol stream.'

Nasher thought Matisse was a Portuguese rosé – 'an arty poof's drink' – and had the same cod-Italian greeting for all waiters and barmen: 'Eh, *bastarrrdos*!' In San Remo, knots of underdressed *signorinas* hovered outside the band's hotel. When he left the place, he'd throw his room key to the best-looking one, pick up another girl later and boot the first out on his return having traded up. Both he and Mark thought it could all end tomorrow, especially as the back line weren't required for recording and were largely ignored by the press. They were hanging by a thread and they knew it so they were milking it for all it was worth. The week before, Mark had flagged down a cab in Notting Hill, taken it all the way to Liverpool and charged the record company. Nasher's motto was 'Take them for everything!' I refrained from mentioning it might be coming out of their advance.

Frankie's front line were two out gay singers: Holly and Paul Rutherford, obsessed with club hits and clothes. Paul had a neat moustache, like a cross between Clark Gable and a croupier. He danced the entire time he was vertical in fluent, graceful little steps, even when being interviewed or signing autographs. Holly dressed either like a theatrical impresario or a club barman on American Depression night, some days an embroidered jacket, white gloves and a silver-topped cane, others a distressed woollen coat and a leather cap worn back-to-front. He'd just got back from Barbados where he'd met Doris Day, the highlight of his holiday. As our minibus sped us from airport to hotel, the band couldn't help noticing giant billboards by the roadside funded by well-heeled rival record companies.

'Sade – welcome to San Remo!' said one.

'San Remo welcomes Bronski Beat!'

'Where's ours?' bellowed Nasher. He wound down the window and stuck his head out. When we overtook anyone, he yelled 'Yer a plank!' at the driver.

Another billboard: 'Have a great San Remo, Duran Duran!'

'I bet *Duran* have got limos,' drawled Holly, still sketching. He talked in a fabulously camp fashion, droll and very self-aware, with long drawn-out vowels and much rolling of the eyes. 'No limos,' he sighed. '*Traaaaagic.*'

Frankie were at that perfect point of their trajectory, still in ascent and still thrilled with the attention while being edged into ever more creative overdrive by the soul-shrivelling tedium of the promotional grind. Everywhere they went, cameras rattled and microphones lunged towards them, and they loved it. They were fantastic to watch, chippy and inventive, effortlessly witty in the grand tradition of their forefathers. Lennon would have been proud of them. Half of what they said they meant and half they didn't, but it was never clear which was which. I wrote it all down in my notebook.

A presenter called Red Ronnie from the Italian TV show *Be Bop A Lula* arrived. He called Holly Johnson 'Frankie' and, in Nasher's view, had 'a face like a welder's bench'.

'*Heeey, evvabaddy,* I'm here with Frankie from Frankie Goes To Hollywood!' said Ronnie, a ghastly vision in three shades of suede. 'Tell us about yourself, Frankie!'

'I've got a pet tiger called Tessa,' Holly twinkled, 'but I don't let it in the living room. I'm buying a church and starting a new religion.'

'How is your album, Frankie?'

'It's a concept record, really,' Mark pitched in. 'Just some covers of songs by Gerry and The Pacemakers. "Two Tribes" was based on Ped's experience in the Vietnam War.'

Red Ronnie wondered what sort of music they liked.

'Vivaldi, Mozart, Tchaikovsky, Billie Holiday,' Holly shrugged. '"Hot For Teacher" by Van Halen, American funk. But I hate clubs,' he said. 'They're just holes in the ground full of mirror-balls.'

'OK, and your favourite group?' gushed Ron.

'The Rolling *Stooooones*,' Holly spat sarcastically. 'I'm not really a musician, I'm an archaeologist.'

'Your least favourite group?'

'Bronski Beat. They're beneath contempt.'

'It's disgusting the way they're making a career out of being "persecuted faggots",' Paul added.

'They're right in line for a pair of steelies,' Nasher warned, swilling his drink and tapping a toecap.

'How is Trevor Horn, producer of your great records?' chirped Ronnie. The press mostly assumed they were just Horn's puppets and the air seemed to freeze around us.

'No idea, mate,' Paul said softly. 'He's just someone we met in an Amsterdam sauna.'

'He's a businessman,' Holly scowled, 'and he's a lot richer than us.' And he turned, beaming, to the camera: 'Hello, I'm Giorgio Armani, and you're watching *Be Bop A Lula*!'

'I love my public and my public loves me!' Nasher slurred at the lens, then bellowed, 'Eh, *bastarrrdos*!' at a distant waiter. 'Four Cokes with Canadian Club! *Viva il Papa!*'

We were poured into people-carriers and driven to the TV studios. I could see why they liked this part of their job, a fizzing, fun-filled pay-back for their lack of artistic involvement. They made good copy and they shook the framework of these dreary pop shows and that, broadly, was all they were required to do, apart from perform their songs. So how was this going to work with no drummer?

'Do you want to play drums?' Mark asked me.

'What – *me*? Drums? Here? Now?'

'Well, Ped's not here, mate, and we need a drummer,' he shrugged and rolled off to talk to the director.

Shamefully excited, pulse racing, my mind tore through a storyboard of thrilling images – charismatic views of my soft cymbal work, a sparkling exchange with Red Ronnie as 'the new-look Pedro Gill' – but as fast as this flame was lit it was cruelly extinguished.

Mark was back. 'Unions won't allow it, pal. Director just said he'd just avoid any shots of the drum kit.'

Among the wobbling plastic palm trees of the TV set, the drummerless Frankie prepared to meet the continent of Europe. On came Village People, a blizzard of leather and bandanas but, sadly, no hard hats or Navajo headgear. Then Sade, still looking like she was going to ask if I wanted the chicken or the fish. Then Chaka Khan in a fearful purple suit, followed by some god-awful Italian proggers called the New Trolls. And now it was Frankie's turn to step out in front of an audience of 40 million people.

Holly peered at a mirror. 'Look at my *crooow's* feet,' he sighed. It was his twenty-fifth birthday. 'Can we have the soft-focus lens? Ooh, I do envy those Wham! boys – twenty-one, still so *young*.'

Nasher, the guitarist, poured another stiff measure of Canadian Club and decided to play bass. 'Shall I be Martin Kemp or Dee Dee Ramone?' he cackled at no one in particular, swaying wildly by the vacant drum stool. Mark, the bassist, strapped on Nasher's guitar – it didn't matter as they weren't plugged in – and out they went in an ocean of dry-ice and cheap lighting, Holly mouthing the words to 'The Power Of Love', Paul tapping a tambourine, Nasher and Mark throwing shapes and tweaking strings, four-fifths of a group with the wrong instruments pretending to perform a record they were barely on in the first place. I watched from the wings with a strange mixture of joy and remorse. Pissed, bored and distracted, they'd somehow got away with it, but what a hopeless old sham it had all become. There was no more hollow sound than a load of acts at a TV festival telling each other how good they were. At *miming*. The more they seemed to be actually singing, the more authentic it looked and the more units they shifted. Miming was a great and valued art, a highly prized skill. Hitting some lip-wobbling top note, hand on heart, brows creased in quavering concentration – while actually making no noise at all: this was what sold records in 1985. This was what people called 'live performance'.

I gazed gloomily at the hair and makeup girls, and the

floor crew with their blinding grins and clipboards, and the artificial trees and the hideous pink textured walls and turquoise nylon carpets, and wondered if the whole pop caper was starting to congeal.

Smash Hits, too, felt like a party that was drawing to a close, its spark defusing, its balloons deflating, its sandwiches curling up at the corners. Back in London, Neil's group had been signed to Sony Music. He was packing his bags and we were going to miss him. Who else wrote such prophetic singles reviews – well, *mostly*: 'We haven't heard the last of British Eurovision entry Bardot!' – or asked question like 'Paul Weller, have you ever had sex with a man?' Columbia had put out his single 'West End Girls', a minor club hit, and EMI were re-releasing it. I liked it a lot – we all did – but we'd had other friends who'd tried to be pop stars. They'd spent several embarrassing years handing out flyers and humping bass amps up pub stairways and not a single one had found the faintest flicker of success. Why should Neil be any different, especially saddled with that hopeless name? It was hard to imagine the words 'Pet Shop Boys' on the cover of *Smash Hits*.

Though a week later, in fact, they were. The magazine had a noble tradition: if someone was leaving you threw a party and, after tipping wine, ash and crisps all over the desks, you presented them with a framed mocked-up edition with their face on the front. This was festooned with cryptic coverlines, in-jokes that made the staff weep with laughter but were incomprehensible to anyone else, in this case written by me. Neil slowly unwrapped his package.

NEIL TENNANT – WORLD EXCLUSIVE!
'How I Left The Party On Paper™ But My "Top" Pop Group Went Totally Down The Dumper So I Rather Swiftly Rang My Old Pals And Asked For My Job Back etc etc – see page 27!"

'Oh, you *shouldn't* have!' He corpsed good-naturedly.

I couldn't imagine how we'd ever replace him. It was a sad day – and there were other distractions too. A letter had just arrived from Karen in the *Whistle Test* office.

Dear Marcus,

Hello! You may have heard that you're to be involved in a small television and radio extravaganza on the 13th July at Wembley and afterwards at Legends. Please find enclosed a running order which will no doubt change. We should be in touch soon.

Best wishes – Karen, production assistant (LIVE AID)

24

Gas, Air And The Midnight Train To Georgia

There were many uses for music. I'd discovered this through years of research. It could be an escape-hatch or an avenue to self-knowledge. It could spark graceless activity on a dance-floor. It could be something to strum while imagining I was Neil Young. It could broadcast my taste and personality – I still mentally carried Chicken Shack's *40 Blue Fingers Freshly Packed and Ready To Serve* whenever I stepped outdoors. It could be a bonding agent – how can anyone in a Ramones T-shirt not have an interesting view of the world? It could be a wage packet or freeze moments in time. It could hold a mirror to guilt, loss and confusion. It could put a roof over my head.

Now I was about to find another practicality. It could be the soundtrack for the mad dash to a maternity hospital.

A lot of thought had gone into this. I wasn't going to be caught on the hop like last time. I'd even prepared a tape to play as we sped to Queen Charlotte's in Stamford Brook. Among its brisk but calming delights were 'The Look Of Love' by ABC, 'Hungry Heart' by Bruce Springsteen, 'Proud Mary' by Creedence Clearwater Revival and, if needed, crisis stress-buster 'Winter Wonderland' from the Phil Spector Christmas album, deeply comforting in any situation. Play these songs – soulful, propulsive, supportive – and the mind stopped spinning, the heart was engaged and the universe seemed vastly improved. But our second child arrived at great speed and, in the blind panic to hustle my gasping wife and two-year-old into a Renault 4, I forgot to collect the cassette from the hall table. And then scrabbled around on the dashboard and slapped in the only thing I could find. Which began with 'Midnight Train To Georgia' by Gladys Knight and The Pips. And it sounded like this.

Gladys Knight: 'He's leaving . . .'

The Pips: 'Leavin'!'

Knight: '. . . on that midnight train to Georgia.'

Pips: 'Leaving on that midnight train – ooh, y'all!'

'Do we *have* to have this?' Clare was breathing heavily.

'It's all we've got.'

Knight: 'Said he's going back . . .'

Pips: 'Going back to find!'

'Isn't there any – *ooof!* – Springsteen?'

'Forgot it, mad rush and all that. Sorry, mate!' to a van-driver. 'Baby about to be on board!'

Knight: '. . . a simpler place and time . . .'

Pips: '. . . and guess who's gonna be right by his side?'

'Tom's crying!'

Knight: 'I'll be with him . . .'

'Ooof!'

Pips: 'I know you will!'

'Red light!'

Knight: '. . . on that midnight train to Georgia . . .'

'Take this off! Where's the Phil Spector album? I'm giving birth in a Renault 4! Ooof!'

Pips: 'Leavin' on that midnight train – whoop-whooo!'

Knight: 'I'd rather live in his world . . .'

Pips: 'Live in his world . . .'

'Knees together!'

Knight: '. . . than live without him in mine . . .'

'Ooof!'

At which point the music merged with other sound effects – the squeal of brakes, the clatter of lifts, the animated talk of 'gas and air'. Pre-natal awareness was a hot topic at the time, the idea that character could be influenced by external forces during pregnancy. The voguish new way to give birth was in a tank of warm water to the soothing, supernatural murmur of whale song. So the first formative experience Robbie Ellen might have had, above the car horns and crashing of gears, was the sound of Gladys Knight's redoubtable Pips – 'whoop-whooo!' – as they tugged their imaginary whistle-cords and rattled down the great railway track of life.

25

'We're On Ninety-Five Per Cent Of All TV Sets In The World!'

It was five o'clock in London, midnight in Philadelphia, and I was sitting at the end of a jetty on the Thames near our house in Chiswick. The tide was low and the dawn breaking over the shingle banks, a cloudless sky above. This was the place I went when I had big things to think about and that day, 13 July 1985, I'd brought along the sleepless mother of all imponderables. It was this. Bob Geldof's idea of extending the Band Aid line-up and staging a charity concert had escalated so rapidly that it was now cloaked in a fireball of hype and hysteria, rebranded 'The Global Jukebox' and billed as the biggest music TV show in history. So how come it was being presented by me?

Geldof's powers of persuasion had been extraordinary. If an act had dragged their heels about taking part he'd remind them that less money would be raised as a consequence and more people would die, many of them children. He stopped short of saying their non-appearance would condemn those helpless Africans to an early grave, he left that hanging in the air, but the vast majority signed up and the few who declined may have spent a chunk of their lives feeling bad about it. Live Aid had expanded so fast he decided the show should be televised and, as his wife Paula Yates presented *The Tube*, he'd asked Tyne Tees in Newcastle to take it on. They said they couldn't handle it and told him to try the BBC, so he'd rung the corporation's rock and roll wing, Mike Appleton at the *Whistle Test*. Mike enthused to Michael

Grade, the BBC director who'd signed off a special transmission of the Band Aid video the previous autumn. With great courage and foresight, Grade cleared a sixteen-hour channel through his weekend schedule, from noon on the Saturday until four the following morning.

I skimmed a few stones and remembered the early conversations in the office at Wood Lane. Could even the might of the BBC *really* lock together this wildly ambitious jigsaw with its perilous links into Yugoslavia and the Soviet Union? And, more to the point, did a handful of people trained on the nursery slopes of *Whistle Test* – whose idea of catastrophe was The Waterboys ending a song a bit early or a no-show by the bassist of Cook Da Books – have the steel nerve and experience to anchor a live global telecast?

'What do you think?' I asked Trevor Dann.

'I think,' he said, scratching his baseball cap, 'that it's like getting Radio Cambridge to cover the election. But who knows? We might pull it off.'

The full *Whistle Test* squad had convened the day before – Dave and I, Andy Kershaw, Janice Long, Richard Skinner and his Radio 1 colleague Andy Batten-Foster. We fidgeted about nervously, unable to take it all in. In view of the scale of the operation, reinforcements arrived in the shape of Paul Gambaccini and *Late Late Breakfast Show* reporter Mike Smith, big guns from BBC1 used to audiences in the region of 10 million. But this wasn't going to be 10 million, or even 100 million. This, we were repeatedly warned, would be the whole wide world. Live Aid was going to be epic. It was going to be a monster. It was going to break every record under the sun. Anything less would be disappointing. We were handed copies of the 'London Presenters' Running Order' and I flicked through mine in reverse picking out strange and extraordinary moments.

21.39 MERCURY/MAY
PAUL McCARTNEY
TOUT ENSEMBLE

21.20 MADONNA/ROD STEWART(?)

21.14 DAVE intro into CAT STEVENS

13.11 INJECT to TRENT BRIDGE (Bob Willis, Ian
Botham, A. N. Other) then ULTRAVOX

The show was peppered with 'injects', live links not just into
Moscow and Zagreb but Australia, Japan, Holland, Austria,
Ethiopia and Germany. It would begin as follows with a
speech by the heir to the throne:

12.00 OPENING CEREMONY
Fanfare
Royal Salute (National Anthem)
HRH Prince of Wales

And the big day had come. I tossed another pebble into the
river and did some deep breathing. The BBC were sending a
cab to collect Kershaw and I – he lived round the corner – and
I wandered back past a paper shop to discover that the race
to overheat our expectations had now entered the stratosphere,
led by the cover of *The Sun*:

BEATLES IN LIVE AID REUNION: Fab 3 plus Julian
The Beatles are poised to play together in a dramatic
reunion tomorrow, with Julian Lennon replacing his
murdered father.

The secret bid to reunite the world's greatest ever pop
group for the finale of the Live Aid concert got under way
yesterday. It started after George Harrison flew into London's
Heathrow Airport.

The Wembley finale – scheduled for just before 10pm

– will include 43-year-old McCartney singing the last Beatle hit, Let It Be.

It will be a moment of rock history if Julian, 22, George Harrison, 42, and Ringo Starr, 45, join him to re-create the famous sound.

I was in the bedroom pulling on my sparkly suit when the taxi pulled up.

'Mark, Mark!' Kershaw shouted, waking the street. 'Have you got your brown trousers on?'

The 'Jimmy Hill commentary box', our base of operations, was a sweltering glass cabin suspended from the rafters of Wembley Stadium, accessible via an obstacle course of ladders and head-spinning metal walkways. Beyond its panoramic window, beneath blue skies, flags and banners, teams of technicians were testing a revolving stage, three segments of a giant wooden disc. One housed the equipment being used by the act performing, the second had the last group's gear being dismantled, the third had the next act's being set up. Round it spun, twenty minutes maximum per set with a traffic-light system telling the musicians how much time they had left. Far below us – take a picture of this – the doors had opened and seventy-two thousand people clutching rugs, picnics and beer-coolers came running from the back, a shimmering carpet of colour, sprinting, shouting, tripping and falling over in their haste to get as near the front as possible. The seats were filling too, the royal stand now heaving with rock aristocracy. Members of Queen and David Bowie in a silver-blue suit filed in behind the stubbly Geldof in his rumpled denim shirt, Paula Yates beside him clutching a cellophane-wrapped bouquet of roses to present to the occupants of the last two remaining chairs, the Prince and Princess of Wales. She'd bought them in a garage forecourt in the Harrow Road. They still had the price tag on.

But the Royal Couple were late. Appleton was in the studio truck below and, at five to twelve, his voice crackled through to the commentary box.

'They're here but Charles won't be making the opening speech. They're going straight to the seating. We need to script another opener.'

Remembering the old Light Programme overture – 'It's twelve o'clock in London, one o'clock in Cologne, and home and away it's time for *Two-Way Family Favourites*!' – Trevor scribbled some words on a piece of paper, which he handed to Richard Skinner to kick off the radio and TV broadcasts. But Skinner's voice was accidentally wired through the stadium as well, an unnerving surprise for all of us. The whole box rattled as he spoke.

'It's twelve o'clock in London, seven o'clock in Philadelphia, and around the world it's time for Live Aid . . .'

What rolled out for the next sixteen hours had a hazy, dream-like quality, as if I couldn't quite believe it was happening, an event with all the shambling hallmarks of a village fête wrestling with the mounting news that the entire universe was apparently watching and dialling in to take part. There was a quaintness about it, a sense of Englishness, of politeness, of stunned and excitable courtesy. The musicians were flown from Battersea Heliport, their choppers landing on a nearby cricket pitch in Wembley where the fielders held onto their hats in the downdraught and a wedding party waved from its wooden pavilion. Wearing a pinny and brandishing tongs, Elton John fired up a backstage barbecue of steak and sausages, adding a veggie-burger to his flaming grill for old pal Freddie Mercury. Elvis Costello scrawled the words to 'All You Need Is Love' on his hand in biro in case he forgot them before asking the crowd to 'Help me sing this old northern English folk song.' Tony Hadley brought along his wife, mother, father, brother, sister and granddad to watch Spandau Ballet from the wings. Asked on-air about the event's impact on her home life, Paula Yates said, 'The phone hasn't stopped ringing, in fact both phones. Very cool, we've got *two* phones!' When the lights fused in the Portakabin during a rushed rehearsal for the finale, twenty-six musicians ran through their lines by candlelight, and when they filed onstage, Pete Townshend announced his presence to the piano-playing Paul McCartney by creeping up behind him and tickling him twice.

Whatever tribe people felt they belonged to, whatever flag they flew, none of it seemed to matter. Members of Ultravox punched the air to Status Quo. Even their greatest detractors cheered The Boomtown Rats. The day's least fashionable act stole the show, Queen's eighteen-minute slot drilled to perfection by three days of military rehearsal. Even Andy Kershaw tried to veil his aversions, though he did tell the TV audience that big-haired pop trouper Nik Kershaw was 'no blood relative', and when interviewing Phil Collins, about to fly to Philadelphia to join Led Zeppelin, he encouraged the drummer to start his trip immediately. 'Will you shove off,' he said, 'and have you got your barley sugars?'

In the all-forgiving mood, the mistakes were what counted most, the kinks, the wrinkles, the idiosyncrasies, the spontaneous bids to forge a sense of occasion. U2's hazardous, high-wire act was an unforgettable piece of theatre. I squeezed to the side of the stage to watch Bono leap down two levels into the pit to get the camera crews to televise the crowd. He then beckoned to a girl to join him but, by the time security had worked out what he wanted and allowed her over the railing, he'd invited another, also wedged at the front. With his precious seconds ticking away, he panicked and waltzed briefly with a third girl, clambering back to the next level to find the first two waiting to dance with him. Baffled, anxious and realising they'd have to cut a whole song from their set, the three other band members ploughed on bravely, The Edge and Adam Clayton just able to see their singer but Larry Mullen, at the back, without the faintest idea what was happening.

But the mistakes weren't so thrilling in the console. The live feed to Trent Bridge to join the ratings-boosting Ian Botham broke down and was abandoned. If we couldn't link to a Nottingham cricket ground, what chance was there of connecting with Yugoslavia or going beyond the Iron Curtain into Soviet Russia?

Live Aid was creating – and then commenting on – its own mythology. Even forty minutes into the show, with the Style Council still onstage, Geldof was already being asked for his emotional reaction. One minute a live performance, the next instant history. 'Everyone was crying around me at the opening ceremony,' he said, unable to take it in. 'I just thought, Christ, what a noise!'

Intoxicating news of the watching world filtered into the box in the roof but we had no way of knowing if it was true. I sat down heavily, my head swimming, a telex beside me hammering out printed messages. The bigger the rating, the more money would be raised – and the more daunting it was for the presenters. I was anchoring the American leg, the six hours starting at ten at night, but Dave and Andy had a few links under their belts and were flying high in a great cocoon of adrenalin. At ten to three, we cut to the national news to discover that 'One and a half billion people are watching Live Aid, more than the number that tuned in to watch a man walking on the moon for the first time.' By four o'clock the Russian anchor said this had risen to *two* billion.

'A Labour MP has asked that Bob Geldof should be nominated for a Nobel Peace Prize,' Richard Skinner announced, 'and Michael Jackson is rumoured to be making a visit to Ethiopia.'

Geldof was in the Jimmy Hill box haranguing the old-school vision-mixers on a talk-back for focusing on a girl in a bikini down the front on her boyfriend's shoulders. The link to Japan crackled into life, as did the one to Australia, but road crews scurried round the stage below as the sound kept cutting out. At three o'clock, 'that most noble of aviators Wing Commander Noel Edmonds' appeared under the lights – he was the Battersea chopper pilot. As the event had now outstripped The Beatles' One World telecast of '67, all it could do was compete with itself. 'You're making more noise than Philadelphia!' he trilled, though to be fair the American show had barely begun. People had run out of superlatives and we were only halfway through: how could you measure something that was off the scale already? Giddy with the size of it, and clearly having a rush of blood to the head, Tommy Vance appeared on screen, my old *Rock On* presenter in his satin jacket and shades. He strolled out and addressed the crowd.

'"Money for nothing and chicks for free" – that was the chorus of one of their songs,' he barked. 'But their hearts are in helping people who are starving – and making great music. From London, Dire Straits!'

'Bob's just told me we're on ninety-five per cent of television sets in the world,' Dave told the universe, 'which makes me feel a little bit ill, actually.'

Nothing could fill the cavernous maw of the media. The outside wanted ever-escalating facts and figures; the inside wanted celebrities of any stripe to help fill the fractious moments between sets. Assistants were sent rattling down the gantries to round up anyone remotely famous and shepherd them to the commentary box for some overawed 'reaction'. Andy interviewed the actor John Hurt for a full three minutes without having a clue who he was. Ian Astbury, the singer with The Cult, was rushed to a cushion beside Dave to pronounce upon the day's events, but when Dave asked the crew to identify him, even *they* didn't know: he simply looked like a rock star.

In the supercharged, tropical heat, the glass box felt like a pressure-cooker, the stadium still glowing from the final bars of Queen's 'We Are The Champions'. Apprehensive and racked with back pains, Geldof settled beside Dave to watch a specially recorded video by David Bowie and Mick Jagger, a crucial plank in his fund-raising operation and another ace in Jagger's bitter rivalry with Keith Richards. Geldof had invited the Rolling Stones to play Live Aid but they'd turned him down, not least because Jagger was pursuing a solo career. Jagger then pole-vaulted onto the cast-list via the duet with Bowie and a collaboration with Tina Turner in Philadelphia. But Richards held the trump card. Bob Dylan had agreed to end the show and, worried as to how one man with an acoustic guitar could round off a sixteen-hour extravaganza without being an anticlimax, he'd rung Richards and Ronnie Wood and asked if they'd help him stage the finale. Jagger appeared on our screens in blue trousers and a blinding green shirt, Bowie in a belted white mackintosh. They high-kicked out of doorways and down fire-escapes to 'Dancing In The Street' but the transmission broke up so badly they were often invisible. Geldof turned to the camera, trembling.

'The Dubai government just gave a million pounds, so thank you, the Dubai government. The other thing is that Mick and David did that video specifically so that you can give something. You know you've got to get on the phone and take the money out of your pocket. Don't go to the pub tonight, stay in and give us the money. There are people *dying* now,' he was shaking, 'so *give me the money!*'

Dave started giving the details for those who didn't have a credit card – 'and not everyone does' – but, maddened with anxiety, Geldof lost his rag.

'No, *fuck* the address! Let's get the numbers cos that's how we're gonna get it!'

Had he delivered this jumble of words at five past seven on any other evening, he'd have been hauled off-air with a shepherd's crook while a long-faced colleague made a hand-wringing apology. But this was the tipping-point. The tide turned. Bob Geldof had spent six months putting this show together and the world was applauding. They'd wired up TVs in their gardens, they'd lit barbecues and opened cans of lager, but not many fancied paying for it. Understandably, he'd cracked. He wasn't cautioned or reproached – in fact, no one even mentioned it. There was nothing but silent sympathy. And from that moment the floodgates opened and the money began pouring in.

Something else flicked the switch seconds later. Onstage below us, David Bowie had cut short his set to allow for a newsreel of starving Ethiopian children, haunting, heart-breaking footage set to a track by The Cars called 'Drive', ironically about the piffling sorrows of a poor little rich girl from Boston. This struck a chord, not least with Bowie himself who'd been shown it the day before and immediately sacrificed four minutes of his show to ensure it was aired. He left the stage as it flooded the screens, went to his cabin and wept. The appeal phones lit up like a pinball machine and production agreed to play it again as often as possible.

Dave back-announced the video, Billy Connolly and Pamela Stephenson beside him on the sofa both dabbing their eyes. He threw to the Pretenders who'd just come on in Philadelphia, Chrissie Hynde flanked by two new recruits, her old guitarist – and now bassist – having famously overdosed and died. We were off-air again and sat watching them quietly.

'The Pretenders,' Billy shivered, subtly changing the mood. He winced and shook his greying mane. 'You wouldn't want to join *that* group.'

'Why not?' Dave wondered.

'Nobody leaves.'

26

Jack Nicholson, Lady Di, Bob Dylan
And Su Pollard

From my cab, the whole of London looked deserted. From Wembley to Piccadilly Circus, there was barely a soul to be seen. Windows were wide open in the blistering heat and I kept catching the sound of the broadcast. Live Aid was blaring from radios in passing cars and parks, and from TVs in pubs, flats and gardens. Sometimes I heard singing, the same song all down the street. The air had the warm scent of smoke and scorched steak.

We pulled in at the Three Crowns off Regent Street so I could use the pay-phone. There was a man outside in a Ford Cortina listening to the show. Twice he pushed the door open to make a dash for it but he couldn't tear himself away. Eventually he jumped out, raced across the empty road, bought twenty cigarettes without taking his eyes off the lounge-bar telly, belted out again, hurled himself into the front seat and snapped the radio back on, cranking up the volume. I could see him sag with relief. He couldn't bear to miss a second. It was extraordinary: those love-affairs we'd all had with scratchy old records made by radicals our parents hated and the newspapers mocked or ignored had somehow blossomed into a mass mainstream movement that could motivate millions of people the world over to feel the same way in the same moment. Pop music had made this happen, pop music and the mechanics of the new media.

But that technology was having its problems at Legends, the sweltering nightclub hosting the last burst of the TV coverage and an aftershow for anyone onstage at Wembley. The British finale had ended, Geldof on the shoulders of Townshend and McCartney, and a flotilla of taxis was now heading to the West End. I was about to face the cameras for the first time, my spangly man-made-fibre suit sticking to my arms and legs.

Communications had been bad enough at the stadium but at least the base of operations was in the same building. Here we were patching highlights and interviews from London around a live performance three and a half thousand miles away, and via some deeply unreliable equipment in both the UK and America. The Who's set was plagued with transmission failure, several of the satellite links had cut out and the show-case stunt of the day had managed comic, almost surreal, levels of epic failure. Heavily trailed for days beforehand, Phil Collins had indeed boarded a supersonic Concorde to the States to appear twice on both sides of the Atlantic, a live on-plane update being the cherry on this ambitious cake. Both huge Tony Hancock fans, Phil and his interviewer Steve Blacknell decided to open their exchange with lines from the comedian's '61 classic *The Radio Ham*. A stock picture of their aircraft appeared on-screen and the much-trumpeted caper began.

'It is are raining not here also,' cracked Blacknell, audibly. At which point, amid squalls of static and turbulence, the link collapsed and was never recovered, a tragedy as Collins's response was heard only by his fellow passengers: 'Send a tray of bread pudding to Kuala Lumpur.'

'How big is the audience?' I asked the crew, as Mike Smith and I were counted in.

'Not big,' the floor-manager said, in a kindly way. 'We're not live into America any more. It's just the UK, northern Europe and Australasia. Coming to Mike and Mark in forty seconds.'

This was strangely calming. On the terror-map of my mind, a whole dark continent had been erased. It was only Britain now. And France and Belgium. And Italy, Holland and Germany. And some bits of the Soviet Union. And Australia. And New Zealand. I had a few friends in America and was far more concerned about *them* than oceans of Europeans I'd never met. I'd imagined them in some New York bar – 'Hey, isn't that Mark Ellen in a bad suit? Must be hot in there. It's round him like a wet towel!'

'So how many people are watching?' I wondered, gearing up for the white-heat of my first link.

'God knows,' he said. 'Two, three, maybe four billion. Stand by, thirty seconds . . .'

'What *is* a billion?' I asked, as if it made any difference, the unit they'd bandied about in ever-escalating sums. I'd wanted to ask all day. 'Is it ten million, a hundred million or a thousand million?'

No one had the faintest idea.

'To Mike and Mark in *three, two, one* . . .'

We linked to a highlights package including a sparky exchange between Geldof and the Princess of Wales, with him pointing at a map of the satellite links.

'Here in New Caledonia,' he explained, 'they're holding their own telethon but I think there's only one phone.'

'They might reverse the charges,' Diana smiled.

'Well, I hope not,' Geldof said, 'as they're not getting their money back.'

Jack Nicholson loomed out of the screens, the main US stage anchor, then Chevy Chase stalking the Philadelphia stage. 'Anyone here have to go to the bathroom?' Chase asked. 'We suggest you just put a towel down and move to the right.' He threw a frisbee into the crowd. It was chaos. It cut back to me so I painted a picture of the empty streets in London – 'like three World Cups on the same day' – while my earpiece fizzed distractingly.

'Going to Jack Nicholson in Philly, no we're not . . . going to a pull-together of The Who, no we're not . . . It's Philly and throwing to Kenny Loggins, no to Rick Springfield, no . . . Back to London, Philly, London and . . . and . . . and cue Mark . . . Mark talking to Sade! Mark to camera, please, in *four, three, two* . . .'

Looking to my left I found Sade, mercifully waiting to be interviewed. She said it 'felt like a school sports day', and I knew what she meant – supercharged lunacy and vicious competition. Brian May then appeared beside me and explained the painstaking rehearsal of Queen's triumphant medley. Somebody found Andy Kershaw asleep on the carpet and woke him up for a link. 'A fireman has shaved his head and raised four hundred pounds for Live Aid,' he blinked, 'and a young lad has just walked in off the street with a guitar. And the name of this minstrel is . . . Cliff Richard!'

Cliff performed a special song he'd just written, clearly pained that he wasn't on the bill or even in the running order, like Cat Stevens who'd spent the day wandering round backstage but seemed more inclined to make a speech than strum a version of 'Wild World' or 'Morning Has Broken'. The actor Robbie Coltrane bowled up and offered his maroon and cream '62 Ford Consul to be auctioned. Jools Holland trundled in, his fellow *Tube* presenter at his side. 'I have my chequebook,' he waved it on-air, 'and I'll pledge another hundred thousand pounds if Paula Yates gives me executive relief.'

There was a strong sense that the best was behind us. The Thompson Twins in Philadelphia weren't holding people's attention, neither was Patti Labelle or Black Sabbath, and the club was filling up fast with self-promoters of every shape and size. The daytime anchors had interviewed Bono and Bowie. I got David Essex, fresh from *Mutiny On The Bounty* in Shaftesbury Avenue, Olympic swimmer Duncan Goodhew and Su Pollard of *Hi-De-Hi!* Coming out of a clip of Costello's sterling afternoon stint, I asked her what she'd thought of Elvis.

She blinked theatrically. 'Has he been resurrected?'

The end was in sight. Hot, tired, still unable to take it all in, we gathered round to watch the last two slots on the big screen at half past three in the morning, Geldof shouting encouragement as Jack Nicholson stepped onto the American stage.

'Some artists' work speaks for itself,' he declared, with a vulpine grin. 'Some artists' work speaks for a generation. It's my deep personal pleasure to present to you one of America's great voices of freedom. It can only be one man . . . the transcendent Bob Dylan!'

In the spirit of the day, a rough-hewn spontaneity now placed its hand on the tiller. Dylan and Keith Richards had gone round to Ronnie Wood's house in New York the day before to 'run down a few songs', much of the time spent gossiping about mutual friends Billy Preston and Mick Taylor and pouring large measures of rum and vodka. They'd planned to travel down to Philly in one vehicle to get more rehearsal time but, as each had his own entourage, they'd ended up in separate cars. The long wait for show-time had been spent in the hospitality tent. Dylan now strolled to the microphone and told the world he wanted to bring on 'Keith Richards and Ron Wood but I don't know where they are'. The pair soon clambered up the steps, cigarettes clamped in their teeth. All three wore black jeans and white tops with varying amounts of chest on show, Ron in a T-shirt, Bob a billowy half-open blouse and Keith in a waistcoat with only one button. But they couldn't hear each other above the massed ranks of USA For Africa who were rehearsing their 'We Are The World' encore behind the stage curtain, deafening a few feet away, inaudible anywhere else. Dylan steered off-road immediately, starting up an obscure tune from *The Times They Are A-Changin'* called 'Ballad Of Hollis Brown'.

'Now I'm a Dylan nut,' Wood told me when I interviewed him two weeks later. 'I know his catalogue better than *he* does. But what was this *Collis Browne*? I honestly thought we were singing about a cough mixture.'

More was to follow. His black eyeliner running in the heat, Dylan swapped his malfunctioning guitar for Wood's in the middle of 'Blowin' In The Wind' and Wood sauntered off to find another, Dylan stopping to retune and Richards trying to keep the whole thing going by himself. But in its own sweet way, it was fitting. An event that belonged in the sixties, the decade that thought it could change the world, had been closed by three people who summed up that shambling hippie optimism, in sharp contrast to the shiny professionals of the new age who'd rolled out the carpet before them. Summoning the spirit of Woody Guthrie, Dylan went into a free-wheeling speech about the dispossessed on his own nation's doorstep, the small-holders who couldn't pay their mortgages, which sowed the seeds of Farm Aid launched two months later.

For a while in the afterglow, I felt the effect of Live Aid. It had jogged the needle right across the Fourth Estate and achieved something the Concert for Bangladesh could never manage: it had motivated people way beyond the reach of music, people who might have turned down the volume for George Thorogood and The Destroyers but still felt moved and involved. For weeks afterwards, the unlikeliest souls of all ages and walks of life stopped me on the street to ask if I'd pass on their thanks to Bob Geldof and 'maybe have a stiff word with Dylan, Keith and Ronnie', as if I'd be seeing them soon. Live Aid changed the power of television, forged a bond between charity and celebrity and revitalised two decades of music, but it fell at its final hurdle. It seemed to have ushered in a return to rock and roll altruism but that was just a blip on the screen of a heart-monitor and things slowly sank back to normal. Soon it was just a warmly remembered, self-contained moment in a time of political selfishness.

It wasn't the beginning of a new era. It was the slamming of the door on the old one.

27

The Endless Pop Soundtrack Of The Mind

Around this time I was at a wedding and the service had just begun. The church was full of tailcoats, women in elaborate hats, and fidgeting teenagers with hair gel or big frocks. I didn't know very many, it was Clare's side of the family, and they'd all started a hymn. It was hot and the organ swelled with its sumptuous, rattling bass notes, and sunlight poured through the stained glass making nice patterns on the flagstone floor. One of our boys was standing on the pew holding my arm, the other asleep in his carrycot, and it was one of those rare moments where time stood still and my mind could fill with any thoughts that might want to fill it. Clare nudged me in a way that said, 'Why aren't you singing "Dear Lord and Father of Mankind" along with the rest of us? It's one of your favourites,' but it was too late: I was floating away. I was thinking about something else.

I was thinking about how the roof reminded me of a magical line in a song by The Drifters where fools fell in love just like schoolgirls, blinded by rose-coloured dreams – 'they've built their castles on wishes . . . with only rainbows for beams' – and I could picture that track as the camera panned across this vaulted ceiling at the start of a movie. I could see other scenes ahead, moments of heartbreak and drama. One had wailing police sirens backed by a luminous image on *The Hissing Of Summer Lawns* where Joni Mitchell sings 'a helicopter lands on the Pan Am roof like a dragonfly on a tomb', a film in itself. Then a silhouette on an empty highway and that flashpoint in 'Ain't No Mountain High Enough' where the chords shift up and Tammi Terrell goes, 'No wind, no rain nor winter's cold can *stop* me, baby!' in a shimmering sky-rocket of purpose and delight. Then I could hear 'Another Girl, Another Planet' by the Only Ones – maybe a plane was taking off – and I was humming every note of the guitar solo and wondering if anyone else in the place knew that Mike Kellie, the drummer, used to be in Spooky Tooth as these things were important.

And then – I just couldn't help it – I found myself playing a round of 'I Wonder What the Grateful Dead Are Doing Now'. On my own, internally. In a church. At a wedding. I was thirty-two years old, for crying out loud. I was grown-up, supposedly. I was a father *twice*. When would this end? And the Dead, for God's sake. Couldn't it be somebody else? They'd only made two *genuinely* great records since *Aoxomoxoa* – which *proper* fans knew was a palindrome – and even *that* was in 1969. Anyway, I'd got as far as Jerry Garcia sitting in a redwood forest playing a mandolin, Bob Weir watching a girl called Sapphire hand-weaving a cape and the absurdly talented Phil Lesh playing a bass in a nine-eight time signature while calculating the number of inches to the moon when I got another nudge from Clare which clearly said, 'Snap out of it and join in as people are looking and, by the way, is that your only tie?' But then a fond tap on my arm and she pointed across the aisle.

'Look,' she whispered, 'there's Jamie, the cousin I was telling you about who's seen Pink Floyd fifteen times. You'll *love* Jamie.'

The reception was under way – fizzy pop, things on sticks, the clatter of cutlery.

'Jamie, this is my husband Mark who likes Pink Floyd too – Mark, Jamie, Jamie, Mark – though he doesn't like

Roger Walters as much as the other Floyders,' she told him brightly. 'I'll leave you two together!' Her work was done.

'One of the great things about the Floyd,' Jamie said, munching thoughtfully, 'was they were at Abbey Road doing *Piper* at the same time as The Beatles were making *Sgt Pepper*. Imagine it. Norman Smith introduced them, apparently . . .'

'The engineer on *Rubber Soul*!'

'That's the guy,' Jamie grinned. 'Took them down the corridor and they watched the Fabs recording "Lovely Rita".'

'I'd love to have been there when McCartney made that track with Steve Miller,' I said.

'"My Dark Hour"! When the other three had walked out cos Paul wouldn't sign the contract with Allen Klein?'

We were in that corner all afternoon. We could have spent the last three decades learning something of value about the share index or geology or surgery or science. But we hadn't. We'd soaked up tons of this useless and pointless knowledge and we couldn't have been happier. 'Come On Eileen' played in the background, people danced around us, heels clattered on the floor, girls shrieked, somebody dropped some glasses. We were miles away, talking about XTC and The Yardbirds.

I left with two key questions high in the mix and they were these. Could rock music be any more absorbing? And when would I ever be free from it?

28

Rod The Mod Plays Away In Milan

It was the first week of January 1986. Dave Hepworth and I were in a little room at number 42 Great Portland Street, planning a new rock magazine called *Red* when we got a call from Reception.

'There's a Neil Tennant here to see you.'

'West End Girls' had been re-released in October and entered the singles chart at number 80. Since then I'd got the impression it was rising slowly but I couldn't bear to look. Neil was downstairs wearing a creaking leather jacket, a white shirt and tie, black plimsolls and expensive trousers with a crease in them. He looked terrific and was grinning from ear to ear.

'We're Up The Dumper,' he said. 'The mid-week sales are in. We'll be number one on Sunday.'

'You're still called the Pet Shop Boys?'

'"West End Girls" by the Pet Shop Boys,' he smiled, 'is the number one record in the country.'

This was overpowering – not just for him, after years of writing songs and watching countless acts pick their way through the minefield of the music business, and not just because he'd dropped by to see us on the day he'd found out: it was overpowering because, for the first time in my life, a friend of mine had achieved something momentous, and done it with such charm and modesty. I was so proud of him. Everything in this daft old world seemed possible. I called up the *Smash Hits* office I'd left six months before and we all went to see the Pet Shop Boys in a heaving club in Soho, a magnificent mix of fantasy and reality. For the howling crowd this was the new godhead-elect of glitterball pop in a pulsing digital landscape. For me it was the bloke who used to help me mend the photocopier onstage in fancy dress.

Dave's basic idea for *Red* magazine was a rock monthly whose stars were the musicians, not the writers. It would take risks and tell stories and was built around albums not singles. We tinkered with this and it slowly evolved into *Cue* magazine – the new-fangled compact disc had to be 'cued up' to be played – but to avoid confusing any snooker enthusiasts we simply called it *Q*.

The CD was the revolutionary new invention. Industry folk on the phone sometimes asked, 'What's your favourite CD?' Your favourite single or album might have made sense but this was absurd. It either meant 'What's your favourite record on this shiny new format?' – and there weren't many available and most of *them* were by Billy Joel – or it meant 'Which of your compact discs fills your Home Entertainment Hi-Fi Centre with the sharpest, most shimmering shards of crystalline sonic fidelity?' which was so monumentally boring it didn't deserve an answer. But people asked it. The compact disc was a national obsession. These 'cutting-edge gadgets' were indestructible, apparently: you could scratch them, stamp on them, cover them with glue, bury them for a thousand years and, if the hardware was still available to play them, they'd play. The cliché was that they were solely for wankers in Lamborghinis as they cost around sixteen pounds apiece, a huge profit for the labels as most were re-releases and, thus, simply analogue tapes turned digital with no recording costs.

But the compact disc had done something significant: it had ushered in a new age of nostalgia. People were buying their record collections all over again. They were reliving the time they'd first heard this music on vinyl and wondering what had happened to their old heroes. And by parachuting back to their teenage years, many felt the magnetic tug of their former selves, a time free from the shackles of mortgages and down-payments on a Volkswagen Golf. Live Aid, too, had played its part, catapulting a troop of supposedly knackered old fools back into the frame – Neil Young, Elton John, McCartney, The Who, the Stones, Zeppelin, most of them past the laughable age of forty. Had it rained on 13 July 1985, it would have dampened more than the charity phone appeal: it would have been the worst possible advert for the rebirth of rock. But the sight of the packed and ecstatic Wembley and the blue sky above convinced a load of hotdog-munching thirty-somethings watching telly at home that the old guard could still deliver, the young guard were more important than they'd imagined, and that maybe it was time to start going to gigs and buying music again. Those daunting stadiums didn't look so bad after all.

I was *Q* magazine's editor and signed up my old *NME* colleague Paul Du Noyer as my loyal lieutenant; he was wise and well-read and had an effortless way with words. The office already spoke in metaphors stretched beyond breaking-point but Paul took this practice to impressive new lengths, a favourite being the wearing of the 'iron hat', a crushing accessory filled with headache and remorse that followed nights of heavy drinking.

'Hey-ho, Paul. Wearing the iron hat this morning?'

'I awoke,' he'd reply bravely, 'to find a wide range of metallic millinery available for my deployment but I've chosen a jaunty beret, fashioned from a light tin-based alloy. Which I'm sporting at a rakish tilt.'

Back at *Smash Hits*, copy had arrived on sheets of A4 stiff with Tipp-Ex, a white paint you dabbed onto the paper so you could retype over the top of it. But *Q* had the latest technology, the Amstrad word-processor, a blurry green screen in a grey plastic moulding that had to be 'booted up' with a series of eerie clicks and hums and had a groove for 'floppy disks'. Writers still hand-delivered their articles but these were now slotted into this contraption and electronically 'flipped over'. Computers, too, were parked invitingly on our desks, dull beige boxes from a company called Apple, the avenue to a brave new world called 'Desktop Publishing', apparently, where magazines would soon be self-made without typesetters having to re-key all the articles. We laughed at this ridiculous suggestion and flatly refused to use them – 'The Amstrad's the way forward!' – and the Apple Macs sat, unloved and ignored, next to the light-box where I peered at transparencies through an eyeglass, our designer, Andy Cowles, beside me forging *Q*'s magnificent red and black logo amid exciting talk of 'dot-gain' and 'web-wander'. Priceless pictures of rock stars would be delivered by motorbike. We hardly dared touch them as they were irreplaceable: if damaged or lost, record labels could charge us thousands of pounds.

So *Q* set out its stall every month with its reams of open-minded album reviews, its charts and lists, and fondly sent up the world around it, its prose rammed with joy-dispensing, mustard-cutting compound adjectives we all thought were hilarious. We didn't yearn for the days when the acts we'd loved still played small venues. We liked it when they were successful and celebrated it. And somehow the magazine made its mark. We seemed to be flying. People understood why it was there. There was a cartoon in *Private Eye* of three figures in a newsagent's, a child reading *The Beano* in 'Kids' Comics', a teenager gawping at *Viz* in 'Youth Culture' and a stubbly type with his shirt hanging out buying *Q* in a new section called 'Second Childhood'. We hired Adrian Deevoy as a staff writer, impressed that he'd interviewed the elusive Bruce Springsteen by simply dialling his office number to find a familiar gravelly voice on the phone. I commissioned a piece about the strange marriage of King Crimson's Robert Fripp to *Smash Hits* pin-up Toyah Willcox and the headline came to Paul in a dream – 'Mr Chalk Loves Mrs Cheese'. I brought my grumbly old pal Tom Hibbert on board for a regular feature in which he grilled pompous egomaniacs or people we just didn't like, such as Bernard Manning, Ronnie Biggs, Freddie Starr and Jim 'Nick Nick' Davidson. 'There are no skeletons in my closet and I've got a knighthood to prove it,' Sir Jimmy Savile bristled when Hibbs probed him about his late-night hospital work.

After a decade of derision from the music press, the stars of the sixties and seventies couldn't believe their luck. Bryan Ferry still imagined he was 'Byron Ferrari', about to be pitch-forked onto a bonfire of old Roxy Music records by cackling imps at the *NME*, but here was a magazine that didn't pull faces behind your back – though Simply Red were always called Amply Fed on the strength of their well-built frontman. We wanted every detailed inch of people's life stories and could now speak to the stars our former titles found hard to reach, though it wasn't always successful. We persuaded Spike Milligan to interview Van Morrison but Van arrived at his old *Goon Show* hero's Sussex retreat to find him galumphing round the lawn wearing a pink, penis-shaped false nose attached with a piece of elastic. Conversation got off to a slow start.

'Are you a Protestant, Van?' Spike asked. 'Don't come near me, I don't want to catch it!'

'I'm not really anything,' Van told him.

'So when I introduce you to people I say, here is Not Anything? This is Van Not Anything Morrison, a singer and Not Anything?'

After months of negotiation I managed to land Bob Dylan and Dave flew to New York for the big encounter, but the record company hadn't dared tell the press-averse prophet it was an interview. After ten minutes, he got up, scratching his head, and sauntered out to find his PR waiting outside.

'How's it going, Bob?' the man from Sony asked nervously.

'There's some guy in there,' he shrugged, 'and he keeps asking me all these *questions*.'

But no one was more wary than Rod Stewart, the raffish soul singer who'd seen more sex than a policeman's torch. Rod the Mod, the satin-shirt rooster of The Faces booting footballs into the crowd at Weeley, had turned into a slappable national laughing-stock, symbolic of everything that had gone wrong with rock and roll, a preening, shameless crumpeteer still believing that if you've got it, you should flaunt it – ideally in a Roller with a 'leggy lovely' on your arm. Not for nothing had *Smash Hits* captioned all his pictures 'It's like punk never 'appened'. Abuse rained down upon this pouting clown not just from the music papers but from galaxies that hadn't yet been discovered. Fans adored him but he was universally despised by the press, which made him all the more fascinating.

'Wearing very tight striped pants, he looked like a bifurcated marrow,' Clive James frowned in an *Observer* review. 'He hopped along like a pensionable cherub.'

But Stewart felt the same way about the media. It was a blossoming hate-hate relationship. If you wanted to talk to him – which I did for *Q*'s second issue – then he was going to make you suffer first. After tortuous arm-wrestling, he eventually agreed to an audience.

'No interview, no pictures,' his tour manager said, when I landed in Milan.

'But the record company said it was sorted,' I squeaked. 'It's the cover story. We go to press on Thursday!'

'News to me, squire. The lad's got to rest his voice.'

I stabbed away at my hotel phone, weighing up the options. The next issue would have to lead with an old live shot trailing a bashed-together 'think-piece' – 'Believe In Rod: The Glory Years Remembered!' or some such hokey. Either that or Fish from Marillion. But after twenty-four hours of being arsed about, I began to get the size of him. An elaborate cat-and-mouse game was afoot, designed to weaken me to the point of nervous exhaustion where I'd be pathetically grateful for any contact with the sly old fox at all. He'd been a gravedigger and an apprentice footballer at Brentford FC, and he'd hauled himself up by his bootstraps, knowing it could end any second and his whole house of cards might come tumbling down. The slings and arrows of the press had been his only major obstacle and he was going to take it all out on me.

The next afternoon, a message arrived from on high. Rod had agreed to meet me: if he liked the cut of my jib there'd be a five-minute interview after the show; if not, forget it. 'Be in the bar of the Hotel Principe di Savoia at seven o'clock,' I was told, 'and don't bring the photographer.'

At just after eight, five rascals came rollicking in, a blur of silk scarves and frock coats, their buccaneer boots clattering on the polished marble floors. They were Rod Stewart's backing band about to take the stage at San Siro Stadium. They hoisted large drinks, shot me pitying looks and hooted among themselves about recent lark-filled antics on the road, handcuffing each other to radiators, supergluing furniture to ceilings and getting thrown out of a Munich bierkeller for their spirited version of 'When Irish Eyes Are Smiling'.

'Any sign of Rod?' I wondered.

'No, mate.' He was famously unreliable. 'Hired a plane the

other day in Berlin and nipped up to Sweden for a knock-about with Björn Borg,' the guitarist told me. 'Only just made it back in time for the gig.'

Fifteen minutes later, Stewart bowled in with his girlfriend Kelly Emberg. He was forty-one, she was twenty-seven. Both had orange skin and shades and were audibly jangling with jewellery, him in a crimson suit and calfskin loafers, her with the impossible physique of a Barbie doll, her blonde hair piled high on her head, a cream mini-skirt, pearl earrings and legs eventually ending in tottering heels that sparkled with gems. Ignoring me, they regaled the band with tales of the day's shopping spree. They'd been ferried round the city in a black Mercedes by a driver with a peaked cap.

'Kel had a top-up with the old sun-ray lamp,' Stewart said, 'then there was a nice little lunch, touch of the Vichyssoise and home-made pasta. Then we motored off to bag a whistle, a nice slice of Armani. Little siesta back at the hotel,' he gave Kelly a nudge, 'and then it's on down to Cartier for *this* bad boy!'

He shook his arm to display a vast, chunky, 22-carat wristwatch. 'Solid gold,' he said. 'Not too shabby. Only fifteen hundred dollars.' He turned and flashed it at me. 'Who *wouldn't?*'

Despite his Spandex buffoonery, his mawkish ballads and his ludicrous Los Angeles lifestyle, I'd always liked Rod Stewart. But all that was beginning to change. Now I was starting to love him. He was just as I'd hoped he'd be, the same offstage as on. He wasn't pretending to be anyone else. He wasn't defined by his art, like most musicians, he was defined by his wealth, and he had so much of the stuff he had to make a conscious daily effort to go out and spend it. It was both awful and strangely touching. He wanted me to envy him. And, like all musicians who claim to hate the press, deep down he wanted me to admire him too. The more the

235

papers tossed their hand-grenades, the more he drew his cash around him like body-armour, the trinkets, the baubles, the trophy wives.

He looked me up and down. 'Want to follow the coach?' he said, and the entourage swept off in a flurry of rattling heels and satin finery, with me bumping along in a cab behind them. I'd passed the first test. Now for the second.

'Stick with her,' he said, pointing to Kelly in the backstage area and, seconds later, a roar from the packed stadium announced he was on. First I was being invited to marvel at the life of Rod Stewart; now I was being allowed to feel what it was like to actually *be* Rod Stewart, squashed next to Kelly Emberg on a flight case in full view of forty thousand baying Italians. Men were howling with rage, some pointing and shouting things that didn't sound friendly. How come this gangly-looking berk in Dr Martens was with this fabulous vamp? They weren't happy and they told me so. From where I was perched, the entire concept of Rod Stewart looked like a riot – the clamour of the amps, the thunder of drums, the raking spotlights, the tented boudoirs, the chilled champagne, the gangsters' molls, the over-cranked theatre of a band trying to reach the wind-lashed bleachers about a quarter of a mile away. And, beside me, a girl who waved when he waved at her, shrieked, screamed, bawled and wailed, mouthed the words to every song – even the lustful old croakers he'd written for other women – then kicked off her heels, leapt on the box and literally *moaned* for an encore. Rod swung by our side of the stage now and again to talk to her, dripping with perspiration.

'Dead loss this crowd, aren't they?' he yelled at us.

'They're great!' she shouted. 'They just don't understand what you're saying, darling.'

'Can't hear a fucking thing!' he panted.

'It'll sound much better out front!' she said supportively.

He did another couple of circuits, punching the air, swinging the mike-stand, sticking his arse out, and was back steaming under the lights.

'Tell you what,' he wheezed, 'I feel fucking old trying to get these Italian bastards going.' And he charged off to the centre, yelling, 'Ladies and gentlemen, the moment you've all been waiting for – The End!'

Now for stage three in the Rod Stewart Rock Hack Initiation Ceremony: the restaurant.

'Eh, my old-ah football boot!' he said to the staff in general and a bevy of over-attentive waiters beetled to his side. They were flattered by this Anglo-Italian greeting and rightly so. Their resident decorated his hotel rooms with the team flags of every city he visited – that night Inter Milan – so 'my old-ah football boot' was the highest compliment imaginable. They told him the seasoned veal shank was the house speciality.

'*Osso bucco*!' Rod enthused. 'Eet taste-ah very goot. Is-ah goot for *you*, is-a goot for *me*, is-a goot for *evahbodee*. It-ah make evahbodee feel-ah verra nice, ah-thanka verra much!'

He sat Kelly on his left, me on his right and 'the lads' from the band all around in a circle, and talked about life in Beverly Hills with his first wife Alana 'Mein Führer' Hamilton where everyone was legless 'and the dance-floor saw some funny goings-on'. Gregory Peck was next door, he said, and Burt Reynolds, Ryan O'Neal, Barbra Streisand, Jack Nicholson and John Belushi down the street. As the bottles of Barolo started piling up, there were fond memories of doing the fandango with Liza Minnelli, much to the chagrin of Mein Führer. His stories were full of nicknames – Freddie Mercury was 'Sharon', Elton John was 'Doris'.

'We were going to form a group once called Hair, Nose and Teeth,' he said, tucking into the cheese. 'Doris was the hair, I was the nose, Sharon was the teeth.'

He'd been rich and famous for twenty years and didn't see why he should apologise. It was all he'd ever wanted. Life was one big rollercoaster, a giant bubble of celebrity he never wanted to leave. He expressed himself with cash and found it hard when people couldn't accept it. He said his mother Elsie had asked for a bottle of Charlie perfume for Christmas, 'awful cheap stuff', but he'd bought her a fur coat instead, 'which she never wears – *and* she goes round my house turning lights off trying to save electricity'. He wore shades whenever he stepped outside, he told me, so he could avoid eye-contact with anyone without appearing to be rude. He loved Robert Mitchum, another working-class hell-raiser aiming for ever-greater wealth. 'Stick with me, sweetheart,' Mitchum told the girls, 'and you'll be farting through silk.' Rod called for the bill – 'My old-ah football boot-ah, the Jack and Jill *eef* ah-you bisso kind' – and then whispered in the waiter's ear and we were all issued with individual tabs, apart from Kelly, each ending with a sobering succession of noughts. But I'd passed the audition. I'd paid in cash, I'd got my round in, I'd bought his early singles. I couldn't be *all* bad.

'Ten minutes at noon,' he said, 'and bring your tape-machine. But don't be a plonker, right?'

The only problem now was what to tell the office. I'd let myself down. I'd let *Q* down. I'd let down the whole of the rock press. I'd got the interview but I'd cocked up and I knew it. I'd fallen for Rod Stewart.

I got back to London to find an ominous message from Mike Appleton inviting me, Dave and Andy Kershaw to lunch, and had a fairly shrewd idea what it was about. The episodes of *Whistle Test* I'd just finished had felt like the last gasp of a steam engine, its rusting machinery clanking as it waited to be shunted to the knackers' yard. The *Old Grey* had overspent so drastically on the series before that, to save money, we'd had to leave Television Centre and pre-record the show using free time in BBC studios in Sheffield, Manchester, Cardiff, Edinburgh and Dublin. The only presenters were myself and Andy; everyone else had gone. I could feel its lifeblood ebbing away, along with its clout and pulling power. The final show featured Wet Wet Wet.

Poking his soba noodles in a restaurant off Great Portland Street, Mike told us the network had appointed a new head of Youth and Entertainment Features called Janet Street-Porter. She'd won awards, he said, for her Channel 4 show *Network 7* and was launching a version called *DEF II* for the BBC – hand-held cameras, computer graphics, rapid edits and such – and this would revolutionise music television. She didn't want bands playing live in the studio and saw no value in our archive of footage. She'd taken *Whistle Test* round the back of the building and dispatched it with a single bullet. Kershaw loosed off a molten stream of invective about this 'lily-livered corporation' and its lack of support for the arts but Dave and I had had enough. We had things to do and magazines to think about and this noble adventure had run its course.

The next day I had lunch with my dear old pa in a chop house near Fenchurch Street station. He'd read an interview with me in *The Times* about *Q*. They'd been impressed with 'the modern guide to music and more' and wished its editor well. And this in *The Thunderer* – there was no greater endorsement. I watched him for a while sawing away at his lamb cutlet, a cloud of memories flooding back. Dad, born in the twenties, sighing at the spectacle of The Kinks. Dad, who loved Mozart, turning down the TV sound for *Magical Mystery Tour*. Dad, the preacher, pretending not to mind that his teenage son had spent Christmas in a hippie commune. Dad, the old soldier wounded in the war, confused and distressed by Frank Zappa's *Hot*

Rats. Dad pushing a copy of *Punch* towards me with encouraging talk of its verve and durability. I could finally see what he'd been through.

'I'm not sure I understand a word of your new publication,' he smiled, between mouthfuls, 'but I can tell many others do. You've lived by your wits and done it off your own bat,' he added fondly, 'and I'm proud of you.'

The press and the sales had made the long struggle worthwhile but nothing mattered as much as this. It meant the world to me. On my way back to the office I found myself in tears. If fathers had been huggable, I would have hugged him.

29

The Terminator And His Bleep Tapes

There comes a point in everyone's life when they feel washed up. Out of touch, over the hill, old and in the way. This sensation tapped me on the shoulder in the summer of 1991. I'd left *Q* to run *Select* magazine. It was my first day in the office. I was thirty-seven years old.

Select had been sold to my publishers EMAP by Express Newspapers and its bewildered staff were ferried by minibus to an office we'd rented in Holborn. It was a monthly rock title that considered itself left-field so their first shock was that they were now owned by the evil print barons behind such mainstream brands as *Q* and *Smash Hits*. The second was discovering their new boss was the prize pillock who'd actually *edited* the insufferable *Q* magazine: me. By the time I'd arrived and met them all, their clunky space-filling Apple Macs were plugged back in and they were trying to finish the issue. I wandered over to the designer, Steve 'The Terminator' Hicks, who was hunched in a corner playing home-assembled 'bleep tapes' at deafening volume through a ghetto-blaster. Cassettes were scattered on his desktop, each with a scribbled label – 'Bleep 1', 'Bleep 2', 'More Bleeps'. He had a wispy beard, like Shaggy in *Scooby-Doo*, and a huge woollen hat emblazoned with the single word 'PERVERT'.

'What's this music, The Terminator?' I asked brightly. He wasn't Steve or Hicks, he was The Terminator.

'Machine-generated noise,' he said, staring straight ahead in the bored, agitated manner of a student addressing a pensioner. 'Bleeps, loops, samples, sounds. This shit's Nosebleed Techno.'

Nosebleed Techno. Even the *idea* was chilling. The top layer seemed to consist of violent, lurching discords and the random interruptions of a smoke alarm. Below that was a fearful queasy bass figure, tuneless and suffocating, and the bottom end sounded like a spin-dryer full of bricks. Its effect on The Terminator was soothing. He tapped a toe as he clicked away at his layouts. He might even have whistled. Personally, I found it hard to breathe. It felt like my nerve-ends were being massaged with a wire brush.

'None of this "Nosebleed" seems to have any words,' I pointed out.

'I hate singing,' The Terminator told me. 'Hate lyrics, hate vocals. And I *detest* guitars,' he announced, enjoying my pain and confusion. 'I've never listened to anything with a guitar on it,' he added proudly. 'Well, not *voluntarily* anyway.'

'What if someone told you what you were listening to had a guitar on it?'

'I'd take it off and tread on it,' he said. 'I *loathe* guitars. They should be killed to bits.'

Next to The Terminator was Lucy O'Brien, a former member of punk band the Catholic Girls wearing a high-visibility anorak. Beside her, in strategically ripped trousers, was Hannah 'Ranks' Ford, the editorial assistant who, at six o'clock, transformed into a tune-spinning club DJ. Then came assistant editor Dave 'The Cav' Cavanagh, sleepwalking through the day after nights of sustained revelry, a black cloud of dissent hovering above his head. Wherever he roamed it stayed with him, as if attached by invisible wires. He'd float in silently with the lugs of his Sony Walkman screwed deep in his ears – Scott Walker B-sides or unreleased outtakes by meandering Bristol collective the Blue Aeroplanes – and hammer out sheets of immaculate prose. His rare speech was peppered with sixties buzzwords deployed with maximum irony – 'I'm splitting the scene but I'll dig you later,' he'd say, if popping out for some cigs. And alongside The Cav was Andrew Harrison, a frantic ball of energy peering through a lank curtain of Happy Mondays hair whose daily rants about one of the groups from his hometown of Liverpool were another kind of revelation. I'd never met anyone under fifty who didn't like The Beatles. People either adored them or admired them and acknowledged their significance. Harrison did neither. He had nothing but contempt for them. His musical twin poles were The Smiths and Kraftwerk – Düsseldorf's 'digital Beatles' – and barely a day went by without one of his sharp, funny and loudly applauded in-office diatribes on the wretchedly offensive, cheese-scented sound of 'the Pre-Fab Four', clearly the bane of his life.

So, yes, people who hated guitars. And singing and song lyrics and The Beatles. *God* I felt old.

But that was nothing compared to their contempt for *Q* magazine. The title I'd fondly edited for the last five years was their benchmark for all awfulness. It reeked of the eighties and was, they told me, for 'yuppies with fitted carpets and two-point-three children' in company cars cruising to the tortuous works of Dire Straits or Eurythmics. It was smug, glib and breezy, they complained, every article about some howling bore with a Fender Stratocaster and filed by 'our man with the All-Access Laminate'.

'The majesty of rock!' they mocked. 'The pageantry of roll!'

This was *Q*'s current slogan – amusing, *I* thought, but guaranteed to make any twenty-three-year-old's blood boil. And here was a room full of them. Mention *Q* magazine and they'd practically form a lynch-mob and rampage through central London stringing up anyone with a Top 40 compact disc while hatching a plot to assassinate Eric Clapton. The nineties, they made abundantly clear, belonged to them – its bleeps, its loops, its samples, its sound-systems, its Moose, Tool, Blur, Cud, Lush, Suede, Felt, Pulp, Curve, Ride, Slint, Hole and countless other groups with one-syllable names – and it was theirs and theirs alone. It certainly wasn't mine.

The final nail in my coffin, even worse than editing a popular magazine, was that I'd presented that dismal last bastion of 'songs', guitars and shagged-out survivors of the rock battlefield, *The Old Grey* fucking *Whistle Test*. They thought of me as the Ancient Mariner, a friendless, grey-beard loon trudging a now-digital landscape with the alba-tross of my Harper-Page disaster hung around my neck. And if I was old enough to have presented that mound of tripe, I could well have been a hippie in the seventies, a paid-up member of that lost generation of sheep-like clots who tapped finger-cymbals to the sound of Fat Mattress. Being an ex-hippie in '91 was one down from a war criminal: you lived in fear of being outed by packs of hyperactive rave-monsters waving glo-sticks, and being force-fed crystal meth and bleep tapes as a punishment. I brought my old student ID card in to prove them right and it was promptly scanned and enlarged into a giant poster occupying most of one office wall, cunningly hand-modified. The words 'TRAGIC HIPPIE' pointed to my yards of lustrous hair, 'British' had been changed to 'Member of the Universal Kingdom of Harmony and Good Vibes', and a thought bubble popped from my tousled head reading: 'Mmmm, Roy Harper's new vinyl outing's a real gas: he's COOKING!'

Strangely, this was all good news. I'd left *Q* to launch other music titles, and the sensible thing to do seemed to be to start a magazine that was the polar opposite for readers ten years younger, and do it fast. And the best way to avoid months of tedious research and test-marketing was to buy an existing one and change it on the hoof. So the temperature lifted when I suggested *Select* should try to destroy *Q* and all it stood for, to topple the great Easter Island statues that loomed over its landscape – The Beatles, The Doors, The Who, Led Zeppelin – and replace them with anyone they reckoned might still be around a decade later, the options including The Wonder Stuff, The Stone Roses, Happy Mondays and, on a bad day, Jesus Jones. The mood switched overnight. I was no longer the evil dictator with a copy of *Brothers In Arms* for a brain but a benign patron of the arts encouraging daft comic invention. And they were no longer dour, mutinous insurgents but a collection of fiercely funny and creative radicals hooting with glee as they tried to hole the good ship *Q* below the waterline.

It was like *New Music News* all over again, but in colour and with some cash. *Select* became a fanzine that went windmilling into any platinum-selling acts who looked pompous and deluded. One feature satirised 'the shady pasts, dreadful lyrics and sickeningly opulent living conditions of today's leading musical entertainers'. We asked bands to take self-expressive pictures of themselves in photo-booths and post us the results, and ran pages of them – Blur, The Farm, The Charlatans, Lush, The Fall. As Creation Records were everywhere with My Bloody Valentine and the Jesus and Mary Chain, we invented group names for non-existent acts they might like to sign – Chodburger, My Cousin Rachel, David Icke In Conversation. We ran flip declarations on 'the burning issues of the day', like Curve's Toni Halliday on the subject of Adam Clayton's penis, controversially pictured on the sleeve of *Achtung! Baby* (her verdict: 'impressively large'). Sales began to lift so we started squandering cash – the set for a photoshoot with Shaun Ryder included some custom-built gold cherubs and his crack-addled revelations in her sparkling profile won Miranda Sawyer a national award. We held a world-trembling 'summit' starring Miki Berenyi from Lush, Peter

Hooton of The Farm and Mark E. Smith – 'I know you,' The Fall leader eyed me narrowly, brushing ash from his lapels. 'You're the bloke who used to do the weather on Yorkshire TV', before he drank nine pints of bitter in four hours, each with a whisky chaser. We ran a stage-diving guide which researched key venues for height of fall, floor composition and levels of 'bouncer aggression', though when a piece appeared about the joys of legal highs – 'Neck four Feminax and a shot of vodka and go cycling in heavy traffic' – EMAP blew the whistle and expensively pulped the entire issue. A new logic had presented itself, as if rock's pack of cards had been shuffled and re-dealt with all the unfashionable bands taken out. We ran blocks of posters in which a handful of old acts the team considered acceptable – early Roxy Music, the Stones, Iggy Pop, Hendrix – sat in perfect harmony beside The Shamen, The Charlatans, Julian Cope and LL Cool J. The headline for an encounter with Alex Chilton of Big Star was 'He Is Risen!' A whole new hierarchy seemed to exist, attached to the main terminals of either Kraftwerk or the MC5.

Rattling down to Somerset a few months later, I was about to get another revelation. Rock festivals had changed too, and so had the reasons for attending them. I hadn't been to one for thirteen years.

'Who are you going to see?' I asked the three hitchhikers who'd just clambered in at a service station.

'Don't know,' they shrugged. 'Who's on?'

I adjusted the rear-view mirror and studied them in turn. One had baggy shorts, a baseball cap and bits of his hair were green. The second had a T-shirt saying 'Happy Daze', with a picture of a gadget with wires coming out of it. The third was very pale and didn't say a word, just stared rigidly out of the window, her eyes swivelling from side to side as if watching a tennis match that only she could see.

'Television, Lou Reed, Teenage Fan Club,' I said. 'Morri
The Orb.'

Silence.

'House Of Love? P. J. Harvey?'

No takers.

'Joan Armatrading? Ozric Tentacles . . .?'

Not a flicker of interest. They were hoping to see Spiral
Tribe, they told me, though they weren't even convinced they
were on – but it didn't matter as they weren't paying:
they were climbing over the fence. Spiral Tribe were a mobile
sound-system on a truck towing a generator who'd staged a
free festival in Castlemorton in the Malvern Hills. Around
twenty thousand party animals and travellers had turned up,
sparking the four-million-pound court case that brought a
new parliamentary bill about 'anti-social behaviour'. They
were also going to a rave called Sugarlump which I'd never
heard of. But I'd got the message: all three were going to
Glastonbury to *hear* music, not to look at it. They couldn't
name a single member of Spiral Tribe and they didn't think
it mattered. I was fascinated, amazed. My entire relationship
with music was based on the personalities of the people
performing it. Every syllable of the lyrics was crucial, every
picture, every quote in the press, every line-up change,
every split second of their public and private lives. Here was
a music with no words or even people, just a sound coming
from a lorry that brought its own electricity. This was about
as far from the Small Faces as it was possible to imagine. A
round of 'I Wonder What Spiral Tribe Are Doing Now?'
would never get off the ground.

Cautiously, self-consciously, I slid into Sugarlump at one
the next morning with my old mate Nick. We stood in the
shadows at the back of the tent, clutching beer cans, feeling
like parents at a house party. In the cascade of spinning lights
and projections we could see the silhouette of a DJ with a

pair of decks on the roof of an American army truck, a heaving mass of people below him waving luminous wands and blowing whistles. They'd taken so many drugs their eyes were like hub caps. They seemed to crackle with static.

'Gimme ten fingers, Glastonbury!' the DJ yelled. Four hundred whistles, eight hundred hands.

The great juddering clamour had two main gears, euphoria and anxious panic. Occasionally the bass would drop away and there'd be twelve bars of unsupported noodling, and everyone would sag, looking helpless and exposed without the warm cocoon of sound around them. Then the sheets of noise kicked back in, fierce and adrenalised, a racing metronomic pulse, like a heartbeat out of control, and the whole place exploded in a ball of light and more whistling. All other music had echoes of its roots – I could work out its origins, I could hear its influences. I couldn't recognise a single note of this. I hadn't the faintest idea where it came from. It was like tapping into another galaxy. It was the newest thing I'd ever heard; strangely liberating, a music with no past. The Terminator's bleep tapes were an office nightmare but the same sound in this packed and steaming marquee with a moon above it sounded magical – even if you hadn't necked a 'Rhubarb and Custard' or some MDMA, just two pints of woolly ale.

But one niggling concern darkened my mood. I thought back to my rain-lashed teenage self peering at The Groundhogs through a rolling fog of fried-onion smoke and came to a mournful conclusion: people were having a better time now than I was then.

I had the same feeling the next day, louder and clearer. The headline act was on and I was in the pit below the Pyramid Stage helping out with the crush. Thirty thousand revellers were wedging down the slope, pressing the ones at the front

Cheery snap for the *Radio Times* to promote my two weeks sitting in for John Peel on his late-night Radio One show. I'm about to tell the nation that 'no member of The Clash can actually sing': big, *huge* mistake.

With Dave Hepworth on the roof of Television Centre, our first Old Grey Whistle Test photo session. We're trying to send up our tortuous press release which claims the show 'takes a sideways look at the rock scene and beyond!'

On set for a Whistle Test New Year's Special with (from left) Dave, 'The Man They Call Richard Skinner', Frank Sidebottom wearing a giant fibreglass head, Andy Kershaw and Ro Newton. The lavish budget runs to balloons and two cans of Kestrel Lager.

The nightmare of Ambleside: with Jimmy Page and Roy Harper at the point where the sheep sound-effects are dubbed on – '*Maaaarrrk! Maaaarrrk!*'

Presenting Live Aid on July 13 1985 to 'four billion people', wondering what a billion actually is.

Levels of expectation are stratospheric: on the morning of the concert the *Sun* claims The Beatles are 'poised to reform' with Julian Lennon in place of his father.

The chaotic interviews, this with Brian May about Queen's show-stealing triumph: next up I had Su Pollard from *Hi-De-Hi!*

Topical 'Wall Street' publicity snap with hair gel and cigars to celebrate *Q*'s off-the-scale success in '87 – (back row from left) Andy Cowles, Paul Du Noyer, Dave, Andy Gill, (front) Nikki Whenham, Adrian Deevoy and John Bauldie. Note stone-age technology.

Eager reporters watching Bob Dylan from a press pen in Hyde Park – (from left) Tom Hibbert, Andy Gill, Andy Kershaw, me and Clare.

Rival titles mocked *Q* for being 'old hippies' so we released this damning snap of the office team at work.

News shot of the *Select* staff under new management (me) in the summer of '91: 'Terminator' Hicks is at the back, 'The Cav' dispensing good-ish vibes below him, Lucy O'Brien centre, Andrew Harrison plotting the downfall of The Beatles (far right).

MOJO's launch marketing reaches my tube station in '93: celebrating with the underawed Robbie Ellen.

The greatest *Q* Awards triumph, Paul McCartney
together with his old Goon Show hero Spike
Milligan, myself and Danny Kelly presenting.

With 'Mister Spector' (*never*
call him Phil): the paparazzi
thought he was Dudley Moore.

Another deathless
moment, Jarvis Cocker
with Bowie and Eno –
'Mister Hunting-Knife,
meet Mister Liver Salts!'

With Dave and Kate Mossman on an early Word podcast, possibly discussing which album it would be least awful to be bumped off by if your entire attic-based vinyl collection fell through your bedroom ceiling.

The final line-up of *The Word* busking in Chapel Market an hour after we'd closed the magazine – (from left) Jon Sellers, Kate, Dave (despairing at a cab firm's punctuation), Fraser Lewry, Magic Alex and 'Seventies' Johnson.

Hilarious and adorable, Lady Gaga with her clothes back on at the
New York photo shoot, October 2011 – 'Hey you, no peeking!'

Epic chaos ahead: Rihanna handing me a $50 beaker of champagne as her cash-melting 777
Tour heads for Mexico City. Five days later the press staged an in-flight riot.

against the barriers. Anyone in distress had to be fished out fast. The security guys had a little routine and we soon got the hang of it. Burly blokes with orange jackets and foam earplugs stood on the folding seats on the inside of the fence and grabbed any outstretched hands, we pulled down sharply on the back of their belts and a steaming sixteen-year-old popped out of the mosh like a cork. We rushed them to a nearby tent – quick check, oxygen, glass of water – then through the exit, round the side and eased them back into the crowd. The giant digital screens above us flashed with blocks of colour and I could smell hot bodies and woodsmoke, warm turf and marijuana. Beats and samples larded with fizzing power chords poured from a stack of winking computers, and images in the flickering strobes – a polka-dot guitar, a peaked cap, flailing curls in the night air – revealed that Lambeth street-prophets Carter The Unstoppable Sex Machine were having their mystifying moment of glory. Beams of light raked across the field catching wide-eyed faces rapt in wonder.

'You fat bastard!' the front row yelled, a key part of the Carter ritual.

And thirty thousand more: '*You fat bastard!*'

The people on the hill now, and in the tents and up the trees: 'YOU FAT BASTARD!'

Waves of sound poured down the hill, roars of approval ricocheted back. And still they came, pressed up against the railings – more hands, more corks, more mercy-dashes to the medical unit. Except . . . hang on. Hadn't I seen this girl before? Trainers, cap, knee-length Jimbob-and-Fruitbat T-shirt? Whatever discomfort she'd bravely endured, she seemed to have made a remarkable recovery. She waved away any bottles or breathing apparatus and dived straight back into the audience.

'Third time!' she yelled to her friend behind her.

'I'm on *four*!' came the cackling reply.

That put the tin lid on it. I gazed around me at this vast canvas city of concert halls, restaurants, clubs, art galleries, theatres, cinemas, circuses and acres of dry, tented suburbs. It was like that vision of Utopia at the end of *Chicken Run*, a cartoon nirvana where symbolic windmills revolve and happy people cavort among the flowers in blistering tropical heat. Everywhere I looked there seemed to be a giant orange inflatable spaceball or a quintet of Charlie Chaplins. There were wind-fired bread-ovens and vats of paella. There were massage retreats and swarming drum workshops. There were solar-powered showers and tea salons. Small boys with painted faces sat on cushions listening to poetry, some in T-shirts saying, 'National Elf'. Kindly paramedics applied bee-sting ointment to little girls in fairy-wings. Handsome mums wearing shades hovered in tank-like cars at the exit gates as if the whole thing was an extension of the school run. Every possible need was being catered for, every element of your comfort and security monitored in this sun-baked Shangri-La – to the extent that anyone feeling the mild inconvenience of a jostling crowd could be hand-lifted to safety and delivered direct to a crack squad of enthusiastic doctors. Even if there was nothing wrong with them. Even if, purely out of boredom, they were just competing with some mates to see how many times they could get over the barrier and back.

This touched some old-fogey nerve and I felt a surge of envy. You bastards, I thought, how *dare* you have so much fun? You don't know how lucky you are! *We* fought this war for you, the shell-shocked survivors of the great campaigns of the seventies, limping home with trench foot and scurvy! *Your* toilets actually look like toilets. *We* sat on wobbling metal poles above a deep, malodorous ditch. Somebody fell in, for God's sake! You've got halloumi. We had salmonella and chips. You've got Orange Mobile 'Camp-Finders' that make your tent light up when you text it. We slept in old fertiliser sacks. You've got Primal Scream beneath a harvest moon, the sky lit up with Chinese lanterns. We had puddles and Van der Graaf Generator.

Young People Today, I grumbled to myself, wandering off to a bar with organic food and wood-barrelled beer. They didn't know they were born. They had no idea what we guinea pigs suffered to drag rock festivals from the boot-sucking quagmire of the Dark Ages.

30

'There's Twelve Notes And Thirty-Six Chords And That's It'

I left *Select* to help cook up a new magazine and on Sunday, 1 October 1995, I found myself talking to Noel Gallagher's mum in a room that looked like a giant meringue. There were marble fittings, starched tablecloths and chandeliers in white plaster ceilings, and a small collection of people were clomping round its polished wooden floor. Her sons' band's label had hired a suite in Pavilion Road, Knightsbridge, and were having a launch party for the second Oasis album. Racks of toast arrived and piles of kedgeree in silver dishes, the air full of the scent of smoked haddock. Champagne breakfast at one in the afternoon, very Creation Records.

Peggy Gallagher spoke fondly of the scooter her youngest lad still kept in their back yard in Burnage, and there he was, Liam, with his stubble, trainers and hoodie, waving from across the room, brandishing a glass of booze. The big time had beckoned and their drummer Tony McCarroll hadn't made the cut; Alan White had taken his place. The rest of the rhythm section were mooching about in the shadows, 'Guigs' McGuigan and 'Bonehead' Arthurs, probably wondering if the Grim Reaper had his evil eye on them too. Noel came by and gave his mum's arm a squeeze – 'It's only the second time she's been to London,' he told me – and wandered off, leaving the two of us staring in silence at the centrepiece of the celebrations, a three-foot block of ice spelling '(WHAT'S THE STORY) MORNING GLORY?' in big letters.

'What's that?' Peggy asked, baffled but intrigued.

'It's an ice sculpture,' I said. 'It's the name of their new record. Made of ice.'

'But it's melting,' she said.

'Well, it's *meant* to melt. It just sort of drips away for a bit and then, I don't know, disappears.'

'What's the point of it, then?'

Good question. Here she was, looking at the waistcoated waiters, the candelabra and wicker baskets of white lilies and thinking – as *any* mum would – that it was all very nice and everything but you could do it much cheaper somewhere else and without all the fuss. And now here was this idiotic thing in the middle of the room, melting. It was barely legible already. Whatever it cost, it would soon be a pool of water.

'Good question,' I shrugged, faintly embarrassed. Seen through the eyes of Mrs Gallagher, the music business looked ridiculous. All I could think of saying was that splashing cash was the standard way of announcing that the last record had sold well and there'd be a lot of muscle behind the new one, though *What's The Story* hadn't got off to a strong start, given such a pasting by much of the press for being overblown and clumsy that I was virtually the only hack invited as I'd been so enthusiastic about the album before it.

Definitely Maybe had appeared in '94, a year after the launch of *MOJO* magazine. We'd been the first music monthly to put them on a cover. I'd done the interview and asked for just the band member who wrote the songs. I was told to meet him in a hotel in Belsize Park and there he was, in a hushed tea-room with the soft chink of china and the rattle of cutlery. Discreet business meetings were taking place, and well-heeled matrons on plump sofas were picking fondant fancies off a tea-trolley. Noel was highly amused by it all, chain-smoking in his leather jacket and drinking bourbon and Coke. He was twenty-seven, fast-thinking and tirelessly funny. He had a chewed George Harrison *circa* '64 crop – it looked like he might have cut it himself – and he rubbed it sometimes with the palm of a hand in deep concentration. He was brash, fearless, transparent, proudly ambitious and utterly without pretension. There seemed no side to him at all. Musicians tend to be cautious and a little calculating, and have aspects of their lives they want to conceal. For all his honesty, even Rod Stewart was cleverly controlling. But Noel Gallagher wasn't remotely bothered about the impression he gave. He told me precisely what he thought and I could make of it what I wanted. Only three of his songs actually meant anything, he said; the rest meant nothing at all and it was monstrous arrogance to pretend they did. He still had a fan's eye view of the world and was besotted with the eighties acts he'd grown up with – The Stone Roses, U2, The La's, 808 State – but he was far enough removed from his *old* heroes to be unsentimental about them. He liked their records from the sixties and seventies and he hated their new ones – 'Ray Davies, Pete Townshend, George Harrison, the Stones and Paul McCartney,' he told me, 'they've all lost it'. And he loved the same ridiculous aspects of rock music I did, the over-amped characters with daft names and terrible clothes. At one point he asked me what happened to Sky Saxon, frazzled leader of garage band The Seeds.

'He made a comeback in 1989,' I told him, 'with Mars Bonfire on keyboards, the bloke who wrote "Born To Be Wild" for Steppenwolf.'

'Mars Bonfire! Fucking excellent name!' he cackled, getting sour looks from the cake-consumers. 'Nearly as good as Ariel Bender from Mott The Hoople. I actually started writing a song called "Ariel Bender". It's that image of this guitarist, tight clothes, long hair and these little wristbands. Ariel Bender

254

. . .' He gazed out of the window. 'What a guy, man, he must have been ace.'

I asked about pivotal moments in his life and he talked about shopping in Doncaster with Johnny Marr. The Smiths were heroes, too, and Johnny had liked a demo tape he'd given him and helped get Oasis a management deal. The two of them had gone to a music store.

'And I'm like skint and on the dole and I'm stood behind Johnny at the counter who's spending nine and a half thousand quid on guitars and I'm thinking, *This* is what it's about! *This* is what it fucking means! Sooner or later *this* is what I've got to be!'

The first Oasis album sounded sulphurous and full of fizz, I told him, and instantly familiar.

'That's because I nick stuff,' he shrugged. 'The New Seekers are suing us for "Shakermaker", the bit that goes "I'd like to teach the world to sing". But you know where we got that song from? "Flying" by The Beatles. Sing the lyrics over the top, that's what it is.'

He didn't mind being sued – quite proud of it, in fact, 'a fair cop' – but he'd rather have been sued by The Beatles than the New Seekers.

'I'd rather McCartney as we'd get more press out of it. He might even turn up in court and I could get his autograph. The people I *expected* to sue us were T.Rex for "Cigarettes & Alcohol", and I would have held my hands up and said, "I'll come quietly." But not a word. "Certain People I Know" by Morrissey is from T.Rex too. U2's "Zoo Station" is from T.Rex. Everyone nicks stuff. Lennon always went on about "I Feel Fine", the first use of feedback but, three weeks before, he saw the High Numbers using feedback and thought, I have to have that first. I understand where he's coming from. I go and see unknown bands and they'll play something and I'll think, I'm a bastard but life's a bitch and that's the way it goes.' He hailed an invisible cab. '*Taxi!* "Start" by The Jam is The Beatles' "Taxman" but Weller never got sued for it. If *I*'m getting sued by the New Seekers then – by fucking *law* – The Beatles should have him. But then McCartney probably thought, Who am I to say? They were ripping people off left, right and fucking centre. They had The Shirelles over on many an occasion, The Beatles. There are twelve notes and thirty-six chords and that's the end of it,' he said, swilling his ice. 'All the configurations have been done.'

No one ever admitted this to me before. Musicians, consciously or unconsciously, stole tunes and chord sequences all the time but if M'Learned Friends got in touch they'd loudly protest their innocence or, if pushed, claim it was 'unconscious' or that composers were mere conduits, the lucky few selected by some divinity to carry ready-made hits from the celestial song-cloud. If they filched the odd melody now and again it wasn't really their fault: they were the humble messenger, not the power in charge.

There was another endearing thing about Noel Gallagher: he was completely honest about the music he liked. He wasn't self-positioning, he wasn't shoring up his own image, he wasn't scoring points or trying to dazzle me with the depth of his record collection. He couldn't have cared less whether he was fashionable or not. When Primal Scream's Bobby Gillespie had made a cassette to give away to *Select* readers, it was all dark, drug-stained and achingly voguish – Patti Smith, Big Star, Marianne Faithfull, Dion, Crazy Horse, Jimmy Reed, Thin Lizzy, Mink Deville – but Noel was having none of this. He believed in the craft of the song as much as the folklore behind it.

'Songs I wish I'd written.' He counted them off on his fingers. '"Don't Dream It's Over" by Crowded House – I'm still trying to rip it off to this day. "Car Trouble" by Adam and The Ants. "Up The Hill Backwards" by David Bowie.

Every Beatles' song. "To Love Somebody" by the Bee Gees. Phenomenal band, the Bee Gees, "Harry Braff" on the *Horizontal* album – "Checkered flag for Harry Braff/ It's so good to see him win the race". "Being Boiled" by the Human League. Weller's "English Rose", The Kinks, The Who, Split Enz, Johnny Marr, Townshend, Sex Pistols. A few by U2. "One" is possibly the most beautiful song ever written. I cried my eyes out when I first heard it. I hate that whole rock critic thing – "Oh, I hate U2." We're now being touted as the U2 It's OK To Like. But why not like *U2*? I saw them at Sellafield and they did "Dancing Queen" by Abba!'

He listened to music with a fierce intensity, madly, deeply, repeatedly. He even bought bootleg versions of songs to see if he could unravel them further. He had a tape of The Beatles singing 'Happy Birthday' to Mike Love of the Beach Boys in India, and an eighteen-minute version of 'Helter Skelter', 'which is where punk rock started, after that you've got The MC5 and the Stooges'. He even had a cassette of Lee Mavers of The La's recording in his bedroom – 'You can hear his mum shouting, "Lee, come and get your tea!"'

This was heartening. This was *MOJO* all over. We'd just launched a magazine about songs, not albums, about the songwriters, not the band itself. It was searching for clues about how the great, deathless records were constructed, and I'd figured it was for people my age. Here was someone fourteen years younger who seemed to feel the same way.

MOJO was formed amid fierce, almost comical levels of secrecy. Any new magazine at EMAP was developed in a 'spook room', a mysterious inner sanctum protected by code locks, and *MOJO*'s was a cramped and cheerless attic in Winsley Street above Oxford Circus. It looked out across the grey slate tiles. Mournful, club-footed pigeons hopped about on the window ledges.

Beyond this heavily guarded portal, furtive experiments were taking place. Dave had a plan for 'a deeper Q', he and Paul Du Noyer were tinkering with it and, now I'd moved out of *Select*, they asked me to join them. For a while it was called 'Zone' and then 'The Electric Times' but Paul had a better idea. We were looking out across the rooftops playing Muddy Waters' 'Hoochie Coochie Man' when, in search of a dark, enduring spirit, the old blues-wailer summoned the voodoo power of 'a black cat bone' and 'a John the Conqueror root', adding, 'I got a mojo too.' That was it: if Q was about acts that were popular and *Select* about stuff that was cool, *MOJO* was about music that was magical and built to last.

Life was good in that little bunker under the eaves. If you'd had a hit magazine – and I'd been lucky enough to have three, *Smash Hits*, Q and *Select* – the world treated you differently. It was like being in a rock band who'd notched up a platinum album and the label couldn't wait for you to get back in the studio. People returned my calls. Marketeers punched me on the arm and laughed whenever I spoke. Senior managers swung by the office and sat on the edge of my desk, loosening their ties and wondering if I could get them free tickets to Mike and The Mechanics. I was sent a hamper at Christmas full of ham and claret. When the media press rang to ask what we were working on, we spread idiotic rumours – titles like *Lunch and Lunchmen* or *Horse & Hovercraft*, or the DIY manual *Underfloor Lagging Enthusiast*.

But something else was in the air. Noel Gallagher wasn't the only twenty-something now deeply in love with the past. Shiny-faced nippers who bought Oasis singles stopped me in corridors and asked if it was true that I'd seen Pink Floyd play *Dark Side Of The Moon*, and Little Feat at the Rainbow, and the final tour of Bob Marley and The Wailers. And they didn't appear to be taking the piss. I wasn't just some superannuated goon born at the wrong time: I was now old and fortunate enough to have seen a few card-carrying rock and roll legends. Some of the hoary, mocked or forgotten acts of the seventies were being readmitted via the back door, and the current ones all talked fondly about their influence. Our packed little attic quivered to new music by Aimee Mann, Liz Phair and The Lemonheads. Paul and I signed up Jim Irvin, the former lead singer of Furniture who'd had a hit with 'Brilliant Mind' then joined *Melody Maker*, and the three of us became obsessed with a long-forgotten record that had all the hallmarks of the new spirit, the second album by The Band. We played it all the time. They'd made it in '69 and its cover was a sepia print of the five of them in a field in upstate New York, their collars turned to the cold and damp, a timeless picture – they could have been ranchers or railroad workers or prospectors panning for gold in the nineteenth century. The songs were as unvarnished as the sleeve, fibrous and wood-stained, full of trombones, fiddles and accordions. You could practically *hear* the beards. It had an outlaw sheen to it, weathered and scuffed, miles from the polished world of the mainstream. They'd recorded it in Hollywood but we imagined them as ornery old buzzards in a shack on a hilltop, taking pot shots at raccoons with a flintlock rifle.

Andy Cowles had arrived, the brilliant designer of *Q* magazine. What should *MOJO* look like? he wondered.

'Hand-crafted and organic,' we said, loftily, 'like The Band's second album sounds.'

He went to a shop in Broadwick Street, bought lino and chisels and carved some graphics that looked like woodcuts, and we worked round the clock, occasionally drifting into a twilight shift we called 'pizzas at dawn', slicing up melting Margheritas with a CD on a biro like a circular saw. Jim, Paul and I threw some desks together to form a creaking hub known as 'Bollocks Island' and the rigours of the real world were never discussed in this wave-lapped whereabouts: for twelve hours a day we talked cliquish nonsense about rock folklore, typed up anything funny or interesting and published it. When we launched, the *Independent* ran an interview with two of us staring manfully from the attic window talking up the joys of our 'hand-made' magazine.

'There's only two types of music, according to editor Paul Du Noyer – good and bad. "*MOJO* readers are still excited by The Clash but not by Andrew Lloyd Webber," he says. "This is a home for honest outrage and crackpot opinions. It's our confirmed intention to pitch a wang-dang-doodle – all night long, if necessary."'

'"We don't subscribe to the *NME*'s Stalinist revision of history where punk rock was Year Zero," says managing editor Mark Ellen, who's enthusiastic and, above all, matey. He talks about their new magazine as if it's a hobby instead of a business.'

We forged ahead in pursuit of arcane tales from uncharted oceans, stories from the darkest, most dust-filled corners of the rock universe. The cover of the launch issue was built around bootleg footage of John Lennon and Bob Dylan careering round Hyde Park in a black cab at dawn in 1966 making stoned and rambling observations. John Peel wrote us a rant about Elvis Presley – 'It might get your office petrol-bombed,' he said mischievously. Our old *Q* and *NME* pal Andy Gill claimed grunge was 'witless posturing, slacker arrogance, morbid nihilism and self-bludgeoning twaddle'. I discovered a lost movie starring Tim Buckley and O. J. Simpson and – in a what *I*'m still calling a bombshell world exclusive – published a revelation about the career of Rose Simpson of The Incredible String Band below a headline my childhood self never imagined he'd read: 'String Band Siren Is Mayoress of Aberystwyth!'

Nobody much bought the magazine until the fourth issue when Frank Zappa died and we played *Hot Rats* in the office on repeat and produced twenty-six pages devoted to his life and art. With his grimy visage sneering from the newsstands, *MOJO* took off and never looked back. The face that had so appalled my father launched another five thousand sales.

With the wind behind us, Paul suggested we start a motoring column with the Bonzo Dog Band's Vivian Stanshall as the man behind the wheel. We planned an illustration of the old duffer bumbling along in a Morgan with a basket of Scotch eggs in the boot, maybe wearing a deerstalker. It was unlikely he had a driving licence and, even if he did, his fondness for the sauce might have removed it, but I wrote to him anyway and so began a strange and sobering correspondence full of calls and postcards and soft insights into what life was like if you'd had your moment in the sun twenty-five years earlier and been largely ignored ever since.

In the sixties, Viv had charged around Soho with Keith Moon gargling cocktails and fêted by all and sundry. When the Bonzos were on the TV show *Do Not Adjust Your Set* and were asked what props they needed, he'd replied, 'Three cardboard boxes, a springboard, a petrol tanker and the largest bath you can find but it needs to be orange', none of which he had any intention of using. He'd developed a posh voice, rich as a fruit cake, created a cartoon cosmos with its roots in the British Raj and sung songs with his psychedelic tea-dance orchestra about gin-soaked colonels shooting tigers out in India. And everyone thought he was genius, especially me. But he now lived in a tiny flat in Muswell Hill whose green walls were hung with theatrical masks and sousaphones, like a shrinking scrapbook of his own past. His preferred tipple was tranquillisers and brandy. He'd read a eulogy I'd written about him and his eccentricities – 'the Peter Cook of rock and roll' – and been touched that anyone still remembered him. There was something both thrilling and desperately sad about hearing his slurred mahogany tones on the telephone, the man whose picture I'd stuck on my bedroom wall now lost and drunk and human after all. Some evenings he'd ring me at home and get my eldest son in his pyjamas, and they'd have a bizarre exchange.

'Dad, Dad!' A hand over the receiver, amused but scared. 'It's *him*, your funny friend!'

'Dear boy,' Viv would begin. 'I've taken enough Valium to stun a rhinoceros . . .'

His last message came in his flowery italic script on a seaside postcard featuring buxom, naked, red-faced maidens cavorting on a desert island, posted from Whitstable:

Dear Mark, Yesterday I swanked on oysters & fish soup. Today: kippers and crab. Tomorrow I ferry to Flanders and swann home on the 3rd. This was supposed to be winkles, whelks and whiting weally but Bernard Manning 'entertains' at the hotel tonight so all is not lost! More grist for the MOJO? Knackered as an onanistic squid! – Viv

31

Music As A Mile-Melter

Around this time, the four members of the Ellen family were driving to the south coast. I'd interviewed Nick Lowe a few years earlier and he'd told me about an invention of his called the 'mile-melter', an idea we'd fondly embraced.

A 'mile-melter' was a long and involved rock and roll story related by himself or a member of his band in the tour bus and spun out to soften the tedium of the endless American highway. I'd extended this to include any form of in-car entertainment that produced participation and prised people from their Sony Walkmans, and made tapes of songs that seemed to enchant the passengers in the back seat. The earliest ones had 'Barbara Ann' by the Beach Boys (impossible not to join in), 'The Love Cats' by The Cure (amusing purring sounds), 'The Equestrian Statue' by the Bonzos (heart-warming tale of a hero's effects on local morale), Moe Tucker with the Velvet Underground singing 'I'm Sticking With You' (because, delightfully, she's 'made out of glue'), 'Come On Eileen' by Dexys (impersonating Kevin Rowland's quavering first entry is a joy at any age), and 'Road To Nowhere' by Talking Heads in the hope that it sparked a philosophical debate about how there was no such thing as a road to nowhere, only to nowhere in particular, as surely all roads have to lead somewhere. And I always included a song by the *Select*-detested Beatles that seemed to chime with how my sons viewed the world at the age they were at the time – 'Please Mr Postman' when they were five, 'I Saw Her Standing There' when they were six ('my heart went boom!'), 'Fool On The Hill' when they were at seven, 'Hey Bulldog' at eight and so on.

This had now given way to a new concept known as the Democratically Elected Car Tape. Each member of the family nominated tracks for a quarter of it and I'd stick them on a cassette, occasionally omitting some of Clare's confrontational Patti Smith dirges as I'd 'run out of room'. She'd suggest bits of her Dylan bootlegs and the boys put forward their latest passions, which, at this stage, were Green Day, NWA and Nirvana – and, very briefly, Menswear, Britpop chancers behind the nerve-shredding 'Daydreamer', but they soon saw the error of their ways. I put on whatever I dared subject them to that seemed worth hearing, Jeff Buckley's 'Hallelujah', or REM or 'Sweet Old World' by Lucinda Williams. But on this particular trip to the coast we had Tom Hibbert on board and his lovely wife Allyce. We sang along to some tapes, then melted the remaining miles with rounds of Who Am I? *You* know it: each person's given a name on a Post-it note which they're not allowed to read and have to work out who they are by asking questions that can only be answered yes or no. If it didn't entertain us, it certainly cheered any cars drawing up beside us at traffic lights and seeing a load of people with yellow stickers on their foreheads – Clare's, on this occasion, said, 'LEONARDO DA VINCI', Allyce was 'JANE FONDA', Hibbs had 'ROKY ERICKSON FROM THE 13TH FLOOR ELEVATORS', Tom was 'ERIC CANTONA' and Robbie 'ACE VENTURA, PET DETECTIVE'. Hibbs and I exchanged knowing looks before the notes were assigned, trying to sense what the other was thinking and we often got it right first time.

'Your turn, Mark-stroke-Dad,' Hibbs declared, thoughtfully tapping his cigarette out of the window so a seventy-mile-an-hour gust could hurl the smouldering tip into one of the children's hair.

'Come on, Dad, *you* remember!' they shouted from the back. 'You've got to start with "Am I male or female?" Or "Am I a real person or not a real person cos I'm in a film or something?" Or "Am I alive or dead and stuff?" Dad!'

'Am I . . .' I asked slowly '. . . am I . . . Alex Dmochowski, bass player of the Aynsley Dunbar Retaliation?'

A furious silence. I pulled off my Post-it note. I was.

'Dad, you're cheating!'

'Dad, you cheat!'

'Mum, Dad's cheating!'

'Look at Dad cheating!'

'*CHEAT! CHEAT! CHEAT! CHEAT!*'

'Fancy a round of Name That Line-up?' I asked Hibbs mischievously.

'Why not, dear fellow?' He grinned, lighting another gasper.

'Alex Dmochowski on bass,' I started, 'Jon Morshead guitar . . .'

'Oh, God, no, *please* not Name That Line-up!' Clare and Allyce slumped back in their seats.

'. . . Victor Brox on Hammond organ,' Hibbs said.

'. . . *and* cornet,' I chipped in.

'Fair point,' he nodded, 'and Aynsley Dunbar, of course, on drums.'

I began singing 'Low-Gear Man' from their criminally underrated second album.

'*DAD!!*'

Sighing adults now stared out of the window and cross boys whacked their headphones on but I felt a great surge of satisfaction. I loved the synchronicity of Hibbs and I jointly guessing our identities – if he wasn't Roky Erickson he'd probably be Big Star's Jody Stephens or Skip Spence of Moby Grape, and I'd be Papa John Creach from Hot Tuna or Lester Square of the Monochrome Set. And if I *did* have an alter-ego in a parallel universe, I'd have been delighted if it was the unpronounceable Dmochowski who, I don't need to tell you, was once a member of Heavy Jelly and played bass on Zappa's *The Grand Wazoo*.

But I'd also managed, magnificently and with a pleasing circularity, to do what my own father had achieved by banging on about opera and ruining *Top of the Pops* – and all fathers should do it: it's their divine right as a parent. I'd infuriated my children with my behaviour *and* my musical taste.

32

Smiling And Dialling

Slowly and steadily, *MOJO*'s sales began to climb and I went off to occupy another attic room beneath the pigeon-stained roof tiles and cook up more ideas. Publishers put their heads round my door to check on any progress, which lurched between the plausible and the terrible – a weekly *Select*, a deeper *Smash Hits*, a *MOJO* for dance music, a 'drinking man's *Record Collector*'. But Dave and I had another enterprise already up and running, born of a sleepless night in '89, and it was my turn at the tiller.

The Brit Awards had been rumbling along since the late seventies, a music-business back-slap that chucked gongs at mostly big-selling acts with international profiles. This usually ended with a hit-filled performance by some grizzled old warhorse like The Who which brought about the scattering of chairs and the uneasy spectacle of Bad Dancing – shrieking press agents kicking off their heels and pissed label execs loosening bow-ties with one hand while punching the air with the other. But in 1989 the Brits dropped a bollock. They put on a show so catastrophic the next day's papers simply couldn't do it justice. It was chaos, they said, a shambles, a disaster, bedlam, a car crash, but I felt they were under-reacting. I'd been out that evening, got back at midnight, rewound to check the video had recorded, glanced at the beginning and sensed something was unmendably wrong. Gripped by a grim fascination, I watched the whole thing from behind a cushion. As a viewer it was deliciously awful. As someone who'd done live TV it was absolute agony.

The combination of presenters was sensationally poor, a media marriage made in hell. On the left, with a bootlace tie and a bouquet of pink hair, looking like a cocktail waitress in a knocking-shop, was 'the Forces' Favourite' Samantha Fox. Every time the nation's troops needed cheering up, the *Sun* ran a picture of their busty page-three glamour girl astride the barrel of a tank. 'Our Sam' had now gatecrashed the music industry by putting out a single, the resistible 'Touch Me (I Want Your Body)'. On the right, a cross between a bloodhound and a lecturer in rare fungi, was the forlorn figure of Mick Fleetwood, the drummer of Fleetwood Mac. But the bright spark who had booked them had failed to detect their difference in height, a massive sixteen-inch chasm. He was six foot five, she was five foot one: when the camera panned in on Mick, you got the top of Sam's head; when it focused on her, you got his chest and some bits of his beard.

In their defence, the teleprompter kept breaking down and people handed them the wrong cards but neither was a natural at papering over the cracks. They fluffed, they dithered, they stumbled through their scripted 'ad-libs'. They forgot to run a message from Michael Jackson. They introduced Boy George as 'the Four Tops'. Whenever there was a pause, Sam would shout 'Woo!' and shake her blancmange-coloured mane, a reflex that became gratingly familiar as the long night wore on. I crawled off to bed but I couldn't sleep. I was haunted by it. Autocue is a trade secret and the audience shouldn't be aware of it. I'd been through the chaos of Live Aid and in TV freefall myself, but I'd never stared blankly at a camera in front of millions of people and said, 'I can't read that thing from here.'

'Somebody *must* be able to put on a better awards show than that,' I told Dave the next morning.

'Us,' he said. 'The trick is to keep it low-key and not do it on telly.'

So we tried it and it seemed to work. The first *Q* Awards were held in Ronnie Scott's jazz club in Frith Street. There were bottles of bright yellow Chardonnay and some sort of curried chicken. The La's, World Party and Paul Oakenfold were on the front tables. Paul McCartney turned up early, hence the unimaginably sweet sight of the man who'd lit my blue touch-paper helping put the napkins out with his wife Linda. It had the loose, convivial air of a wedding party in a village hall full of excited nieces, plastered nephews, cheery aunts, two small children and the odd grumbly old uncle on his best behaviour, everyone keeping the lid on any family tensions. Bill Wyman bowled up in a black suit and a splendid silk waistcoat. I'd just read his memoir, which recorded a pre-Paul fling with Linda, and couldn't help introducing them. There was a brief, very sixties, flicker of recognition – *did we or didn't we?* – before she gave him a squeeze and announced they were 'old friends'.

Dave ran the next three years, each bigger and better, then handed the baton to me. But awards shows at that level were a whole new ball game. Shepherding musicians into magazines was tough enough and full of complications – the timing wasn't right, they hated the writer, they'd only discuss the new album, they wanted picture approval, it had to be the cover, no mention of drugs, divorce or the time the guitarist copped off with the bass player's girlfriend. I'd long since learnt to separate my personal and professional opinions as a wistful singer-song-writer could turn out to be a tedious prima donna. Huge amounts of arm-wrestling were required as an editor, digging deep into reservoirs of tact and diplomacy.

But awards shows were ten times worse. The magazine's readers and a judging panel voted for the winners and I'd tell the artists they'd been nominated. Surely all they had to do was turn up, fork down some rubbery food, sink some booze and deliver a heartfelt speech if they'd won, and three hundred people would whoop uncontrollably and make them feel loved and wanted. And the papers would write nice things about it. But it wasn't as simple as that. The musicians saw it differently. The room was a minefield beyond their control, a bear-pit of complex social intercourse. They might bump into the hacks who'd savaged their last album, or the upstart new acts who'd slagged them off in the press, or the chief executive who'd kicked them off the label, or the band who'd nicked their drummer. Queues of people might want their autograph. They could be sat next to someone they were suing. The vegan option might contain nuts. Liam Gallagher might throw cheesecake at them in full view of the tabloids.

For the next three years, I ran the *Q* Awards with the magazine's publisher Delyth Chapman. I sorted out the people onstage and presented it, and she booked a spangly Mayfair ballroom and organised the red carpet, the Fleet Street columnists and the budget-stretching seared scallop medallions in a balsamic *jus* with a medley of seasonal vegetables. But it was like a game of Bash The Rat. Every time I thought I'd got it fixed, someone would stick their head up and announce they were pulling out. And then another. And another. Then the first one was back in – and out again. Del and I developed our own coded language. The drumming up of a room of rock stars was called 'smiling and dialling'. If someone agreed to come they were 'on the bus'. If they couldn't they were 'a try-me-next-year'. If they wouldn't they'd 'given us the swerve'. If they agreed and then pulled out, they'd 'flounced', an expression that conjured up largely accurate images of U-turns, hissy fits, diva tantrums and heel-spinning dashes to the exit.

Del would pop her head round the door. 'Any joy with Pulp?'

'They were on the bus yesterday,' I'd say, 'perfectly happy, sharing a sandwich with Lou Reed, mooning with Jarvis Cocker out the back window. But we've had to make an emergency stop,' I'd sigh. 'They've flounced.'

Every stage of these tortuous negotiations – every call, every letter, every message – I logged meticulously in my notebooks. Arrangements with Phil Spector alone took forty-two phone conversations and 117 faxes, all carefully recorded. They told an illuminating tale, those books. There was something fascinating about these unguarded insights into the protected worlds of the rich, famous and, occasionally, over-employed.

19/07 MADONNA – 'not available', having a baby.

20/07 REM – Bill Berry and Mike Mills playing golf tournament in Las Vegas on 7 Nov. Buck won't travel, wife just had twins. Only person available is Stipe who 'doesn't want to fly'.

21/07 GENESIS don't want what they're calling the 'gold watch award' as they're 'back next year with a new singer'.

31/07 JOHN LEE HOOKER – unlikely to come, 'medical probs, high blood pressure'.

18/08 KEITH RICHARDS is a granddad – 'Marlon had a kid on Saturday. May now stay at Redlands for three weeks which will use up all his UK time.'

1/09 ERIC CLAPTON *ON THE BUS!* – but will be late as receiving OBE on morning of Awards from Queen at Buck Palace. Bringing daughter. Won't sit anywhere near [Warner's chairman] Rob Dickins.

19/09 PHIL SPECTOR – Fax from Norma [Phil's PA]. 'Phil must be referred to in all communications as Mr Spector.'

19/09 ROD STEWART *ON THE BUS!* – 'Try Eric Cantona to present. He'd be happy with Ruud Gullit.'

29/09 RUUD GULLIT – 'Ruudy can't leave training till 12.30 p.m. but get a chopper and he's up for it. Can land on the Chelsea training ground. Anywhere to land in Green Park?'

29/09 BOB DYLAN – Fax from Jeff [manager]. 'Bob's not big on promotion and I have to say *Q*'s not our favourite magazine but I'll play the trump card and offer Concorde.'

1/10 THE CLASH – Faxed Joe Strummer in Chile. Faxed back something about 'desert and guns'. Can't tell if he's coming or not. *POSSIBLE SWERVE!*

1/10 THE WHO – Ken Russell fine to present the award but John Entwistle says, 'Tell him not to wear that awful sequined denim waistcoat.'

1/10 IGGY POP *FLOUNCED!* – Robert [press] says 'dental reasons'. Manager says, 'Iggy's failed his medical MOT and he's taking the rest of the year off.'

7/10 U2 *ON THE BUS!* – Suggested presenters: Liam Neeson, Damon Hill (a neighbour), Björk, Tricky, Michael Stipe, Pavarotti, Father Ted. *SMILING & DIALLING!*

9/10 PULP *ON THE BUS!* – Kate Moss 'not committing' to present award. Trying Michael Caine, Charlotte Rampling, Norman Wisdom, Mrs Merton, Albert Finney, Scott Walker, Oliver Reed. 'Won't have Skinner or Baddiel.'

16/10 BLUR – Damon *FLOUNCED!* 'Now filming gangster role in Ray Winstone/Robert Carlyle movie.'

21/10 MANIC STREET PREACHERS *ON THE BUS!* minus Nicky Wire who 'can't fly'. Suggested presenters

– Morrissey, Prince Naseem, Linford Christie, Joe Strummer, Stuart Pearce of Notts Forest.

22/10 TONY BLAIR – Message from Alastair Campbell: 'The former lead singer of Ugly Rumours is keen to meet Pink Floyd, Kinks and Noel Gallagher but can't be photographed with Damon Albarn or the tabs will headline it 'TONY BLUR' and run some bollocks caption about lack of focus re New Labour strategy etc.'

22/10 MANIC STREET PREACHERS – Strummer can't present award. Suggested Shane MacGowan or Richard E. Grant. They faxed back: 'We want Kylie!'

23/10 PHIL SPECTOR *FLOUNCED!* – 'Mr Spector has a major copyright case lawsuit that's waited two years to come to court. Under oath, perjury etc.'

24/10 THE PRODIGY – Keith won't present an award as Goldie did last year and Keith rubbished him in the press for it. Coming but 'can't reconcile his principles'.

31/10 PHIL SPECTOR – Mr Spector just played Norma 'an electronic Hallowe'en song down the phone'. Good sign, apparently.

31/10 ELVIS COSTELLO *ON THE BUS!* – Burt Bacharach sending telegram. Chrissie Hynde to read?

2/11 PHIL SPECTOR – 'Mr Spector arrives Sunday a.m., staying at the Savoy. Six-seater Mercedes. One security not enough. He's all yours now!'

6/11 THE BEATLES – Voice message from Derek Taylor [Apple head of press]: 'George considers himself retired from showbusiness. He doesn't go anywhere and hopes you understand. He won't be able to come, or be on the end of a satellite or any damned thing that might help you and I pull this thing off, so I *do* regret it as I've enjoyed our communications. Would like to meet you sometime when this whole bloody war is over. God bless – Derek.'

Show days were extraordinary. Delyth sorted out some crash barriers and our press man tipped off the paparazzi, and we'd watch the whole thing unfold with a combination of pride, terror and vague disbelief. Cash-hungry snappers would start to grumble and look at their watches but the rock fraternity were past masters of the late entrance. Like a cloud of butterflies, expensive cars would suddenly descend on the Park Lane Hotel, doors flapping open to deliver their newsworthy cargo. And so began that glorious dance with the press, a seamless charade where the stars got the exposure they wanted while managing to give the impression they were doing the photographers a favour, charging purposefully up the carpet – to mounting shouts of 'Rod!' or 'Keith!' or 'Matey With the Hair From The Prodigy!' – then turning round at the doorway in a blizzard of flashbulbs with an oh-all-right-then-just-the-one shrug before vanishing back into their huddle of WAGs, pals, PRs and personal minders. Phil Spector's limo hovered in the backstreets of Mayfair until assured that both Pete Townshend and Paul McCartney had already arrived, his thunder-stealing manoeuvre somewhat dented when he leapt out to a baffled silence broken by a cry of 'Fucking hell, it's Dudley Moore!' at which point the motor-drives clattered afresh.

I was the onstage host and, while the videos of the shortlists played, I'd gaze into the crowd picking out faces from my past, a strange and moving sight, all those acts that seemed so separate thrown together in a soft haze of cigarette smoke. I'd sat up all night playing Pink Floyd's *Echoes*, waiting for it to hand me the keys to eternal wisdom, and there was Dave Gilmour on table eight. I'd counted the days to seeing Ray Davies's crumpled grin on the telly, and there he was on table ten, though in the corner of my eye I noticed his brother Dave, that once-foppish threat to society, being bundled back up the stairs by his own minder for being drunk and objectionable. There was Mick Jagger, mercifully unaware that Liam Gallagher had just strolled past and tapped ash in his hair. There was Morrissey on table six, another voice that had sung my son to sleep. And here beside me was McCartney, who'd lain awake as a teenager listening to *The Goon Show* spirited in from the ether, and Spike Milligan was clambering up to give him a hug and sing his praises.

At one point the whole event took the warped, softly comical shape of a surreal and magical dream. Long months of fragile protocol had finally landed a triple-header, David Bowie and Brian Eno accepting a gong for their Berlin Trilogy of the late seventies.

'. . . and to present the award,' I announced, 'please welcome Jarvis Cocker!'

'*Danke schön, meine Damen und Herren,*' Pulp's sticklike mainman began. 'You all right? I'm not too bad myself, thanks. I'm going to give you some *more* clues as to who the two people are that are winning this award. Some would say they're the Morecambe and Wise of conceptual music, which is better than being the *Cannon and Ball* of conceptual music, and one of their career highs together was also' – long pause – 'a *Low*. And my final clue is if I was to introduce these people to each other – which I don't have to as they already know each other but if I *was* – I would say . . . Mr Hunting Knife meet Mr Liver Salts!'

I sank deep into an armchair at the aftershow in a great sentimental heap, glowing with strong drink. I tried to picture my childhood self discovering that, around some distant bend of the river, I'd throw a party and members of The Kinks and The Beatles would turn up. All that affection I'd channelled their way, all those thoughts and imaginings, all those posters and singles, and now, thirty years later, this highly charged moment of happiness.

But let the record reflect there was one substantial fly in this ocean of ointment, a guest who gave a whole new dimension to the word 'curmudgeon'. Listening to his early music, I'd pictured him as a mystic pilgrim with simple provisions in a knotted handkerchief – pies, potted herrings – striding across the blasted heath on a Celtic soul-odyssey, pausing occasionally to read aloud from worn volumes of Keats and Shelley. His songs were full of nightshirts, gypsies and campfires, and he roamed the elemental landscape on a poetic quest for knowledge. So I was surprised to discover he was a surly old goat with a chip on both shoulders, a cantankerous grouch it seemed impossible to please. If a greater gap existed between someone's artistic image and the person they were in real life then I was yet to encounter it. The name of this man: Van Morrison.

There appeared to be two types of people in the world, those who liked Van Morrison and those who'd met him. He added fuel to my theory that stars were often frozen at the emotional age when they first became famous as, from that moment on, many character-moulding responsibilities were whisked away and they were allowed to freewheel in a cocoon of cotton-wool, performing, recording and being their self-promotional selves while a team of forgiving and put-upon drones did the boring stuff and swept up after them. Neil Tennant first appeared on *Top of the Pops* when he was thirty-one, a fully formed, socially integrated adult. Michael Jackson, however, was a celebrity at the age of eight and, when acquiring untold wealth years later, blew a lot of it on a fairground full of monkeys, merry-go-rounds and machines that made candy-floss. Ozzy Osbourne was twenty when he made the headlines and spent his time off arsing around on quad bikes. The fifty-year-old

Van had a hit as a teenager and still behaved like he should be sent off to tidy his room.

I should have seen the signs. For a start, despite our devoted and generous support for his chequered catalogue, Van referred to *Q* and *MOJO* publicly as 'comics'. And he was breathtakingly anti-social. He was an early adopter of the mobile phone and, if walking alone, would call associates at any time of day or night and witter on for hours so no member of the public could come up and talk to him. My fax machine melted with his demands – cars, hotel suites, copies of the seating plan (when he ate out, he'd book the corner table and position people either side of him so no passing diner could get near enough to tell him his *Moondance* album had changed their lives). For three long years, Van had been attached to the socialite Michelle Rocca, a former Miss Ireland, and he told me the sight of the two of them together would spark such pandemonium in the photographic rank and file that he'd only attend if smuggled into the building through a secret passage. The moment he'd got his award, he said, they'd be leaving. I fired off a cloud of faxes confirming my cunning plan: the hold-the-front-page rock Romeo and squeeze would be delivered by car to the hotel's back entrance in Brick Street where escorts with walkie-talkies would rush them down the service stairs, through the kitchens – past tempting pies and, possibly, potted herrings – out of the side-door and into the ballroom, a well-drilled military operation that made that siege-busting raid on the Iranian Embassy look like a trip to the zoo.

This was deftly executed and the couple delivered to their seats by the stage. Every one of his whims had been catered to, every insistence met, fine foods assembled and arch enemies vaporised to distant tables. But still all wasn't well on Planet Van. He didn't like the house wine. Waiters scattered hurriedly and returned with a leather-bound list arranged in escalating order of price. The thirsty troubadour turned several pages before plumping for a bottle from so deep in the Park Lane cellars it had dust on it and cost £520. He enjoyed it enormously and ordered another.

And so the long day rolled out. Over six hours later, the guests had drifted off and I wandered up to the balcony to take a last look at the place. And there, with his shirt untucked, his hat removed, a glass of glossy red to hand, the house lights up and two waiters hoovering around him, was Van Morrison. With his arms round my two Irish bosses, he was singing a rousing chorus of 'Danny Boy'.

33

A Wormhole In Time

The awards shows and magazines allowed me to see my old heroes in a variety of different lights. They could be sages, seers or prophets. They could be rocks of reliability or quicksands of disappointment. They could be godheads on a pedestal: courageous, unimpeachable. They could be fallible objects of envy and adulation or beacons of light in times of darkness.

But in the autumn of '96, I discovered another perspective. They could be fellow parents at a Year Seven Meet-the-Teachers Evening.

There he was, just across the room, it *had* to be him. He had a slightly too-bright shirt and a cream linen suit with the sleeves bunched up to the elbows, good-looking in a weathered sort of way, suspiciously tanned. I think there was an earring. Everyone else was dressed in the low-key manner that allows the impossibly youthful head of Middle School to deliver bad news about a child's maths coursework without feeling challenged, but he had a look that said, 'I'm the bassist in the band that were possibly the *premium* vendors of the twin-lead-guitar rock format of the early seventies who the critics hated but who shifted some units and are still lumbering on with the occasional tour of Europe,' and he'd registered on nobody's radar but mine.

I was in a right old state. I'd fallen through a wormhole in time and landed back at the age of sixteen. Bonds with your heroes are set in stone, like relationships with form masters or elder sisters: they'll always be above you and you're always slightly overawed in their presence. I edged forward, offering a nervous handshake.

'Are you . . .?' I started.

'Martin Turner,' he said, 'of Wishbone Ash,' as if it was a PR firm or a petrochemical company. He could have said Bell Pottinger or Shell Oil. He looked cautious but unmistakably thrilled. Members of Wishbone Ash were used to only two reactions – 'Never heard of you' or 'Didn't I once see you supporting Robin Trower some time in the seventeenth century?' To be met with paw-gripping, boyish enthusiasm was way off the map. 'Guilty as charged!' he said. 'Just finished a tour, as it happens.' He was getting friendlier by the second.

My mind was racing. I was back at school listening to their first album with my band and deciding it was a work of genius, though the freckle-faced Socks said the cover was a bit rubbish as it just had a burnt wishbone on it. I was remembering the shock of seeing their new look in *Melody Maker* – drummer Steve Upton had gone for a crew-cut, which had wreaked havoc with my entire belief system. Don't mention you saw the Ash at Bracknell Sports Centre *and sat at the foot of his mike stand trying to work out the bass part for 'Phoenix'* as that would look sad and unprofessional. *And don't call them the Ash* . . .

But it was too late. I could hear a voice and it sounded like mine.

'I saw the Ash at Bracknell Sports Centre!' I said. 'Got right up the front. My school band had "Phoenix" in the old set list and I wanted to work out the bass part! And now we've both got kids in Mr Orme's history class. What are the chances? Ha!'

'Great days,' he said bravely, though this had backfired a bit. For me, Bracknell Sports Centre was the top of his curve, for him pretty much the bottom. 'No Madison Square

Garden, that place,' he said breezily. 'Which we played a few years later, of course. Winterland, too.'

Already I was starting to think this was hopeless. We were locked in the eternal tussle of the rock star and the early admirer and I felt sorry for both of us. He wanted me to acknowledge that he'd moved on – changed, evolved – but I wanted him to have stayed where he was. I still had him in Cuban heels and a cheesecloth shirt. I didn't want this craggy older version who might or might not dye his hair; I wanted the twenty-four-year-old Martin Turner frozen for ever in the cheap, spangled lightshow of a sports complex just outside Woking. And maybe for five minutes *I* wanted to stay the same too, plunged back into a world free of the complications of adult life, like work and tube strikes and Year Seven Meet-the-Teacher Evenings. But this was his career. What right had I to think it was a bit undignified and he should have knocked it on the head? Rock musicians *can't* knock it on the head. None of them ever retire, even the most successful. It's impossible. Being in a rock band's the most exciting thing that ever happens to them and no amount of money, fame or critical applause can replace the sound of even a modest crowd hearing a song that once got on Radio 1, even if they shout, 'Do some old!' when you play the new album. Musicians are locked in this cycle and they can't let go. They don't *want* to be anything else. There's always another record deal just round the corner. Or a possible tour of Norway.

We clapped each other awkwardly on the back and made noises about forming a team for Quiz Night, and I wandered home trying to imagine the perfect picture of graceful retire-ment. A silver disc above the telly. A battered tour jacket on the back of a door that Grandpa pulls on to amuse his students at the Music Academy's Christmas party. A couple of framed pictures with David Bowie when his group supported him once in Stafford. And Gran saying, 'Hey, kids, come and look at these photos of Gramps and the funny clothes he used to wear!' And they swarm around his armchair, clamouring for those fond old stories about the time he ran away to join the rock and roll circus. And how he escaped in the nick of time with the girl on the flying trapeze. And isn't still stuck there plodding along with the elephants.

34

The End Of An Era

I passed the *Q* Awards on to another poor soul who didn't mind getting his nerve-ends welded together, then started a job with the embarrassingly grand-sounding title of editor-in-chief. I kept an eye on *MOJO*, *Smash Hits*, *Select*, *Q*, *Kerrang!* and *Mixmag*, along with the company's men's, film and teenage magazines. The first week I went to an event where they gave me a misspelt laminate so for a while I was the 'editor-in-chiel', but the music wing soon cooked up a name of their own and I was touched and proud of it: 'Editor Of Cheese'.

Q no longer cruised at its peak of 270,000 copies a month, and *Smash Hits* was a long way from its million-selling days, but the publishing world was still firing on at least three cylinders despite the arrival of a computer-linked communications network known as 'the information superhighway'. Confused early users wondered if they should cruise this 'digital infobahn' under the influence of alcohol, but shrewd observers saw its early impact on print and record sales. If reliable reviews, the engine of the music press, now appeared free on the internet, was there as pressing a need to buy magazines? And why pay for music if you could copy a friend's CD or steal songs from a file-sharing site? But singles still went gold, albums went platinum and publications tore up trees to feed the presses. If an editor landed a commercial cover – Michael Stipe, Kylie, Morrissey, Kate Bush, Metallica, the Chemical Brothers – they'd always send the same gag through our new-fangled email system: 'Dear Cheese, can we up the print-run? If so, please fell extra square miles of virgin pine forest.'

I opened up a garage on the second floor for titles needing an oil change, a car wash or an MOT, a little retreat whose walls were plastered with design experiments and mocked-up front covers. Tired and overworked editors would come by for a few days and eat biscuits, and we'd get under the bonnet and tinker. The most fascinating were the ones I'd never worked on and knew least about, the heavy-metal weekly *Kerrang!* and the dance bible *Mixmag*. In fact, they had a lot in common: their molten core was a riotous cartoon fantasy, an escape-hatch from the rigours of real life. They weren't about sitting alone in bedrooms waiting for music to unlock life's mysteries, they were about going out and getting absolutely hammered – 'putting the beer goggles on' as *Kerrang!* called it, or getting 'mashed, munted or gibboned' in the saucer-eyed argot of rave-world. *Kerrang!* had usually shaken off their hangovers by lunchtime. *Mixmag* would go out on Friday nights and come home forty-eight hours later. By Wednesday they'd regained the power of speech.

I'd wander down to visit both offices and never want to leave. *Kerrang!* was full of Gothic girls with nose-rings clanking around in steel-plated boots, and stubbly blokes with names like Krusher in T-shirts with pictures of 'Eddie', Iron Maiden's blood-gushing zombie mascot. All day long they played deafening music, dark industrial rackets like Nine Inch Nails or Marilyn Manson, and swapped hoary old tales of excess and pandemonium that got ever more ludicrous and usually featured Geezer Butler, the bassist of Black Sabbath, whose trainers fellow band members would apparently fill with mayonnaise. Sometimes they'd leave a turd in a shoebox outside his hotel room, light the cardboard, shout 'Room Service', and run away. Without fail, the simpleton would open his door and stamp hard to put out the flames. *Mixmag* was made up of pale, slightly nerdy arts graduates and girls who always had Polaroids of themselves pinned to their computers looking sunburnt in Ibiza and dancing on a bar-top in shiny gold shorts and fairy wings. The whole place shook to pumping, bass-heavy beats spun by a bloke on the payroll whose sole job was to mix 12-inch singles on a twin-deck in the corner. *Mixmag*'s hair-curling tales from the battlefield usually started with a club full of foam and ended with someone either in a hospital emergency ward or stumbling round Munich at four in the morning dressed as a leopard.

This age of prosperity, this magical hay-making episode of my life, showed no indication of ever ending. But, in the way of the world, things changed. It ended very suddenly indeed.

Fired by a sense of omnipotence, EMAP began filling its upper corridors with highly paid strategists hell-bent on evolution. They brought with them a whole new language that was hard to comprehend. They were 'drilling down' and 'rolling out' in pursuit of 'low-hanging fruit'. The opinions of magazine readers were 'end-user perspectives'. Investments were 'war-chests' with our 'tanks parked on the lawn' of our main rival IPC, the publishers of *NME*, *Melody Maker*, *Vox* and *Uncut*. It was the testosterone talk that clever – often slightly dull – business people employed to make the mechanics of their job sound windswept and creative. This progressive and fun-filled publishing company, the greatest place to work imaginable who'd backed us and allowed us so much freedom, was being infiltrated by wiry creeps in designer shirts. The heads of editorial were packed off on bonding exercises to 'free up our thinking' in which ambient Scandinavians slid us into role-playing scenarios where fathers defended sons who'd kicked footballs through neighbours' windows, or made us rearrange mystifying piles of coloured plastic cones in a hotel car park. The whole world seemed to have gone completely fucking mad.

The new management decided to turn the music magazines into 'multi-media content platforms', each with its own digital radio and TV channels. Advertising would now be sold, not by each title's passionate advocate, but by a group sales force working across the board from the teenage titles to *MOJO*. The magazines themselves would be removed from their gloriously noisy, self-contained bunkers and pushed together in one giant open-plan space, a four-foot partition separating *Smash Hits* from *Period Living & Traditional Homes*. And the place run, not by publishing experts, but by the company's radio division.

From where I was sitting, a large percentage of this scheme appeared to be a huge heap of horse manure.

My new boss was a tiny little man who looked like Mr Burns in *The Simpsons*. He took me to Chez Gérard restaurant in Charlotte Street and blithered on for hours about how much he liked Steely Dan, which was heart-breaking as I did too. At one point he kicked off his loafers, turned sideways on his bench and put his feet up, pressing a hand to his brow as if the dim light-bulb of inspiration was about to flicker into life. As, indeed, it was.

'These five-star reviews in *Q* magazine,' he said, 'they seem very valuable.'

'They are,' I told him.

'Why?' he asked.

'Because there are so few of them. How many albums deserve five stars?'

'But the music business loves them.'

'Of course they do. They sticker the albums as it sells: *Five Stars! – Q Magazine*.'

'Then why don't you give more of them?'

'You can't give a three-star CD five stars.'

'Why not if they matter so much? Think what they're worth. You could sell them to the record labels.'

'Sell them?'

'Sell them.'

'*Sell* them?'

'Sell them.'

I don't remember much more about this occasion, just wandering back feeling dizzy and depressed. What kind of people had ideas like that, even if this one was never tried? Within days I'd been labelled 'change-resistant'. Had you opened my copybook, you'd have found an indelible blot. Sure enough, at 11.30 a.m. on Friday, 14 January 2000 – my diary records a café in Winsley Street – I was summoned to a meeting by the new second-in-command, an enormous woman who put away a steaming baked potato with cheese to help with her hangover. She looked up from this feast to tell me that, going forward, I didn't fit into their vision of the future.

'It's time you thought of going freelance,' she said darkly, before inspecting the puddings.

Happy New Year. Happy New Decade. Happy New Millennium.

I stumbled off to find a phone box and ring Clare. It smelt of piss and was full of cards from call-girls. I felt woozy and my head was spinning. I thought I was going to be sick. Of *course* they wanted me out. Why *wouldn't* they? I was 'change-resistant'. I thought their new plan would damage the magazines and the atmosphere in which they were created and I'd told them so. But what hurt the most – a real searing actual physical pain right across my chest – was that EMAP's cowardly chief executive, the man who'd sung my praises in speeches to the shareholders, who'd claimed to value my nineteen years of work, who'd called me a key plank in the company, hadn't got the decency to walk me round the block and tell me himself that he wanted me out. He let his henchmen do it for him. Huge respect was being extended to the people moving the giant chess pieces round the company's chequered board. Slightly less respect to those who'd created those chess pieces in the first place.

Old friends in another division threw me a line so I cleared my desk and moved there, but the bubble had burst, the spirit was gone and the great days were over. Appalled by events, Dave Hepworth left to start his own company. A few months later I resigned and joined him.

35

A Media Feeding-Frenzy

Mark Ellen's last office was a chrome-and-glass structure with panoramic views of London. He was a senior executive at the publishing giant EMAP. Up on the eighth floor, with two decades in magazines behind him, he couldn't get much higher in the publishing world. But he quit. His new office is small and grubby with a radiator that doesn't work properly. 'And it's got a broken window!' he says excitedly. 'We've had to mend it with gaffer tape.' Four other EMAP defectors share the office. Together they are launching *Word*, a new entertainment magazine.

Perhaps kindly, the reporter from the *Independent* left out some key details here. Yes, there was a taped-up window and the radiators dripped into coffee cups but she never mentioned the fraying power cable sticking out of the plasterwork. Or the mousetraps.

Ellen and Hepworth enthuse about losing the perks of their previous jobs, like taxis, expenses and motorcycle couriers. They've also jettisoned market research, unheard of in the publishing industry. '*We*'d buy it,' they insist. 'All good magazines start as fanzines.' Coming from two maestros of the magazine world, this can't be naïvety. But could it be wilful stupidity?

'Magazines are like fast food these days,' says Hepworth. 'There's no steak. This magazine will provide the steak.' 'The steak,' Ellen adds, '*and* the sizzle.'

EMAP refugees came thick and fast and the old band was back together again. Dave's business partner was our former publisher, the splendid Jerry Perkins, a Glastonbury regular who worked out budgets on the fire escape in pouring rain just so he could smoke a Marlboro. Paul Du Noyer signed up for our mouse-filled Islington boot-hole, the *Q* and *MOJO* survivor still sporting his 'iron hat'. Andrew Harrison was on board, fizzing and inventive former *Select* editor, along with *Q*'s designer Keith Drummond, who cycled up the canal towpath from Greenwich every day, dodging bricks dropped from bridges, and tried to slip a mention of Luke Haines of The Auteurs onto every page. The final piece of the jigsaw was the great Jude Rogers who'd launched the London fanzine *Smoke* and came from a country she proudly called 'Welsh Wales'.

All of us arrived at the office plugged into the latest piece of technology. Every paper I'd worked on had coincided with some transformational new format or gadget. The early *NME* had surfed the shift from singles to albums. For *Smash Hits*, it was the video. For *Q* it was the compact disc. For *Select* it was the mix-cassette. For *MOJO* it was the box-set boom. For *Word* it was the digital music-file and, crucially, the sexy, pocket-sized slab to play it known as 'the Great White Wonder', a device that separated tracks from their packaging and left them floating in a characterless sound-cloud with no sleeve notes or mythology attached. The iPod allowed people to listen to more music, but if they didn't buy it or own it and stare at its cover, would they ever feel the depth of affection that might make them want to read about it too? And would they ever stumble across those B-sides and obscurities that could tip them into lifelong, hopeless devotion, the vanishing equivalents of The Kinks' 'She's Got Everything' or 'Acquiesce' by Oasis or Elvis Costello's version of 'Psycho'? I prodded my new toy's nubby little buttons with the same adolescent joy as I'd first fiddled with a transistor, but I couldn't work out if it was a blessing or a curse.

As we neared the launch and the long, cold nights closed in, I thought I'd done something insane. Joe Strummer had died and we were playing *London Calling* on repeat: its thunderous theatre made me wonder if some inevitable doom lay up ahead. Maybe it *was* wilful stupidity. How could we take on goliaths like EMAP and IPC? I could feel the shadow of those mass-market 'publishing giants' looming above me as we loaded our little sling-shot with pebbles. All I had was the belief that *Word* was worth pursuing and that enough people my age might feel the same way. In my forties, music wasn't about contrivance or gimmickry. It wasn't about being dazzled by spectacle or made to feel awestruck or envious. It was about distraction, warmth and reassurance. It was about songwriters who might echo my own life – the knowing fallibility of Nick Lowe, the restless expeditions of Lucinda Williams, the crumpled optimism of John Prine.

We pitched *Word*'s tent off the beaten track, miles from the mainstream, and covered anyone on the same wavelength, anyone gnarly and idiosyncratic, square pegs in round holes. Everything we published was meant to chime with Billy Wilder's first commandment: 'Thou shalt not bore!' Dave knocked up a strapline – '*Word*: At Last, Something To Read!' It was as far as we could get from the cold marketing analysis we'd left behind. A grim gallows humour emerged as we passed the first issue's final pages, a Dunkirk spirit in our darkest hour. We began talking in a ludicrous business-speak to lampoon the opposition and convince ourselves we were right.

'What do we think of our top-end media product?' Dave asked, poring over the proofs.

'With a paradigm shift in higher-order thinking,' I told

him, 'it ought to peel back the customer-centric onion and get the octopus back in the paper bag.'

'Though we probably need to up the eyeball traffic,' Paul said, 'in terms of a synergistic relationship with platform-neutral regulations. While boiling the ocean.'

But there was still a dusty, romantic flavour to the whole adventure. Andrew said it was like being asked to join The Magnificent Seven. Times were bad and the village needed defending – its values, its beliefs and principles – and a few older gunmen had come out of retirement for one last job. In our hearts we knew we were headed for a chest full of lead but people would sing songs about us and the most beautiful girl in the village would wear black for the rest of her life. If *Word* died, at least it would die with its boots on. I organised a lunch and knocked up an invite.

YOUR chance to play a key role in the triumphal ascent
of the new independent publisher Development Hell and
applaud the miracle birth of . . .
WORD MAGAZINE
at its low-key yet intimate
LAUNCH PARTY
at The Finca, 96/98 Pentonville Road, N1 9JB on Tuesday
February 4 2003 at half twelve
Ale • Lovely people • Exotic Spanish food • No ice
sculptures • Live music from the purely delightful
ED HARCOURT

Word appeared but seemed to be dying like a louse in a Russian's beard. Sales were poor and there was a mountain to climb. Independent publishing was like a corner shop battling with the vast promotional clout of the megastores. The third issue was riddled with problems: we came to work on a Wednesday morning, saw the sun set and rise again, and went home late on Thursday night, a forty-hour stretch

292

broken only by manic laughter, the patter of mice on the water pipes and Keith heading out to buy a fresh pair of socks, putting the old ones in a knotted plastic bag and tossing them into a bin. After three hours' sleep I switched on Radio London but found Danny Baker's optimism hard to share.

'Good morning, everybody!' Baker began, unforgettably. 'The snail's on the thorn, the lark's on the wing, the rainbow's around our shoulders, the hat's on the side of our head and everything is for the best in this best of all possible worlds. The first marmalade fingers of dawn creep across the lawn as a gardener leans across a tree playing a harmonica . . .'

Yet very gradually over the next few months, the lark – if not actually in ascent – started sitting up and taking solids. Sales began to lift, various cover stories – Morrissey, Joni Mitchell, Paul Weller, the White Stripes – sold in ever larger numbers, and previously untroubled swathes of pine forest began to fear the logger's axe, though a rogue edition with Dido on the front was both nailed *and* glued to the shelves – 'dead as a Dido', as we darkly observed. Pursuing the vanishing tales of rock and roll, I had fish and chips with Pinetop Perkins, the piano-player in the Muddy Waters band, still flint-eyed and devilish at ninety. Howlin' Wolf, he told me, was a looming physical presence, six foot six and 300 pounds, and had a powerful put-down for hecklers: if someone barracked him, Wolf would shoot back the worst insult he could muster – 'Man, you ain't got 'nuff money to burn a wet mule!' Now forgiven for my Radio 1 shifts, I wrote a piece about John Peel and stayed overnight at his house in Stowmarket. I watched him broadcast from his home studio, then we drank red wine and played singles till three in the morning. At one point he dug out 'Frankie And Johnny' by his great hero Lonnie Donegan, 'the English Elvis, the man that pushed the button that started it all'. He'd been to see him in hospital two weeks before, 'frail and full of pain-killers, just sitting in his dressing-gown', and he'd died three days later. Peel stood in the kitchen while his scratched old copy played, spellbound, trembling, tears running down his cheeks. 'Some records are elemental,' he said, raising a glass. 'There's nothing you can add or subtract to improve them, they just *are*. That one is almost hewn. You could dig it up.'

Word had a spirit that struck a chord with musicians and I could reach a few big names directly through email. This was a reply from Robert Plant:

> Dear Mark you fucking old drunk. There's not enough Polyfilla on the planet to warrant my visage on the cover of your estimable periodical, but of course the answer is 'yes'. Hope you're steady on the sensitive questions other-wise I'll get a repeat bout of amnesia – RP

The more we sold, the more I got offers to promote it on radio shows. Mild controversies would rage about Pink Floyd refusing to 'unbundle' their albums into separate sound-files, or whether Led Zeppelin should re-form, or the earth-shaking revelation that Ringo Starr was now refusing to sign autographs, or some rock legend would pass away, and the editor of *Word* would be invited to give an opinion, the kind of publicity money can't buy, particularly magazines that hadn't got any money in the first place. The best times were the rolling news stories. Monthlies can only react days – if not weeks – later to any bombshell event so it was fascinating to be caught in a feeding-frenzy. I was in bed on Thursday, 29 June, when the phone rang: a researcher from Radio 4's *Today* programme.

'Mark Ellen?' she asked.

'It's eleven at night,' I said. 'Somebody's died?'

'Michael Jackson . . . possibly. There's a rumour about it on the TMZ website.'

'Where's Paul Gambaccini when you need him?' The veteran broadcaster was top of the network's Rolodex for any big news in the music world.

'He's not picking up,' she said briskly. She was scanning her contributors' file. 'You did the last ever interview with Jacko, right?'

'In Britain, yes, but that was 1982 and . . .'

'I've got a car for you at half six in the morning.'

'But what am I going to say? That's he's not feeling too good?'

'The cab's booked. I'll get confirmation.'

'I didn't actually *meet* him. It was forty minutes on the phone . . .'

'But the *last* interview, right?'

'I guess it was.'

'We'd be *so* grateful if you'd be available,' she said softly. 'Ring you back in five!'

She rang back in two. 'Confirmed. See you at Wood Lane, quarter to seven.'

I got up and went to the computer to watch the reports roll in, the net already clogged with clammy, high-handed, hysterical rants about 'Wacko Jacko', the boy genius gone wrong, the freakish surgical experiment in his friendless Disneyland, the human horror-show imprisoned by drugs. For years our house had rattled to the sound of *Thriller* and *Bad* with small, one-gloved children skating about in their socks trying to moonwalk, but my view of Michael Jackson had altered too. I'd never forgiven him for the day the boys came back from school, aged eight and six, and asked me to explain what he'd been up to at a sleep-over that the playground was whispering about. When pop musicians let me down as a child, I learnt to live with it; when they let me down as a parent, I wasn't quite so compassionate. I still had a fondness for his music but the man behind it seemed sad and repulsive.

The kids next door were having a party in their back garden and I stood and watched them, wondering how they'd react when the news filtered through. I remembered being their age when I'd heard about Brian Jones, tiny fragments of information it took months to piece together about a chilling death with all the hallmarks of a murder mystery. I remembered the school assembly where some ancient teacher in his early thirties mentioned 'the loss of James Marshall Hendrix' – he couldn't quite stretch to 'Jimi' – and feeling even worse as he'd belonged to *us*, not them. An eerie hush descended the other side of the fence. The music cut and I heard the swell of *oh-my-God* voices shrieking with shock and disbelief. Minutes later someone found 'Billie Jean' on a laptop, but it didn't make any sense with nobody dancing so they clicked it off and went back to Lily Allen.

My car pulled up at Television Centre to find the whole place humming. Every screen had Jackson's haunted face on it, covered with screaming captions. Aerial views of his house flicked up and shots of his personal physician. The story was huge and getting huger by the second. Every outpost of the BBC's news network was leading with it. I was rushed to *Today*'s green room with its Styrofoam cups and comforting smell of coffee and muffins. A Fleet Street writer was gearing up for a piece about the dangers of asbestos and a priest adjusting his Thought for the Day. Whisked straight to the studio, I watched, awestruck, as the day's main anchor, the steel-nerved Sarah Montague, googled statistics while speaking to the editor on talk-back and coolly spreading marmalade on a piece of toast. With five million listening, she then leant into a microphone and gave a politician a hard time.

'Tributes are pouring in for Michael Jackson, who died

last night at his home in Los Angeles of a suspected heart attack,' she said. 'The pop icon was treated by paramedics at the scene and later pronounced dead at the nearby Ronald Reagan Medical Center on the eve of his fifty-first birthday. I'm joined now by the editor of *Word* magazine, Mark Ellen, the last person to interview Jackson in the British music press. He was a complex man, Mark, plagued by sex scandals and medical issues, but have we forgotten his music?'

'Well, Sarah, I believe we have. Every report I've heard so far has focused on this element of human tragedy, the car-crash that's threatening to overshadow his legacy. But he brought a huge variety of American roots music to a world market – soul, R&B, gospel, hip-hop – and was the biggest event since Elvis Presley or The Beatles . . .'

'And when you talked to him . . .'

Don't mention it was a phoner, doesn't sound great.

'. . . back in 1982 . . .'

Brilliant.

'. . . did *you* feel, as people have suggested, that he was locked in some kind of lasting childhood as a result of finding fame so early?'

'Well, he seemed pretty clued up on the business aspects of his life, very aware of the way the *Thriller* album was being mixed and marketed, but for the rest, yes, he *did* speak in a strange child-like voice about the "magic" of fairy stories, and told me he watched Disney cartoons obsessively, and *The Wizard of Oz* and Charlie Chaplin. He seemed happier in the past than the present . . .'

And on we rattled in the giddy, supercharged way of live radio. I was shepherded out to find a scrum had gathered in the passage. Rumours of my Jackson connection were circulating fast and already getting bent out of shape. Here in the building was someone who'd not only *met* Michael Jackson . . .

Guys, it was on the phone!

. . . but watched the way he worked and could *shed light on the superstar's untimely demise*. No one on God's earth appeared to have got within a country mile of the reclusive pop idol but this Mark Ellen fellow had *actually interviewed him*. It wasn't a question of *whether* I'd be on their programmes, just *when* – in fact, an efficient girl seemed to have taken charge and was working out an order. I felt for her. In a couple of hours I'd be doing the same thing. I'd be back in the office ringing round, trying to pull a story together.

'I have with me the editor of *Word* magazine, Mark Ellen, who conducted the last interview Michael Jackson ever gave in this country.'

This was World Service radio, going out to Asia, Africa, the Americas, Europe and the Pacific. More coffee, more muffins.

'Mark, from your perspective, what are the main factors that have contributed to this extraordinary icon's tragic death?'

We were off again. I was sprung out of the door and back into the throng, Efficient Girl propelling me down the corridor. 'Radio 2 want a piece,' she said, 'and Radio 1, of course, the locals can lift something out of that, and then . . .'

'Where's Gambaccini?' I asked. This was insane.

'No sign yet,' she said, tight-lipped. 'It's BBC 1's *Breakfast* next – that's the UK only. Let's get some powder on you.'

I was flung into a dressing-room where a makeup team came at me with combs and sponges and rushed to the dazzling scarlet sofas of a TV set where two presenters were linking to some footage of an ambulance outside Jackson's house in North Carolwood Drive. One of them waved, the other gave me a wink.

'It's now eight thirty and we're joined by Mark Ellen . . .'

From *Word?*

'. . . from *Word* magazine . . .'

Nice!

'. . . and one of the few people lucky enough to have met, interviewed and got some understanding of the complex life of Michael Jackson, the record-breaking star whose death last night is still shrouded in mystery.'

Away we went again, at one point cutting to a reporter in light drizzle in a field full of tents who claimed, 'Everyone here, too, at Glastonbury Festival is in mourning for the self-styled King of Pop', though this rang a little hollow as the acres of damp canvas behind him said the place was still asleep. Back out in the passage it was clear the Jackson story had erupted into a firestorm devouring all in its path. Anyone with the faintest connection to the man or his music was being hauled in front of a microphone. I was so lit with adrenaline I felt invincible. I'd reached a level of surging self-confidence where nothing could faze me. If they'd asked me to *present* their TV shows I'd have swapped chairs immediately. I was *flying*. I was important and in demand! The appetite was so ravenous that someone who'd had a phone conversation with Michael Jackson twenty-seven years ago was being catapulted all over the globe. The whole thing was becoming farcical. Who needs Gambo? Bring it on! I couldn't wait for the next one.

'America's next,' Efficient Girl said, shunting me to another studio. 'Live world news. Goes right across the globe but mostly the States.' She squinted at my brow and started dabbing with a tissue. 'More slap over here, please, Suzie!'

'Gambo?' somebody asked her.

'Stuck in traffic,' she hissed.

More powder, more hair-calming and back in another blinding 'comfy area' with two orange-skinned TV anchors with immaculate teeth. American media had famously underplayed the death of another doomed recluse, Elvis Presley. They weren't going to make that mistake again.

'We're still across this Michael Jackson story AS it rolls out, helping YOU sift the facts FROM the fiction to get TO the heart OF a life that had gone SO right and yet so tragically wrong. WITH us now, someone who met AND spent time with him and became close TO the troubled singer . . .'

Pur-lease!

'. . . Mark Ellen, who edits a magazine called *Word*. Mark, thanks for joining us . . .'

I was beamed to people in Chicago bars and chewing steak in Idaho truck stops – and possibly health spas in Hong Kong – then rushed out and ferried down another passage to do something for Radio 5. But somehow the world seemed less hectic, the pace a little slower and the gaggle was melting away. The red light was already on when I got there and a soft, familiar east-coast accent emanating from the guest seating area.

'. . . one of the greatest stars of recorded music,' the voice was saying, 'Jackson would be in the Top Ten Of All Time, regardless of who the other nine people were. The trilogy of albums he made with the great Quincy Jones, of course . . .'

An arm came across the doorway, a producer on the end of it. He looked tired and embarrassed.

'You're off the hook, mate,' he said. 'Gambo's in the building.'

36

When Good Nights Turn Bad

My ten-year-old self, if I'd clambered back and asked him, might have made a point about my changing relationship with rock stars. They'd once been people whose lives I'd imagined while wearing out the grooves of their records. Then they were gods I'd gazed at through clouds of dry ice. Then prophets, whose sayings I'd scribbled down on tour buses. Then legends I'd asked to awards shows or talked about on television.

But the strangest of all these arrangements – the daftest, most strained and bizarre – was this.

Some time in the middle of *Word*'s wobbling trajectory I went to a literary dinner. This was in a wood-beamed private room at the top of an expensive restaurant in Islington and laid on for the scriptwriter Paul Schrader. I was invited as they hoped I'd give it some publicity. The great author of *Taxi Driver* was three seats to my right and, between us, the playwright and novelist Hanif Kureishi and the screenwriter Andrew Davies. Opposite me was Robert Wade, who'd co-written the last two Bond movies and, to his right, some nice people from *Esquire* magazine. On my left, an empty chair.

I pulled heavily on my glass of fizz and took it all in. Waiters hovered attentively, delicious scents wafted from a clattering kitchen, clever people were saying interesting things and I was about to be filled with nice food. Wade was suave and affable, quite Bond-like in his roll-neck shirt, and the two of us were getting on famously. The menus arrived and he went for the chorizo sausage and the lemon sole. I put in for the most carnivorous combination on the planet, ordered with one of those simpering *shouldn't-really* shrugs, implying I was normally a pumpkin-tartlet-with-spinach-and-gorgonzola kind of guy but tonight, hey, I'm feeling a little crazy! I went for the rare rack of lamb preceded by the *pâté de foie gras*.

I know, I know, I *know*. I did a bad thing. On the chart of Terrible Crimes Against The Animal Kingdom, it's one above bashing veal calves on the head with a shoe and pan-frying them for Jeremy Clarkson. But I'd had a couple of drinks and I fancied it. What was the worst that could happen?

The worst that could happen was this. The door at the far end burst open and a figure in a denim jacket and black jeans exploded into view, heading straight for the chair beside me. She sat down in a crotchety fashion, just as the waiter slid a thimble of French onion soup in front of us, and shook back her low, dark fringe. For crying out loud, it was Chrissie Hynde. She sniffed her *amuse-bouche* suspiciously, clearly unamused.

'This got beef stock in it?' she barked. Like I was supposed to know.

I flagged down the *maître d'*, who dashed off to investigate, only to return with some controversial news. 'Zer is, Madame, zer *teeenieeest leeetle beeet* of zer most *deleeecious* biffstock in zis . . .'

Hynde recoiled in horror – he might as well have told her it was radioactive – and it was whisked away smartly and returned to the kitchen. We chatted in a slightly stilted manner about onion soup in general and the ruinous cost of rock tours, and I thought the ice was starting to melt. I'd met her enough times to know that, in the great cricket match of life, you don't want Chrissie Hynde batting against you. *The Face* magazine had packed me off to Paris in '81 to write a profile of the Pretenders' singer and I'd sat, quivering, in her hotel room while she hurled a blistering barrage of abuse at her bass-player and guitarist – both former boyfriends – and I'd made a mental note: never, *ever* get on the wrong side of this girl. And that was when she was on the way up. Rock stars who've made it tend not to go for those sorts of niceties. They have self-belief. They know they're right. They give it to you straight. Heaven help the fool who incurs their wrath.

I looked at Wade. Wade looked at me. We were both thinking the same thing. I was in deep shit here, the unspeakable in pursuit of the inedible. The world's most militant animal-rights activist – a woman, let's not forget, who'd chained herself to railings and been *jailed* for her hands-on demonstrations against the fur trade and McDonald's, who had once advised me 'Never kick in the windows of a police car' – and I'd ordered a large, possibly still pulsating, steaming great slab of *pâté de foie fucking gras*. Its arrival was seconds away. If this was announced by a troupe of weeping geese holding banners declaring my barbarous hors d'oeuvre to have been a close blood relative, I honestly don't think the situation could have been any worse.

Suddenly I had a fantastic idea. *Wade* could help me! And he wasn't blame-free himself, bang-to-rights with his sausage starter. We were firm friends, best pals – he was the brother I'd never had. He'd sprung James Bond out of all sorts of scrapes with his charm and his way with words. Old Wadey would have a cunning plan! I waited till Hynde was deep in conversation and conveyed my blind panic. He tapped his nose and gave a comforting wink.

'Worry not, me old pal,' he whispered. 'This I shall handle!'

I slumped back in my seat, exhaling deeply, and took another long draught of the bubbly. What it was to have allies, chums you could trust, old muckers in your hour of need. He'd say it had come to the wrong table, I imagined, and could they get my salad as soon as possible. The swing doors smacked back open to admit a trail of waiters rattling dishes. 'One courgette fritter, the roast goat's cheese and pomegranate, the chorizo with prawns, one *pâté de*—'

'*Pâté*, did you say?' Wade shrieked fiendishly, just for the hell of it. '*Pâté . . . de foie gras*?' He was standing up, the whole table was looking. 'I *think* you'll find that was ordered by our friend sitting . . . over *here*!' And he stabbed his finger in a look-at-this-clown, we're-all-sensitive-literary-dinner-types-having-the-mushroom-risotto sort of way.

It all went horribly quiet. If I'd been a cartoon character I'd have had a wavy line for a mouth. And I'd got the lamb to come.

Hynde looked at Wade, then at me and my mound of seared offal, then at Wade again and – clearly reading this as a set-piece cooked up by the pair of us to take the piss out of the world's leading vegetarian campaigner – turned back to *Esquire* and never spoke another word to us all night.

37

Waiting For Gaga

Barring the odd literary dinner, all was not well on the good ship *Word*.

All wasn't well in the music business either. Sales were collapsing, advertising drying up, stores and studios closing, small labels going to the wall and the record giants of my youth, the cornerstones of the industry, were merging and shedding staff. Even EMI, unsinkable home of Pink Floyd, Radiohead and The Beatles, had been taken over by a private equity firm. The idea of paying for music was so devalued by the internet that the old model was turned on its head. In the past, bands often lost money on the road but earned through sales of the album they were promoting. Now they gave their music away to reach as many people as possible, hoping enough would pay handsomely to see them perform it. So the acts toured constantly and lost some of their magazine-selling mystery in the process, and those who still had any became cautious in the way they controlled it. On the rare occasions Bob Dylan allowed himself to be interviewed, he hired a friend to talk to him and released the carefully edited results on his website – which is advertising not editorial.

And how much mystery did some of the new acts have anyway? An appalling television programme called *The X Factor* was changing the perception of singing. Warbling wannabes risked public humiliation to appear to be *feeling* the soulless tracks they delivered – 'lungs of a whale, tears of a crocodile', as Dave Hepworth put it. I'd interviewed Christina Aguilera backstage for VH-1, a doll-like creature who'd started life as a mouseketeer on a Disney children's show. Her idea of self-expression was to wobble her lower lip while emitting shrill, melismatic streams of notes in a fashion first coined by Whitney Houston. This wasn't singing, it was showing off. She was just a technician, but the more the hollow vocal fireworks, the more people thought she was a genius. The big sensation was Adele, another product of the new stage-school circuit, a hot-house that trained teen-agers for the rigours of stardom, even teaching them how to be interviewed. Her mother sat in the front row of her shows and she mostly used collaborators, seasoned professionals who helped her explore her big emotional pivots and write songs about them, the dramatic peak of this sheltered life being the hit single 'Chasing Pavements' on which she runs back home in a certain amount of turmoil after having a row in a pub with a boyfriend.

I tried my best to make *Word* sell but the main engines of the publishing world – news, reviews and information – were now freely available, and anyone with a passion for an act could rapidly burn it away by gorging on available links and YouTube rather than waiting, patiently, for fresh revelations from magazines like ours. A rare big-seller with Leonard Cohen on the cover brought a lugubrious email from the great man himself – 'Very kind of you to have devoted so much space to my shabby career' – and another featured the briefly beguiling Libertines' songbird Pete Doherty, so deep in his tunnel of drugs that his sole representative was a shadowy figure who arranged to meet me in a King's Cross boozer. He wore a pork-pie hat so I could identify him, like something out of a spy thriller. Damp, stubbly and with a bad attack of the shakes, he scribbled down Doherty's address on condition that I let him use the office photocopier and make him a tea with six sugars. Our brave reporter, Sylvia Patterson, rang later to let me know she was out and still alive.

'A crack den,' she told me from a Shoreditch backstreet. 'Adoring teenage girls, pale and very thin, lying around on sofas. Poor wee things, I wanted to make them some soup. The carpet crunched underfoot with used needles. At one point I asked Pete why he painted blood all over the walls and he said, "I just *do*" . . . and sang the rest of his answer.'

I threw everything I knew into the pot but I couldn't raise the circulation. In one dark hour, Dave, Jerry and I decided to change the title from *Word* to the more assured *The Word* but it didn't make any difference. In one even darker hour, we toyed with the absurd notion of changing it back again.

It wasn't a great time to be in magazines.

One morning I got a call from the number two at Apple Corps asking me for lunch in Kensington. I assumed this was an excuse to push some steak round a plate while he filled me in on the next Beatles' release but, two drinks later, we were joined by Neil Aspinall, a muscular, weather-beaten man in a sleeveless quilted jacket. The band's roadie when they'd played the Cavern Club, he'd risen through the ranks to become Apple's chief executive, chasing down their pictures and recordings and masterminding the compilations that secured their legacy. Not for nothing was he still known as 'the fifth Beatle'. I managed to stop myself asking breathless questions about the times he drove their old Commer van but told him I'd kept my phone messages from their publicist, the great Derek Taylor, when I was running the *Q* Awards. I echoed the soft cadence of his voice, like a resigned James Mason – 'I'd love to meet you,' he'd sighed, 'when this whole bloody war is over.' But Derek had died and we'd never hooked up.

These days, Neil explained, The Beatles were a business comprised of Paul McCartney, Ringo Starr, Olivia Harrison and Yoko Ono, and Apple had lucrative film and record projects stretching way into the future. 'We need someone to write the press releases for the next set of albums,' he told me, 'and generally talk the whole thing up. Apple needs a new publicist.'

'A new Derek Taylor!' I pointed out.

'A new Derek Taylor,' he said. 'How about you?'

'*Me?*' I hadn't seen this coming.

'You.'

He walked me over the road to the Apple HQ with its thick carpets and signed concert posters framed on the walls, its platinum discs, its jukeboxes, its statuettes from *Yellow Submarine* on polished wooden shelves. I couldn't picture a place that screamed 'prosperity' any louder. In a beleaguered music business, The Beatles led the shrinking number of acts still guaranteed to make any money. And now they needed a publicist.

'*You*,' he said, and he patted me on the shoulder.

I wandered back to the *Word* office and stared at the place uncomfortably, its still-active mousetraps, its broken radiators, its kettle that only worked if you jammed a CD under the base. It was a constant struggle to keep our heads above the water. Life on the magazine felt like *The Raft Of The Medusa* on the cover of the Pogues' album, *Rum, Sodomy And The Lash*, where ragged souls with tattered sails battled an aggressive ocean.

It wasn't a great time to be turning down a job as The Beatles' PR.

But I did and I didn't give it a second thought. I could hear the words of Anton Corbijn back at the Roach Motel when I'd been offered that job at Island – 'You're writing and I'm taking pictures,' he'd told me. 'This is what we do.' I couldn't leave this noble boat and its magnificent crew, and I still believed our sails would fill and that magical wind was on the horizon.

★   ★   ★

But the publicists' world was no bed of roses either. A regrettable quote, a damaging snap or a copied sound file could live on the net forever, so they'd clamped down hard in a vice-like attempt to control the press. Every negotiation seemed like a tug-of-war. A few years earlier I could live with an established artists' new album for weeks before writing a considered review. Now I had to trundle obediently to a play-back studio along with the world's assorted hacks, hand in my phone, sign an agreement not to tweet my opinion, and hear it once in the hawk-like gaze of a publicity chief. Access to musicians was just as restricted. Homes were out of bounds, thought to be too revealing. Major interviews were conducted in characterless hotel rooms with publicists attempting to 'sit in' on the conversation to ensure it didn't stray 'off-message'. I was supposed to feel overjoyed to have ten minutes to touch the hem of some rock star's garment and dutifully jot down the same PR-chiselled waffle they'd just given a bunch of rival titles on the same one-day promotional junket. It was harder and harder to paint a fresh and original picture. I thought back to the early eighties when I'd knocked on Sting's door to find him padding about in his socks making tea. His press girl had simply given me his home address in Hampstead and told me what time to turn up. He'd had four British number ones, three US top tens, colossal sales the world over – The Police were the biggest act on the planet – but there wasn't a PR, manager or even a childminder in sight. It was just the two of us, me and him, two dogs called Steerpike and The Prune, and his five-year-old son Joe scooting about on a toy car.

I hadn't realised how far-fetched these levels of protection had become till I got a call from *Elle* magazine.

'Hi, Mark, it's Annabel Brog. Do you want to talk to Lady Gaga for us? I wondered if I could put your name forward as a possible interviewer.'

'For God's sake,' I howled, 'stick me on the list!'

The world-slaying diva was *way* beyond the reach of *The Word*. A lot of the readers wouldn't have liked her anyway but I thought she was fascinating – ambitious, theatrical, bonkers, a hugely talented musician and songwriter. I'd just watched her Monster Ball wedged among a baying crowd of twenty thousand zombies, Goths, cross-dressers, fashion statements, fembots and Bacardi Breezer-gargling caners who looked like they'd steamed in from a Tim Burton theme night or a hen weekend in Magaluf. She called them all her 'Little Monsters' or 'The Underdogs Of Love'. She'd clambered into the drum kit and started laying about the cymbals. She played piano with her feet. She appeared in drag, with fake sideburns and stubble, fuelling the delightful rumour that she wasn't actually a girl at all – recent stage photos had suggested a much-trumpeted 'penis'. At one point she dressed like a giant candle with tassels and then lurched out of a crashed tube carriage in transparent sheeting with plasters on her nipples, her right hand a mutilated claw. Then she appeared covered with blood in a wedding dress and rustling electronic wings. A girl at the front tossed a Christmas gift onto the stage, a two-foot Santa Claus, and Gaga tore it in half, stamped on its felt-filled corpse with a stiletto and performed the next song with its decapitated head on the top of her shroud.

It was a night of all-round splendidness. What kind of madman *wouldn't* want to meet her? 'But why me?' I wondered. They'd spent a year negotiating this. 'Why not somebody *her* age?'

'You've interviewed all her heroes,' Annabel said sweetly, 'The Beatles, the Stones, Bowie, Queen, Elton, Sting, Jacko. She's barely met any of them. She'd be interested. It's different. She might go for it.'

It was and she did. I was booked for a meeting 'to see if we got on'. If I passed this acid test, I'd be flown to New

York for stage three. A week later, I was summoned to the sumptuous Lanesborough Hotel on Hyde Park Corner where 'The Garg' had taken her usual top-floor suite of rooms, a high-security eyrie overlooking its back courtyard and the rooftops of Knightsbridge. News of her arrival had spread from her Twitterfeed, and a round-the-clock gaggle of Monsters now occupied the space below in the hope of a regal wave from a distant window. This devotion ran both ways: motorcycles arrived at four in the morning delivering them pizzas and boxes of pink, sugary macaroons, all on the Garg's bottomless tab. I kicked about in the foyer for three hours adjusting to 'Gaga Time' and was eventually rushed to a narrow stairway leading to the hotel's wine cellar, a brick-arched Gothic vault deep in the bowels of the building. Dimly visible in the flickering candlelight, racks of dust-covered bottles behind her, was a tiny figure on a throne-like chair, an anxious PR beside her. There was a strange, heady scent of perfume and hot wax. I looked at her, blinked, and looked again.

She was wearing a thin turquoise dress on a flesh-coloured body-stocking and blue shoes with clumpy great brick-like stacks. She had two-inch fingernails. Her long, mint-green hair was so straight it seemed to have been ironed. Her face was ghostly white, like porcelain. Extravagant painted cat's whiskers sprang from her eyes and back across the sides of her face, like a space-age Cleopatra. In one slow, constrained movement, she extended a hand and I wondered if I was meant to kneel down and kiss it. She could barely move for fear of snagging a cobalt-coloured nail, or knocking over the candelabra, or shifting her plank-like wig. How much time and effort had gone into this? How much thought and planning? How many stylists had scrambled into action so this pocket-sized luminary – all five foot one of her – could remind me I was in the presence of greatness? It was adorable. You didn't get a lot of *this* with Eddie and The Hot Rods. She spoke in a fabulous east-coast accent with a big twist of Valley Girl – anything theatrical she called *derr-rummah*, underwear was *lan-djer-aayy*. I asked her about London and the Little Monsters outside, with their pink hair and painted faces, and she asked me about The Beatles and Queen and Elton John, and then the voice in the corner said it was time to go.

'You've passed the audition,' Annabel told me. 'New York on Monday.'

Four days later I was in a voguish brick warehouse on the Upper West Side waiting for Gaga. The room crackled with the supercharged, stay-calm energy of a mega-starlet's boudoir set to 'high anxiety'. Dresses were being freshened with steam-hoses. Monstrous, teetering shoes were being readied for action. Acres of wigs, hats and jewellery were being laid out for inspection. Caterers piled in with trays of steamed fish and tofu. Juice-bar operatives hurled carrots into blenders. Gently carbonated water flowed like the Hudson four floors below us. Nineteen people fidgeted about – photographers, chefs, stylists, makeup, steam-hose personnel – preparing to keep this multi-million-dollar meteorite looking luminous and sparking on all cylinders. According to the schedule, the cover shoot would follow my eighty-minute interview but the Garg and her people were already four hours late. Tension was being punctured by camp buffoonery from the fashion menfolk.

'*Oh. My. Actual. God!*' one declared, waving his hands about. 'We're out of summer berries. *Stay* positive, people! *Stay* focused!'

Like gentle rainfall, a shower of texts pattered through the room, suggesting the cavalcade was drawing near. Minutes later, the Garg and entourage sprang from the lifts and she headed straight to the dressing room, emerging fourteen inches taller, wobbling bravely on a pair of preposterous platform shoes, an assistant holding either arm and followed by a video crew. The Pet Shop Boys began pumping from a sound-system, then Soft Cell, Blondie, Garbage and Fleetwood Mac, the lights flared up and she clambered onto the set and threw shapes for the camera in the teeth of a wind-machine. Whenever there was a pause, she pulled hard on a Marlboro. She checked each shot as it popped up on the screens, referring to herself collectively.

'We hate it.'

Click.

'We like it.'

Click.

'We look good.'

Click.

'We look great! We look like *a sexy watermelon*!'

I followed her through the backstage curtain where another flurry of clothes, gloves, wigs, hats and rings was being presented for perusal. It was how I imagined the life of Marilyn Monroe, or maybe the court of Marie Antoinette with some ginseng energy drinks. As the shoot was so far behind, I suggested I just hover about in the dressing room and grab any available time to talk to her.

'Okay,' she said, 'though right now I gotta get naked.' And she shooed me out.

Seconds later I was beckoned back through the curtain to find the Garg wearing a fringed platinum wig, like a blonde Liza Minnelli, and a tiny and completely transparent slice of paper-thin chiffon. Beneath that, nothing. Nothing at all. Not one square inch of her hallowed frame left to the imagination.

'This is so funny,' she said, with a mischievous smile, inspecting her eyes in a little mirror. 'I sent you out a minute ago cos I was getting naked and now I have this see-through dress on!'

You *could* have called it a dress but it was, in fact, Lady Gaga in the raw plus an invisible veil. She popped a straw in her mouth and sucked dark-green liquid from a plastic beaker. 'You know how I keep my energy up?'

I didn't, no.

'Lots of orgasms,' she said. 'Orgasms and spinach!' She stirred her pressed vegetable juice, rattling the ice cubes.

I was all over the place. The last time I'd seen every inch of a twenty-five-year-old girl was when *I* was twenty-five, and she hadn't had a mythical creature inked on the side of her arse. I found myself prodding it with a finger-tip.

'That's my unicorn,' she giggled. 'Everyone needs *one* funny tattoo. And this is my white rose, this is my swan, this is my musical note, these are my daisies . . . and this,' the Gothic text on her left arm, 'is from the poet Rilke,' and she translated it, looking straight ahead as if performing *Hamlet* – though I wasn't really listening, to be honest, I was miles away. '"In the deepest hour of the night, if you were asked if you would have to die if you were forbidden to write, look deep into your heart for the answer spreads its roots, and ask yourself – *Muss ich schreiben?* – must I write?"' She paused and, with an impish *oh-silly-me* look of cartoon horror, retrieved a tiny white rumpled thong from the floor by her ankles and rolled it back up her thighs as if it had dropped off by itself. Then wandered over to the rails and tried on a dress, topless.

'Hey you,' meaning me, 'no peeking!'

I couldn't work it out. Was she a shrewd, calculating operator or a total moon biscuit? Was this a set-piece cooked up between her and the management to bag some extra publicity? Was she just 'on' all the time, one of those people who wilt, like a flower out of water, if not the centre of attention? Was it a Gaga-the-naked-truth caper to put the mockers on the penis allegation? Was she so profoundly kooky she hadn't even been aware she was *sans* thong? Was it a high-risk spontaneous mood-swing from a bored and unmanageable genius, or just a minxish manipulator trying to rattle the only male heterosexual in the room and remind him who was in charge? It was one of the above but I couldn't tell which. When I'd interviewed big stars in the past, I'd usually been left alone with them so we could figure each other out, but the music writer of the twenty-first century was given a series of storyboards and had to sieve the facts from the fiction.

'I don't compare myself to anyone,' she told me as a team of stylists fiddled with her next frock. 'All the nice things you've said about me today, like how I've stolen Madonna's thunder, they make me want to pee my pants but I don't compare myself to anyone. I'm a separate magical entity unto myself. My fans don't care what I am and that's what I like about them. They don't care if I'm a boy or a girl or an in-between or a phoenix or a mermaid or a unicorn . . .'

'Do you wish you'd been born a boy?' I asked her.

'How do you know I wasn't?' she said.

'Because I'm the only journalist who's seen you naked.'

An inscrutable smile and she swept back to the shoot. Pausing to hitch up the front of her dress and flash the video camera.

38

Scritti Politti And A Jar Of Chutney

Back in London, *The Word* stumbled along on a shoestring. When we'd started there'd been six of us and two part-timers; now it was just me and the tremendous Kate Mossman, with Dave and our two-man production team arriving for the layouts.

Some small characteristic often tipped me into hiring staff on music magazines. I'd been impressed at *Smash Hits* with our junior writer's hair when we'd first met him, a vertical clump in the style of Mac McCulloch of the Bunnymen, held aloft, he revealed, with raw yolk and orange juice – though he once used electric curlers which had made it look like egg-fried rice. With Kate it wasn't just her vast knowledge of music or her touching devotion to Queen – she'd left forlorn graffiti on Freddie Mercury's brickwork at the age of eleven – it was what she had for lunch that convinced me. I interviewed her in a Chapel Market café. When her cheese omelette and chips arrived with a large salad garnish, she pushed every last shred of the lettuce to the side of the plate where it stayed, untouched. '*Greens*,' she sighed, and gave a little shiver.

The office fizzed with the thrilling new music of Gotye, John Grant and The Decemberists – and, when only Kate and I were there, lost recordings of fevered sixties jazzers Colosseum – while *The Word* found itself a new lifeline. The same digital world that was denting our sales had bunged us a shiny new toy: the podcast. Dave and I recorded the first in his attic on a Dictaphone wrapped in an overcoat to dampen the echo, and these reports from the rock and roll trenches started pulling a crowd. Podcasts were like conversations in a pub. On radio you always had to cut to the news or key up a track or worry about explaining yourself. This was different. Nobody listened by accident. They'd sought you out. You were among friends. You could talk. We could start by saying, 'So Keith, Brian and Anita were driving to Marrakesh in a Bentley . . .' and people either knew what we were on about or liked the idea we *assumed* they knew and were up for the ride anyway. We shot the breeze, launched screwball theories, told hoary old anecdotes and put the world to rights in the manner of two tragic souls who'd wasted chunks of their lives they'd never get back again in sticky-floored dives while Ducks Deluxe were doing a soundcheck. I once admitted the sheer weight of my record collection had cracked the spare-room ceiling, concerned that a ton of vinyl might crash from the attic and a slumbering guest be decapi-tated by Gong's *Camembert Electrique*, and this sparked a lively debate about the best and worst albums to die by. Dave had the genius idea of fading the podcasts in at the start and out at the end, as if you were eavesdropping on a constant exchange.

'How was Bob Dylan last night?' he asked on an early one, rubbing his hands and stirring a cup of tea. He'd had the sense to abandon the old buzzard's stage shows years ago but Clare and I weren't giving up without a struggle. 'It was, what, the thirty-sixth time you'd seen him?'

'Thirty-ninth,' I admitted, 'and even by *his* standards it was a shocker. He only played guitar once and it wasn't plugged in. The rest of the time he prodded a keyboard. He'd start a song nobody recognised – least of all the band – and, presumably maddened with boredom, try and sing it all on one note, emphasising different words, which gave it a whole new meaning – "Where have you been, my BLUE-eyed son?" as opposed to his other optically flavoured offspring. "Once upon a time you dressed so fine, threw the BUMS a dime", this particular cash-distribution including the gentlemen of the road, et cetera. Maddening! But Clare put on a brave face and said he had a nice pair of shoes. It was a disgrace, a scandal, a travesty, a mockery of the great legacy of the sage, seer and prophet who was the godfather of modern music.'

'But you're going again tonight, right?'

'Of *course*! Come with!'

The Word Massive, as the listeners called themselves, all knew the feeling and posted on our site with a series of lovable pseudonyms – Pencilsqueezer, Drakeygirl, El Hombre Malo, Backwards7, Burt Kocain, Captain Underpants, Bob-The-Blogger-Formerly-Known-As-Idiotbear. They'd been there too. They understood. They were lifers, just like us, saddled with rock stars they couldn't abandon who were written through them like a stick of rock. Following Dylan for me was like supporting a football team. He'd won the Premiership year after year and several FA Cups, but in the early eighties he'd dropped through the ranks to the Championship and no amount of investment or new players could lift him from the relegation zone. Like matches, his live shows chimed with the gentle rhythms of real life. There was something as dependably comforting about his epic failures, his missed chances, his fluffed shots, his inconceivable rottenness, as there was about the rare moments he still pulled some magic out of the bag. He could be breathtakingly dreadful but he was still Bob Dylan, the man who had given me 'North Country Blues' and 'The Lonesome Death Of Hattie Carroll'. I'd sat up till dawn dropping the needle on them again and again when I was fourteen and they'd changed my life completely. I could still smell the vinyl as it slipped from its sleeve, and the warm tubes of the Dansette. They might have meant little to him, those songs, but they meant

they were doing the same for us and brought ale and homemade cakes. I read out some messages from corners of a foreign field where the soft, shrugging Britishness of *The Word* must have felt like a postcard from home, this one from Elvis Costello:

> Dear Mark, very sorry to hear about the demise of your august organ. It could always be found, pride of place, alongside the pickled onions and Jaffa Cakes in the local 'English produce' shop in Vancouver. It made me laugh and featured some music that might otherwise have been overlooked for which you should be applauded. I especially liked Hepworth's grumpy columns. In the words of Mort Sahl: the future lies ahead. Onward and God Speed – EC

How perfect, and how touching, that the person present at my first nervous excursion into this whole caper should have been spirited into what I assumed was my last. Thirty-five years down the line, the man whose manager had thrown me out of the Nashville Rooms for having long hair and a velvet jacket was wishing me God speed. The future lay ahead and I hadn't the faintest idea what it would bring.

Until the phone rang and it was Annabel from *Elle* again, bless her cotton socks.

'Rihanna is playing seven concerts in seven countries in seven days, travelling on a private jet, a 777. She's plugging the new album. We need a piece about twenty-first-century stardom. Inside the life of the planet's biggest pop star. Maximum bling as the music biz struggles. The diva's diva. The gin, the jetlag, the jewellery. It'll be a hoot! You *have* to do it and you *know* you want to.'

One last hurrah. One last roll of the dice.

39

One Last Roll Of The Dice

A week later I was on a flight to Los Angeles to join the Rihanna tour. I was gazing out of the window, stirring a drink and contemplating The Glamorous But Impossible Lives Of Musicians. Hers, I suspected, would be even more impossible than most. No matter how alluring a star's world seemed to be, or how charged I felt to be in their orbit, I hadn't met a single one I envied. I wouldn't have changed places with any of them. Because their lives are impossible. They live impossible lives.

And this is why. No matter who you are – McCartney, Morrissey, Beyoncé – people resent it when you change, and their mental image of you is always pegged younger than you actually are, which was my problem with old matey from Wishbone Ash. They expect you to be just like you seem in your songs, charming, charismatic, even if they run into you at a luggage carousel at five in the morning. They know everything about you and you know nothing about them. They've invested so much time and money in your life and music they feel they *own* you.

It's an impossible arrangement.

And what about *you*, the rock star? Achieving success is hard enough but sustaining it is even harder. You claim to make records to please yourself but lie awake worrying about chart positions. I asked Paul McCartney in '82 why he'd put back the release of his single and he said darkly, 'You don't want to go head-to-head with Abba or the Human League.'

Meeting other musicians is agonising as you have to remind each other of the pecking order and you may both see it differently. Watching – or even listening to – your rivals' music is painful as you spot things you wish you'd done first. No matter how many houses you have, you don't want to sell any as you can't bear your perception of 'you' to be shrinking. One less home is a blow to your personal pride and you need a bolt-hole the fans don't know about – not for nothing did George Harrison have signs around his Friar Park estate saying, 'Private: Keep Out!' in ten different languages. You're used to living at a certain altitude so anything less is a step down, and without the insulation of chauffeurs and first-class travel, you'll have to rub shoulders with your adoring public. Every private party you attend is both made and simultaneously wrecked by your overpowering presence. The gap between the sum of your parts and the magic you've created has sparked an appetite so vast that people you've never met build the tiniest available details of your life into complex psychological theories that apparently 'shed light on the real you'. Your profile is part fantasy and part reality – and those confusing them die early – but your sense of self-worth hinges on this popularity. If your ticket sales dip, so does your confidence. That's how you measure yourself. And when you come off tour you can't relax: every night at eight, you're still programmed to perform and great surges of unscheduled adrenalin pump through your body while you're trying to switch from being a towering giant bathed in the validating roar of a stadium to just another owner-occupier required to squint at a school report, a gas bill or a demand from the Inland Revenue.

All that is impossible too.

Two particular moments had given me a taste of The Glamorous But Impossible Lives Of Musicians and this was one of them.

On a rainy night in the autumn of 2005 I climbed into a jeep behind the stage of a basketball stadium in Boston. The other passenger was already on board, The Edge of U2, his stage clothes steaming in the night air. Twenty-one thousand people were stamping their feet and howling for another encore, a deafening racket. I could feel the vibrations through the floor. Suddenly there was a wail of police sirens, a metal gate clanked up like a portcullis, and our motorcade of eight shiny jet-black vehicles leapt out across a ramp, down a steep track and straight onto the expressway.

The Edge glanced at his watch. 'I'm timing it,' he said. 'We call it doing a runner.'

We snaked over bridges and plunged through tunnels, the neon glow a smear on the windscreen, the roar of the engines beating back off the wet road. Police with light sabres waved us through red signals.

'Is this good as runners go?' I wondered. 'Marks out of ten?'

'I'd give it . . . ooh, nine-point-two,' he said, sending it up. 'You can gauge the degree of affection in a city by the level of back-up you get,' he added, 'and Boston have always looked after us. This is better than Barcelona where they drive at a speed that's actually life-threatening. And better than Italy where the cops bang on your roof with batons.' He wiped the condensation with his sleeve and waved at Larry Mullen in the car behind. Motorcycle outriders gunned ahead to man the next lights. 'And it's better than France where they're *too* relaxed. One of the Paris bike guys drew up alongside us at forty miles an hour to discuss the finer points of the escape route and leant an elbow on our driver's window.'

In exactly six minutes ten seconds – 'Fantastic!' – the cavalcade barged into Boston's Logan Airport and screeched to a halt on a part of the runway reserved for private planes. Small and polished Learjets stood on the tarmac, new and sparkling Gulfstreams beside them. There at the front, dwarfing them all, was a customised sixty-seat Airbus 320 emblazoned with the black and orange logo of U2's Vertigo Tour. We piled out, bundled up the gangway and fell into our seats, mine next to the supermodel Christy Turlington who was part of the band's sprawling retinue of friends and celebrity revellers. There were tables with bouquets of roses – though when they'd borrowed the Sultan of Brunei's jet, the taps, light fittings and toilet seat were made of solid gold. The band's new press officer had never been to America and sat up front with the pilot so she could see Manhattan from the cockpit. It seemed like a glorified car journey: once we were all in, they just slammed the door, started the engines and off we took. We touched down thirty-three minutes later, another platoon of cars waiting at the stand. My abiding memory was of a stewardess hauling herself gamely up the centre aisle balancing a tray of drinks, the lights of Massachusetts falling away behind her. She was clinging to the seat-backs, the aircraft in steep ascent.

When the tours ended and the band returned to Dublin, Bono's wife Ali did a sensible thing, forged from the hard-won wisdom of being married to a rock star for nearly twenty-five years: she booked him into a hotel for a few days to 'decompress' before he came home to the family. But can you ever really readjust? Clearly this is preferable to playing half-filled sports centres in Bracknell where I'd seen U2 in '81, but was it a vicious circle? The concept of 'Bono' was a blank canvas onto which an alarming number of people projected their hopes, fears and fantasies, and the private planes were a compensation for having to sustain it. Being Bono is what paid for it all but it was entirely possible that he didn't *want* to be Bono a lot of the time and wanted to be plain old Paul Hewson, though if he began to slide or fade away then he'd be the bloke who *used* to be Bono and that might be worse.

Would *you* want to be Bono? Think about it. Whatever he did his fans believed in it implicitly and his detractors took the piss as publicly as possible, and both could play havoc with your head. When he'd appeared at Live 8 three months earlier, his charitable contribution was applauded by his supporters but the rest had another recollection. Giant screens had broadcast the concert in various parks around Britain. At one point, a pre-recorded appeal flashed up to convey the scale of the disaster featuring Bono snapping his fingers every three seconds.

'Every time I click my fingers,' he began, 'a child in Africa dies . . .'

And someone in Glasgow shouted: 'Well, stop fucking *doing* it, then!'

And being on tour, of course, brings a second cargo of head-warping problems. This is where my other view of The Glamorous But Impossible Lives Of Musicians fits in.

A few weeks earlier I'd got as near as I'll ever get to the onstage experience. Robyn Hitchcock was playing the Village Underground in Shoreditch, a birthday show with guest appearances from 'heavy friends' – Green Gartside of Scritti Politti and the comedian Adam Buxton were on backing vocals, Kimberley Rew of the Waves playing guitar. Hitchcock had been the leader of Cambridge psychedelicists the Soft Boys, who'd supported Costello that night of my first review, and he'd made records since the late seventies for a small but loyal following. Clare and I had known him for years. One of his songs, 'Clean Steve', mentioned us by name in the lyric, the celebrated Steve arriving at a party later with 'a Nick Lowe cassette'. As Nick and I were both neighbours, Robyn asked us to help perform this track, the three of us running through it in his kitchen the night before. Nick worked out some vocal harmonies and guitar frills for me and they recorded us and played it back, nodding sagely. Me and Nick Lowe coming out of the same speaker – *I know!* I tried to look relaxed and professional. I bowled up the next night and joined the breezy talk about foot-pedals and foldback. I thought this would be like being onstage with any of the amateur acts I'd been in but it wasn't. It was something else entirely. Even rammed to the rafters there could only have been seven hundred people there but the sensation was overpowering – the intense heat, the crackling of monitors, eyes looming from every angle, sound bouncing off the arches. I could see silhouettes of people straining to get a view, on tables, on railings, wedged at the back on the stairs.

'I'd like to bring on another guest,' Robyn announced, flinging his arms about. 'From west London's swinging Chiswick district . . . Mr Mark Ellen!'

There was a ripple of recognition from 'Clean Steve' owners, I charged on to join Nick and we were counted in. But I was finding it hard to focus. I was trying to remember the things I had to play and sing while consumed by the boyish thrill that Nick Lowe was the first rock musician I ever saw and here I was, forty-three years later, sharing his microphone. I was having an out-of-body experience. I could see myself from the audience, the three of us in my tragic imagination looking like The Beatles doing 'Please Please Me' – Robyn was John and we were Paul and George to the left on the backing vocals, a childhood fantasy times ten. I had to stop myself shaking my head and going 'woooh'. But then – and this was what threw me – I saw the sea of upturned faces. Rammed against the stage, jammed, crushed, pressed up, people were mouthing every word of the set, mostly handsome girls in their twenties and thirties with interesting clothes. They smiled their knowing smiles, their limpid eyes gazing at Hitchcock as if only he understood them, and only they understood him, as if they were inside his head and knew every syllable he was about to sing, as if his songs wore the luminous glow of every dream they'd ever had.

Then one turned her high-beam lamps on me. She was clutching a present but couldn't get near enough to pass it to him so I got the pleading look. Big eyes, *huge*. Chords, harmonies, heat, lights, noise, and now a girl at my feet mouthing, *Can you give this to Robyn?* I glanced at the others – Green, Kimberley, Tim, Terry on keyboards, Jen, Lucy, Nick – and they smiled back encouragingly. Nothing fazed *them* and why would it? This was what they did for a living. Nick could fill the Albert Hall. He'd conquered America with Rockpile. He'd played the Bottom Line with Keith Richards. This was their office. This was where they worked. They were working. *My* office was a computer with some records playing. Imagine going to work and finding an explosion of light and sound and gorgeous women with presents. I became fixated by the package. What was in it? Gifts from people you don't know are peculiar. I'd sat in Rufus Wainwright's dressing room once in Montreal and watched him unwrap the parcels delivered to his stage door, all linked in some strange way to his lyrics. Among them – this is insane – were two copies of the art fanzine *Fish Piss*, a bag full of fir twigs, a DVD of *The Golden Girls*, a bowl of silver-coated almonds, a complete guide to the recordings of Maria Callas and two boxes of Ferrero Rocher chocolates, one of them half eaten. Hitchcock knew about such levels of obsession too. He once wrote some songs about seafood that caused an overheated American to travel ten miles to one of his concerts with a live lobster he wanted the startled musician to sign. Fans being as competitive as the people they worship, this might have been to show other supporters they were lightweights. I glanced down at the wrapping paper and thought I saw it move. Maybe it was a spider crab or some whelks.

So, yes . . . riffs, fills, chords, heat, harmonies, lyrics, lamps, noise, foot-pedals and foldback – and now this to deal with, the stunning girl with the eyes and the present. Jesus Christ, I thought, *this* was what it was like. This was the kind of lunacy rock stars went through, delusive love from complete unknowns that they need to make them feel valued. And this was *Robyn Hitchcock*, who'd never had a hit in his life. It wasn't Bono. It wasn't even Rufus Wainwright. How corrupting could this be? How destabilising? How fundamentally bad for you? What kind of self-obsessed, narcissistic fool might this breed? What idiotic mistakes might you make if total strangers half your age routinely wanted to sleep with you? And thought you held the keys to the universe? And gave you a packet of prawns?

As we touched down in Los Angeles, I remembered something Roger Waters told me about how all successful musicians have 'holes in our psychology' which only adulation can fill. They have vast egos needing full-time maintenance. You *had* to, he said, if you wanted to be as big as Pink Floyd. If you didn't have this burning thirst to win, you never would. So you ask for this devotion and you feed and encourage it. It's what you always wanted. But how the hell do you cope if it arrives? And what kind of monster might it produce?

I climbed aboard the 777 for Mexico City. I was about to find out.

40

Seven Days On The Struggle Bus

The 'Bling Airbus' took off four hours late, at around three in the afternoon of Wednesday, 14 November 2012.

The rough layout of this customised Boeing was as follows. Up the front, in the high-sided first-class pods, were Rihanna, some of her friends and family, her six-piece band and their sound, light and laser technicians, her tour controllers, her creative director, her choreographers, her videographers, her film unit, her bodyguards and personal assistants, the 'Glam Crew' (costume designers, wardrobe mistress, hair and makeup stylists), her chef and dietician, her massage therapist, her press directors, her hospitality liaison girl, some senior personnel from her record label, Island/Def Jam, and the president and other high-ranking officials from her management company, Roc Nation. A total of eighty-one people. In the middle section of the fuselage were deal-makers from the tour's three main sponsors, along with 150 members of the media – journalists, news reporters, gossip hacks, bloggers, compulsive tweeters, and radio and TV presenters from every patch of God's Earth where Rihanna topped the charts which, barring a small slice of Brazilian rainforest, was everywhere. She normally appeared in stadiums but this week she'd be playing small clubs while her passengers linked her to a world audience. At the back of the aircraft were thirty-five super-fans, the 'Rihanna Navy', who'd won competitions to be on board. They'd been told they'd meet the object of their affection and get a chance for a photo.

Most of the writers had been promised a brief encounter, too, and a couple of quotes. The might of *Elle* magazine had fixed me a ninety-minute interview in Paris two weeks later so I was just along for the ride, to get some background colour, file daily blogs from the front line and tweet the hell out of anything that moved. For me, no pressure at all; for the others, quite a bit.

The kite was barely into the clear blue skies above California before the intercom crackled to life: the unmistakable voice of Rihanna.

'This is an emergency! Welcome to 777. Make some noise, people, and let's get drunk!'

I looked up to find her personal assistant charging down the aisle handing out plastic beakers. Rihanna was behind her in a black dress and shades, pouring $300-a-pop gold bottles of Ace of Spades champagne, a thicket of lights, TV cameras and flashing iPhones springing up around her.

'And if you *really* want to black out,' her PA shouted, 'we got cognac!'

The entourage and its well-refreshed press corps spilt onto the baking tarmac of Benito Juárez Airport and into a flotilla of people-carriers which barrelled through the lively traffic of Mexico City to a packed dance-hall where six hundred punters and seventeen anxious film crews were waiting. Rihanna was due onstage in thirty minutes and, three hours later, the show began. We got to the airport at one in the morning and piled back on the jet, but no flights were allowed out past the midnight curfew – take off any later and you faced crippling financial penalties. We couldn't have left anyway as she wasn't on board: she was still in Mexico City, chilling in her backstage area, eventually rolling up on the runway at three. At which point the tremors from a nearby six-scale earthquake kept us rooted to the strip until a quarter to five.

Already I was starting to see a pattern emerge. She was perpetually late. She was so late onstage in Mexico that we were six hours behind leaving for Canada. She was so late in Toronto, we bust the midnight barrier for Sweden. She was so late in Stockholm, we missed our slot for Paris. As some of the European shows were sponsored live broadcasts, I could feel the problems piling up. The whole thing was costing $3.6 million as it was, with various vital cash-earners logged in the schedule. She was getting £400,000 alone just to turn on the Christmas lights at London's Westfield shopping mall but what if we were six hours late into Heathrow? Nothing could stop her lateness. On it went, with a knock-on effect like a line of tumbling dominoes, a whole daisy-chain of disaster leaving maddened airport officials, vexed crowds and fretting media partners in its wake.

And exasperated hacks. What had been sold as a monumental jolly, a week of scooting round the globe, seeing the sights, occasionally hanging out with the star of the show and filing reams of quote-packed prose, was turning into an insomniac nightmare. We had sumptuous rooms booked in Canada but had to check out an hour later. We now seemed to be living on the plane, or in a gridlock on the way to the concert, or shuffling through endless security queues while the only staff still on duty at two in the morning grumpily put us through Customs. I'd had eight hours' sleep in four days and felt pretty chipper but some of us had notched up none at all, despite hard self-medication with bottles of Ace of Spades and 'American gin and tonics' (no tonic).

Since her lavish drink distribution on the Mexican flight, Ri had slunk back into her heavily guarded lairs and was invisible. She made a brief filmed appearance at Toronto Airport in a tracksuit and pink baseball cap to give the impression she handled her own luggage, but otherwise we'd only seen her onstage – no interviews, no press conference, not even a grip-and-grin photo-call or a 'walkabout'. She tweeted some snaps of herself smoking weed and turned up in a roped-off nightclub area with P. Diddy, Pharrell and Akin. Apart from that, nothing. To fill the vacuum created by the daily posts, we interviewed her band, chef, stylists, hairdressers, masseuse and spiritual adviser, who vouchsafed the divinely west-coast logic that 'It's great that she loves herself enough to want someone to take care of her.' Video crews were filming each other to paint a picture of frantic media action. Lone bloggers barked reports into their iPhones. News columnists took selfies with the cabin crew and swapped buffed-up facts and figures. Frazzled fashion stringers filed each other's multi-climate style tips – 'From scorchio Mexico to Great *Brrrrr*itain: what to wear and how to wear it!'

The bloke from Budweiser in the row behind was in a terrible state. Only one member of Rihanna's band actually drank his sponsorship brew and was prepared to be photographed doing so, the heavily inked, singlet-sporting former leader of Extreme, guitarist Nuno Bettencourt.

'What's wrong with that?' I wondered.

'It's off-brand,' he sighed. 'We're trying to move *away* from tattoos right now.'

Starved of Instagram material, I loosed off snaps of the Rihanna socks and the 'genuine conflict-free diamond' we'd each got in our bulging goody-bags and, at one low point, of a complimentary tray of nougat. The *really* desperate were posting 'Drunkstagrams' – blurred snaps of photos on other people's phone screens of key moments they'd missed because they were asleep or in a bar. Everywhere we went, there was a mad race to find a signal and be the first to fire off pictures of a stage door, or a set-list, or an empty dressing room, or one of Rihanna's shirts on a hanger, or tweet the news that she'd had Bajan jerk chicken for lunch, or that she's 'not good around vegetables', or double-tweet that 'Tonight #777RihannaTour Ri's wearing an oversized Adam Kimmel for Carhartt denim jacket, a vintage leather and gold-encrusted Chanel belt with . . .' – tweet two – '. . . a Chanel nameplate chain and plastic pop-art shades, denim American Apparel shorts, black Tom Ford heels and a white see-through Wolford body-suit (no bra)'.

Another classic feeding-frenzy. The press pack had whipped up the expectations of the outside world and the outside world was watching and wanted more. The problem: after four days with no access to the girl there was the thick end of sweet fuck-all to write about.

But how did we get here? How was this kind of pop star allowed to evolve? At the very pinnacle of his tantrums and tiaras, even Elton John wasn't so self-centred or as surrounded by people who'd put up with it. This was *epic* lateness. This was lateness on a superhuman scale. No one – not even *royalty* – would be this late or care any less about it. There was a good reason her support acts were both DJs: bands can't play for hours on end; DJs just stick on another record. We seemed to spend every waking moment waiting for Rihanna. One night we boarded at one in the morning and she sashayed in at 03.14. They shut the door, we taxied out and were in the air two minutes later. The crew referred to the 777 as 'Airforce One'; the press called it 'the 666', a byword for booze-plied, sleep-deprived, demonic, nerve-shredding madness. We'd begun to wonder if we weren't taking part in some bizarre new version of *The Hunger Games* where 150 hacks were put through a series of punishing physical and mental tests and the last one awake got the world exclusive. And slept through all five minutes of it.

But when the Elton Johns of the past were at the top of their curve, broadly all that was required was they do a bit of press, play a stadium and get completely hammered afterwards. The twenty-first-century world was bigger and more complex. From the moment Rihanna woke up, someone wanted a slice of her. Film projects and merchandise deals were on the table, new songwriting partnerships and lucrative fashion endorsements, crucial offers that funded the vast army around her. The old music business dictated the pace at which you operated but the leeching, accelerated appetite of the digital world meant Rihanna had to embrace every chance at once, quick, before the bubble burst. On top of this she had a show every night and nobody wanted to be the one who 'negatively affected her performance'. You wouldn't want to get the blame for upsetting her by trying to hurry her up. So her whole world was layered with ways of reducing the chance of unhappiness. She was like a spoilt child with over-attentive parents waiting for her to eat, poop or sleep. To sidestep the possibility that she didn't like her food she had a personal dietician. She couldn't be stressed so she had a masseuse who doubled as a soothing Buddhist philosopher. She couldn't dislike her surroundings so her hospitality liaison manager rushed ahead in each city to 'Rihanna-ise' her backstage area. Her band might be cooped up in a neon-lit brick bunker every night but the queen bee had an identically styled, low-lit private boudoir hung with black curtains and filled with diva-approved fur rugs, soft furnishings and her favourite calming 'accents of pink' – pink scented candles, pink lilies and embroidered lengths of pink Chinese silk. Being in this room was her big moment of power, the helpless dependent world spinning frantically around her, a million eyes beseeching her to start the show, and she extended it for as long as she could.

And when she *did* eventually step onstage, her clothes with the sweet tang of marijuana, her lips a slash of crimson, her huge feline, hazel eyes radiating a cute and impossible innocence known only to the heroines of Disney cartoons, the sense of relief was so gigantic I instantly wanted to forgive her. We *all* did – men, women, teenage kids, the band, the crowd, the entire crew of Airforce One. There was a loud collective sigh. It was the same any time of day or night in whatever room she entered. The agonising cycle of anxiety and release was finally over. The thing that was waiting to begin could begin.

For me, the whole caper started falling apart in Paris. I'd travelled fifteen thousand miles in five days on a total of ten hours' sleep and finally entered the condition my little gang called 'being on the Struggle Bus', a delirious state of goofball stir-craziness. For once we had hotel rooms and time to occupy them. Within seconds of scattering possessions round my suite and dialling room service, I caught sight of myself in a ceiling mirror – a gibbering, stubbly, red-eyed, naked maniac floating in a bath, drinking gin and tonic through a straw and staring blankly at a French sitcom while eating chips and topping up the water with my toe. I felt like my brain had been replaced by a blancmange. I looked at myself and laughed out loud. This unbounded lunacy was still strangely entertaining.

Rihanna was starting to unravel a bit too.

'Let's hear it for our sponsors!' she said when she finally got onstage at Le Trianon Club for the night's live broadcast. 'Lemme hear you say River Island!'

'River Island!' Paris dutifully shouted.

'Lemme hear you say Bud-weis-serrrr!'

Oh, for fuck's sake.

'Lemme hear you say HTC! I got one HTC phone to give away tonight,' she added, waving the gift aloft. 'What's the French for one?'

But the next day was the killer. That was when the wheels came off.

'Hey, it's *hot* in here! What's the German for hot?'

It *was* hot – and possibly hotter for the audience. They'd been standing in a sweltering rave-barn called E-Werk near Berlin's Checkpoint Charlie since seven o'clock, expecting a show at eight. At ten to midnight – oh, yes – and with loud booing now audible backstage, Ri emerged from her smoke-filled compound to join the nightly ritual known as 'The Prayer', the band's way of finally getting her to 'commit' so there was nowhere to go but onstage. The seven of them locked arms in a circle – group hug! – and the chant began, led by Adam, her teetotal Bible-packing bassist.

'Dear Lord,' he yelled, 'bless this band! Bless every beat of its drum, bless every note it sings. Bless the guitars and the tunes they play. Bless us all and the sound we make. We love you, God!'

'Seven-Seven-Seven!' they all shouted. '*BERRRLIIIIIN*!!'

And they charged out into the lights, hit the first chord and looked around to discover . . . Rihanna was still in the wings, another last gasp of relaxation. For three whole minutes they lumbered on until the spotlight picked out a tall, slim figure strolling casually to the microphone.

Knackered, shredded and babbling incoherent nonsense, the press corps were ferried to the 777 after the show and began another long, curfew-busting wait for the big gun to bowl up too. Still no interviews or press conference. Editors back home were threatening to spike their reports if there was no contact with the star. Seven days on a plane for nothing but a bad attack of the shakes and the head-grating grandmother of all hangovers. I settled back in my seat as we eventually took off for London, fairly sure there was now only one person on board still enjoying themselves, the mad-eyed man from *Elle* magazine: me.

At the back of the jet, the Rihanna Navy were on the verge of full-scale mutiny, worn down by six days of texts from friends wanting pictures of them and the object of their dying affection. Super-fandom was getting less super by the minute. The all-round mood was fractious, the cabin staff pouring down the aisles to douse angry passengers with cognac and fizz.

'Wayne's World!' someone sang, weakly.

'Wayne's World!' A few more. 'Party time. Excellent.' But their hearts weren't in it. They'd lost the will to live. A chant of a different kind started in the bowels of the aircraft.

'Save our jobs! Save our jobs!'

Louder now and starting to build. With rhythmic banging of tray-tables.

'SAVE OUR JOBS! SAVE OUR JOBS!'

And another: 'Just one quote!'

'JUST ONE QUOTE! JUST ONE QUOTE!'

Then a third, a cunning ruse to tempt the dope-friendly diva down from the sharp end: 'We've got weed!'

'WE'VE GOT WEED! WE'VE GOT WEED!'

Utter chaos broke out. One hundred and fifty hyperventilating souls leapt from their seats and started punching the air in a forest of microphones, TV crews barging round the plane.

'Free The Rihanna One-Fifty!'

'FREE THE RIHANNA ONE-FIFTY!'

Panicked officials from Roc Nation came tumbling through the blue curtain to appeal for peace.

'*People, we need you back in your seats!*'

'Occupy Seven-Seven-Seven!'

'OCCUPY SEVEN-SEVEN-SEVEN!'

'*Guys, in the interest of your comfort and security—*'

'Save our jobs!'

'SAVE OUR JOBS! JUST ONE QUOTE! WE'VE GOT WEED!'

Had Rihanna appeared at this point, posing for photos and dispensing *bons mots*, there'd have been such a stampede from the tail-end the whole crate might have gone arse-over-tit and corkscrewed into the English Channel. Roc Nation couldn't stop the riot. The only way to stop it was to give the press something to write about and they wanted the girl beneath the blanket in the first-class sleeping-pod. Feeling we'd reached flashpoint, an Australian DJ called Tim, the spit of Michael Hutchence of INXS, slipped thoughtfully into a toilet cubicle and reappeared stark naked. Legs akimbo, his long ginger mane flying behind him, he streaked round the aircraft pursued by cameras and batteries of lights, men hooting with joy, girls marvelling at the magnificence of his all-over tan. At last we had a headline. The 777 Tour had been such a nerve-fraying nightmare, such a strength-sapping endurance test, a fact-finding mission so free of facts, that some selfless soul – the stitchless Tim – had fallen on his sword to give us all a story.

Now the race was on to get it out. But at 10,000 feet, no one could get a signal.

'Tweet! Tweet! Tweet!' one guy whimpered, stabbing feebly at his dial.

Phones aloft, arms in the air. 'TWEET! TWEET TWEET!' came the manic mass chorus.

Gradually it all died down. One by one the lamps winked out and the place returned to darkness. I started tapping out an account of it, about nude protests and near-plummeting planes. A kindly steward saw my light on and swept back down the aisle.

'Can I get you something, sir?' he said gently, a hand on my shoulder. His voice was camp and comforting.

'What have you got?' I whispered.

'We do a great Bloody Mary.'

'*But it's six in the morning and I don't know where I am!*'

He had a soft bedside manner. He was there to soothe and assist. 'Think of it,' he said, 'not as the first drink of the day but the last drink of the night.'

'Bloody Mary, please.'

'See?' he cooed. '*That* wasn't so hard.'

I lifted my little window shade. The dawn had begun to glow on some curved horizon and the creaking portals of my mind had opened and issued one last mud-stained memory. I was thinking about what Nick Lowe had told me, years before, about that concept of the 'mile-melter', about the various ways he'd devised to puncture the tedium of motorway travel and stave off the rigours of real life. One of them was this. Before they boarded the tour-bus, Nick and his band would choose a front wheel, each write their name on a wheel-nut and throw twenty dollars in a hat. Ten hours later the coach would pull up outside the dance-hall they were booked to play and they'd all pile out and rush to the front. Whoever's wheel-nut was nearest the venue got all the money.

On the great mile-melting tour-bus of life, anyone older always told me I'd been born too late, that the music I was hearing was just an echo of some Big Bang in a distant past. And anyone younger shook their head saying I'd missed the action too, that theirs was the best age to be. But I'd been old enough to watch singles rattle down the spindles of record-players and young enough to see the most extravagant expressions of where all those thrills would lead, and I wouldn't have missed it for the world.

Whose wheel-nut was nearest the venue? For one brief and glorious moment, I was starting to think it was mine.

For more exclusive images relating to this book visit
www.RockStarsStoleMyLife.com

Do you wish this wasn't the end?

Join us at www.hodder.co.uk, or follow us on
Twitter @hodderbooks to be a part of our community
of people who love the very best in books and reading.

Whether you want to discover more about a book
or an author, watch trailers and interviews, have the
chance to win early limited editions, or simply browse
our expert readers' selection of the very best books,
we think you'll find what you're looking for.

And if you don't,
that's the place to tell us what's missing.

We love what we do, and we'd love you to be part of it.

www.hodder.co.uk

 @hodderbooks

 HodderBooks

 HodderBooks

so much to me I'd pay a fortune just to be in the same room as the man who'd written them. Strangely, I didn't want him to play them anyway, and stretch them out of shape and massacre them with his new-found monotone. Only the original versions could fire my childhood self. I wanted to hear the new songs that keyed into my fifty-year-old self – planed-down, wry and removed, like 'Po' Boy' and 'Floater'. We were growing old together.

Hopeless, steadfast, uncritical devotion became a running theme and *Word* writers piled onto the podcast as if going to confession. Kate's unshakeable fondness for Glen Campbell would have baffled psychologists. Rob Fitzpatrick had once made a clay pig in pottery class emblazoned with the logo of prog-symphonists Rush. Andrew Collins was still besotted with Carter The Unstoppable Sex Machine, not least because they had a single called 'The Only Living Boy In New Cross'. Digital editor Fraser Lewry talked warmly of years in the poodle-haired grip of Faster Pussycat and Mötley Crüe. Production chief 'Seventies' Johnson pined for David Essex and The Stranglers. For me there was something redeeming, too, about the admission of failure, about publicly apologising to a sympathetic audience for appalling past errors of judgement. I'd chosen the Ozark Mountain Daredevils over David Bowie as the path to follow – wrong, *very* wrong. I'd spent hours listening to Wishbone Ash and Roy Harper, and this now seemed like laughable madness. I'd shot records by ELO with a rifle that I now considered masterpieces. And there was something delightful in talking about music as the framework of everyday life. About how banjos put a spring in my step. About the fragile rhythms of Feist making the outside world evaporate. About how no one could possibly hear 'Heart Like A Wheel' by Kate and Anna McGarrigle and not end up in a pool of tears. About how I never tired of Boz Scaggs doing 'Don't Cry No More' if it swung into my earphones. About my boundless admiration for Syd Barrett and the words his tangled mind invented – 'she straggled the bridge by the water'. About how the swelling chords of Brian Eno's 'Fractal Zoom' made everything seem achievable, a movie for the ears with its propelling drums and ghostly choirs. We'd end monologues about music with the same ludicrous flourish – 'This isn't a discussion, it's a statement of fact!' – as if personal taste could never be wrong.

'What's the greatest record ever made?' we asked each other regularly.

'Don't tell me, I *know* this one!' the other panicked, as if it was a quiz with only one right answer. The greatest record ever made changed all the time, depending on the mood we were in, though part of me wondered if my eight-year-old self had been right all along and it was still the impeccable 'Hole In The Ground' by Bernard Cribbins.

When the advertising finally vanished and we closed *The Word* after ten magnificent years, the Massive flew their digital flag at half-mast and blew their ceremonial trumpets. We even made the national TV and radio news. There was an outpouring of grief and I found it very moving. Anyone on our wavelength seemed to have loved our spirit of adventure. Kate and I had made monthly videocasts of the two of us talking about each new issue. On one of the last ones Fraser, behind the camera, announced the subjects we'd covered while she held up the pages and I played 'Singing In The Rain' on guitar. 'The only magazine with a musical contents page,' the *Guardian* noted, in their fond farewell. The Massive threw a party for us in a pub in Foley Street. We'd put on shows for them in the past, a cross between a club gig and village fair where you could win some cupcakes or a pineapple or a jar of chutney in a shambolic 'prize draw' before Wilko Johnson or the Blockheads or Scritti Politti came on. Now